SPRINGFIELD COLLEGE READER

Edited by Anne C. Wheeler

Kendall Hunt
publishing company

SPRINGFIELD
COLLEGE

Cover images © Springfield College

www.kendallhunt.com
Send all inquiries to:
4050 Westmark Drive
Dubuque, IA 52004-1840

Published in the United States of America

CONTENTS

PART 1

Welcome to College Writing at Springfield College!

Introduction

Dear Student,

Welcome to College Writing at Springfield College! The College Writing program plays an essential role in preparing students for reading, writing, and thinking at the college level. Over the course of the year, you will practice reading and writing in a variety of contexts. You will also engage in the writing process, and through multiple drafts and revisions, you will develop your rhetorical and mechanical abilities. The goal of the College Writing program is not for you to "master writing," but rather to develop a strong understanding of how the process works and to become a flexible writer who is equipped to respond appropriately to a variety of writing situations.

This reader is intended to support your journey toward becoming a well-developed writer. It is divided into three sections:

Section 1 consists of an anthology of exemplary texts that have been carefully selected by the Springfield College writing faculty. Topics in this anthology range from the cultural meaning of popular toys to an investigation into Major League Baseball's recruiting system in the Dominican Republic. They also represent a selection of the same writing styles that you will be trying out over the course of the year including, but not limited to, narrative, analytical, and argumentative. Collectively, the anthology also provides you with a variety of methods for conducting research and integrating sources into your projects.

Every year, the College Writing program sponsors an annual contest. **Section 2** of this reader contains six award winning essays written by your predecessors in College Writing 1 and College Writing 2. These essays are not only great reads in their own right, they will also give you a sense of how real students interpret the kinds of assignments you will encounter in College Writing.

Finally, **Section 3** is all about style. It provides you with comprehensive guides to the MLA and APA citation systems, which are the two primary systems used here at Springfield College. It also includes a variety of resources to refresh you on the rules of grammar and usage so that you can do a better job of proofreading your own work.

Because writing will be a cornerstone of your educational experience, the College offers students Writing & Reading Support Services to assist you with all aspects of the writing and reading process. To learn more about Writing & Reading Support Services, please feel free to visit the Academic Success Center, located on the third floor of the Learning Commons, or visit their website for additional information.

I encourage you to take advantage of the strategies and techniques that your professors and writing tutors offer you. I am so excited to see the work that you do!

Sincerely,

Anne C. Wheeler, PhD
Assistant Professor of Composition & Rhetoric
Writing Program Director

PART 2

Anthology

Burke's "Unending Conversation" Metaphor

Kenneth Burke writes:

Imagine that you enter a parlor. You come late. When you arrive, others have long preceded you, and they are engaged in a heated discussion, a discussion too heated for them to pause and tell you exactly what it is about. In fact, the discussion had already begun long before any of them got there, so that no one present is qualified to retrace for you all the steps that had gone before. You listen for a while, until you decide that you have caught the tenor of the argument; then you put in your oar. Someone answers; you answer him; another comes to your defense; another aligns himself against you, to either the embarrassment or gratification of your opponent, depending upon the quality of your ally's assistance. However, the discussion is interminable. The hour grows late, you must depart. And you do depart, with the discussion still vigorously in progress.

From *The Philosophy of Literary Form* p. 110–111.

Shitty First Drafts

Anne Lamott from *Bird by Bird*

Now, practically even better news than that of short assignments is the idea of shitty first drafts. All good writers write them. This is how they end up with good second drafts and terrific third drafts. People tend to look at successful writers who are getting their books published and maybe even doing well financially and think that they sit down at their desks every morning feeling like a million dollars, feeling great about who they are and how much talent they have and what a great story they have to tell; that they take in a few deep breaths, push back their sleeves, roll their necks a few times to get all the cricks out, and dive in, typing fully formed passages as fast as a court reporter. But this is just the fantasy of the uninitiated. I know some very great writers, writers you love who write beautifully and have made a great deal of money, and not one of them sits down routinely feeling wildly enthusiastic and confident. Not one of them writes elegant first drafts. All right, one of them does, but we do not like her very much. We do not think that she has a rich inner life or that God likes her or can even stand her. (Although when I mentioned this to my priest friend Tom, he said you can safely assume you've created God in your own image when it turns out that God hates all the same people you do.)

Very few writers really know what they are doing until they've done it. Nor do they go about their business feeling dewy and thrilled. They do not type a few stiff warm-up sentences and then find themselves bounding along like huskies across the snow. One writer I know tells me that he sits down every morning and says to himself nicely, "It's not like you don't have a choice, because you do—you can either type, or kill yourself." We all often feel like we are pulling teeth, even those writers whose prose ends up being the most natural and fluid. The right words and sentences just do not come pouring out like ticker tape most of the time. Now, Muriel Spark is said to have felt that she was taking dictation from God every morning—sitting there, one supposes, plugged into a Dictaphone, typing away, humming. But this is a very hostile and aggressive position. One might hope for bad things to rain down on a person like this.

For me and most of the other writers I know, writing is not rapturous. In fact, the only way I can get anything written at all is to write really, really shitty first drafts.

The first draft is the child's draft, where you let it all pour out and then let it romp all over the place, knowing that no one is going to see it and that you can shape it later. You just let this childlike part of you channel whatever voices and visions come through and onto the page. If one of the characters wants to say, "Well, so what, Mr. Poopy Pants?," you let her. No one is going to see it. If the kid wants to get into really sentimental, weepy, emotional territory, you let him. Just get it all down on paper because there may be something great in those six crazy pages that you would never have gotten to by more rational, grown-up means. There may be something in the very last line of the very last paragraph on page six that you just love, that is so beautiful or wild that you now know what you're supposed to be writing about, more or less, or in what direction you might go—but there was no way to get to this without first getting through the first five and a half pages.

I used to write food reviews for California magazine before it folded. (My writing food reviews had nothing to do with the magazine folding, although every single review did cause a couple of canceled subscriptions. Some readers took umbrage at my comparing mounds of vegetable puree with various ex-presidents' brains.) These reviews always took two days to write. First I'd go to a restaurant several times with a few opinionated, articulate friends in tow. I'd sit there writing down everything anyone said that was at all interesting or funny. Then on the following Monday I'd sit down at my desk with my notes and try to write the review. Even after I'd been doing this for years, panic would set in. I'd try to write a lead, but instead I'd write a couple of dreadful sentences, XX them out, try again, XX everything out, and then feel despair and worry settle on my chest like an x-ray apron. It's over, I'd think calmly. I'm not going to be able to get the magic to work this time. I'm ruined. I'm through. I'm toast. Maybe, I'd think, I can get my old job back as a clerk-typist. But probably not. I'd get up and study my teeth in the mirror for a while. Then I'd stop, remember to breathe, make a few phone calls, hit the kitchen and chow down. Eventually I'd go back and sit down at my desk, and sigh for the next ten minutes. Finally I would pick up my one-inch picture frame, stare into it as if for the answer, and every time the answer would come: all I had to do was to write a really shitty first draft of, say, the opening paragraph. And no one was going to see it.

So I'd start writing without reining myself in. It was almost just typing, just making my fingers move. And the writing would be terrible. I'd write a lead paragraph that was a whole page, even though the entire review could only be three pages long, and then I'd start writing up descriptions of the food, one dish at a time, bird by bird, and the critics would be sitting on my shoulders, commenting like cartoon characters. They'd be pretending to snore, or rolling their eyes at my overwrought descriptions, no matter how hard I tried to tone those descriptions down, no matter how conscious I was of what a friend said to me gently in my early days of restaurant reviewing. "Annie," she said, "it is just a piece of chicken. It is just a bit of cake."

But because by then I had been writing for so long, I would eventually let myself trust the process—sort of, more or less. I'd write a first draft that was maybe twice as long as it should be, with a self-indulgent and boring beginning, stupefying descriptions of the meal, lots of quotes from my black-humored friends that made them sound more like the Manson girls than food lovers, and no ending to speak of. The whole thing would be so long and incoherent and hideous that for the rest of the day I'd obsess about getting creamed by a car before I could write a decent second draft. I'd worry that people would read what I'd written and believe that the accident had really been a suicide, that I had panicked because my talent was waning and my mind was shot.

The next day, I'd sit down, go through it all with a colored pen, take out everything I possibly could, find a new lead somewhere on the second page, figure out a kicky place to end it, and then write a second draft.

It always turned out fine, sometimes even funny and weird and helpful. I'd go over it one more time and mail it in.

Then, a month later, when it was time for another review, the whole process would start again, complete with the fears that people would find my first draft before I could rewrite it.

Almost all good writing begins with terrible first efforts. You need to start somewhere. Start by getting something—anything—down on paper. A friend of mine says that the first draft is the down draft—you just get it down. The second draft is the up draft—you fix it up. You try to say what you have to say more accurately. And the third draft is the dental draft, where you check every tooth, to see if it's loose or cramped or decayed, or even, God help us, healthy.

Is Google Making Us Stupid?

NICHOLAS CARR

WHAT THE INTERNET IS DOING TO OUR BRAINS

"Dave, stop. Stop, will you? Stop, Dave. Will you stop, Dave?" So the supercomputer HAL pleads with the implacable astronaut Dave Bowman in a famous and weirdly poignant scene toward the end of Stanley Kubrick's *2001: A Space Odyssey*. Bowman, having nearly been sent to a deep-space death by the malfunctioning machine, is calmly, coldly disconnecting the memory circuits that control its artificial "brain". "Dave, my mind is going," HAL says, forlornly. "I can feel it. I can feel it."

I can feel it, too. Over the past few years I've had an uncomfortable sense that someone, or something, has been tinkering with my brain, remapping the neural circuitry, reprogramming the memory. My mind isn't going—so far as I can tell—but it's changing. I'm not thinking the way I used to think. I can feel it most strongly when I'm reading. Immersing myself in a book or a lengthy article used to be easy. My mind would get caught up in the narrative or the turns of the argument, and I'd spend hours strolling through long stretches of prose. That's rarely the case anymore. Now my concentration often starts to drift after two or three pages. I get fidgety, lose the thread, begin looking for something else to do. I feel as if I'm always dragging my wayward brain back to the text. The deep reading that used to come naturally has become a struggle.

I think I know what's going on. For more than a decade now, I've been spending a lot of time online, searching and surfing and sometimes adding to the great databases of the Internet. The Web has been a godsend to me as a writer. Research that once required days in the stacks or periodical rooms of libraries can now be done in minutes. A few Google searches, some quick clicks on hyperlinks, and I've got the telltale fact or pithy quote I was after. Even when I'm not working, I'm as likely as not to be foraging in the Web's info-thickets' reading and writing e-mails, scanning headlines and blog posts, watching videos and listening to podcasts, or just tripping from link to link to link. (Unlike footnotes, to which they're sometimes likened, hyperlinks don't merely point to related works; they propel you toward them.)

For me, as for others, the Net is becoming a universal medium, the conduit for most of the information that flows through my eyes and ears and into my mind. The advantages of having immediate access to such an incredibly rich store of information are many, and they've been widely described and duly applauded. "The perfect recall of silicon memory," *Wired*'s Clive Thompson has written, "can be an enormous boon to thinking." But that boon comes at a price. As the media theorist Marshall McLuhan pointed out in the 1960s, media are not just passive channels of information. They supply the stuff of thought, but they also shape the process of thought. And what the Net seems to be doing is chipping away my capacity for concentration and contemplation. My mind now expects to take in information the way the Net distributes it: in a swiftly moving stream of particles. Once I was a scuba diver in the sea of words. Now I zip along the surface like a guy on a Jet Ski.

I'm not the only one. When I mention my troubles with reading to friends and acquaintances—literary types, most of them—many say they're having similar experiences. The more they use the Web, the more they have to fight to stay focused on long pieces of writing. Some of the bloggers I follow have also begun mentioning the phenomenon. Scott Karp, who writes a blog about online media, recently confessed that he has stopped reading books altogether. "I was a lit major in college, and used to be [a] voracious book reader," he wrote. "What happened?" He speculates on the answer: "What if I do all my reading on the web not so much because the way I read has changed, i.e. I'm just seeking convenience, but because the way I THINK has changed?"

Bruce Friedman, who blogs regularly about the use of computers in medicine, also has described how the Internet has altered his mental habits. "I now have almost totally lost the ability to read and absorb a longish article on the web or in print," he wrote earlier this year. A pathologist who has long been on the faculty of the University of Michigan Medical School, Friedman elaborated on his comment in a telephone conversation with me. His thinking, he said, has taken on a "staccato" quality, reflecting the way he quickly scans short passages of text from many sources online. "I can't read *War and Peace* anymore," he admitted. "I've lost the ability to do that. Even a blog post of more than three or four paragraphs is too much to absorb. I skim it."

Anecdotes alone don't prove much. And we still await the long-term neurological and psychological experiments that will provide a definitive picture of how Internet use affects cognition. But a recently published study of online research habits, conducted by scholars from University College London, suggests that we may well be in the midst of a sea change in the way we read and think. As part of the five-year research program, the scholars examined computer logs documenting the behavior of visitors to two popular research sites, one operated by the British Library and one by a U.K. educational consortium, that provide access to journal articles, e-books, and other sources of written information. They found that people using the sites exhibited "a form of skimming activity," hopping from one source to another and rarely returning to any source they'd already visited. They typically read no more than one or two pages of an article or book before they would "bounce" out to another site. Sometimes they'd save a long article, but there's no evidence that they ever went back and actually read it. The authors of the study report:

It is clear that users are not reading online in the traditional sense; indeed there are signs that new forms of "reading" are emerging as users "power browse" horizontally through titles, contents pages and abstracts going for quick wins. It almost seems that they go online to avoid reading in the traditional sense.

Thanks to the ubiquity of text on the Internet, not to mention the popularity of text-messaging on cell phones, we may well be reading more today than we did in the 1970s or 1980s, when television was our medium of choice. But it's a different kind of reading, and behind it lies a different kind of thinking—

perhaps even a new sense of the self. "We are not only *what* we read," says Maryanne Wolf, a developmental psychologist at Tufts University and the author of *Proust and the Squid: The Story and Science of the Reading Brain.* "We are *how* we read." Wolf worries that the style of reading promoted by the Net, a style that puts "efficiency" and "immediacy" above all else, may be weakening our capacity for the kind of deep reading that emerged when an earlier technology, the printing press, made long and complex works of prose commonplace. When we read online, she says, we tend to become "mere decoders of information." Our ability to interpret text, to make the rich mental connections that form when we read deeply and without distraction, remains largely disengaged.

Reading, explains Wolf, is not an instinctive skill for human beings. It's not etched into our genes the way speech is. We have to teach our minds how to translate the symbolic characters we see into the language we understand. And the media or other technologies we use in learning and practicing the craft of reading play an important part in shaping the neural circuits inside our brains. Experiments demonstrate that readers of ideograms, such as the Chinese, develop a mental circuitry for reading that is very different from the circuitry found in those of us whose written language employs an alphabet. The variations extend across many regions of the brain, including those that govern such essential cognitive functions as memory and the interpretation of visual and auditory stimuli. We can expect as well that the circuits woven by our use of the Net will be different from those woven by our reading of books and other printed works.

Sometime in 1882, Friedrich Nietzsche bought a typewriter—a Malling-Hansen Writing Ball, to be precise. His vision was failing, and keeping his eyes focused on a page had become exhausting and painful, often bringing on crushing headaches. He had been forced to curtail his writing, and he feared that he would soon have to give it up. The typewriter rescued him, at least for a time. Once he had mastered touch-typing, he was able to write with his eyes closed, using only the tips of his fingers. Words could once again flow from his mind to the page.

But the machine had a subtler effect on his work. One of Nietzsche's friends, a composer, noticed a change in the style of his writing. His already terse prose had become even tighter, more telegraphic. "Perhaps you will through this instrument even take to a new idiom," the friend wrote in a letter, noting that, in his own work, his "'thoughts' in music and language often depend on the quality of pen and paper."

"You are right," Nietzsche replied, "our writing equipment takes part in the forming of our thoughts." Under the sway of the machine, writes the German media scholar Friedrich A. Kittler, Nietzsche's prose "changed from arguments to aphorisms, from thoughts to puns, from rhetoric to telegram style."

The human brain is almost infinitely malleable. People used to think that our mental meshwork, the dense connections formed among the 100 billion or so neurons inside our skulls, was largely fixed by the time we reached adulthood. But brain researchers have discovered that that's not the case. James Olds, a professor of neuroscience who directs the Krasnow Institute for Advanced Study at George Mason University, says that even the adult mind "is very plastic." Nerve cells routinely break old connections and form new ones. "The brain," according to Olds, "has the ability to reprogram itself on the fly, altering the way it functions."

As we use what the sociologist Daniel Bell has called our "intellectual technologies"—the tools that extend our mental rather than our physical capacities—we inevitably begin to take on the qualities of those technologies. The mechanical clock, which came into common use in the 14th century, provides a compelling example. In *Technics and Civilization*, the historian and cultural critic Lewis Mumford described how the clock "disassociated time from human events and helped create the belief in an independent world of mathematically measurable sequences." The "abstract framework of divided time" became "the point of reference for both action and thought."

The clock's methodical ticking helped bring into being the scientific mind and the scientific man. But it also took something away. As the late MIT computer scientist Joseph Weizenbaum observed in his 1976 book, *Computer Power and Human Reason: From Judgment to Calculation*, the conception of the world that emerged from the widespread use of timekeeping instruments "remains an impoverished version of the older one, for it rests on a rejection of those direct experiences that formed the basis for, and indeed constituted, the old reality." In deciding when to eat, to work, to sleep, to rise, we stopped listening to our senses and started obeying the clock.

The process of adapting to new intellectual technologies is reflected in the changing metaphors we use to explain ourselves to ourselves. When the mechanical clock arrived, people began thinking of their brains as operating "like clockwork." Today, in the age of software, we have come to think of them as operating "like computers." But the changes, neuroscience tells us, go much deeper than metaphor. Thanks to our brain's plasticity, the adaptation occurs also at a biological level.

The Internet promises to have particularly far-reaching effects on cognition. In a paper published in 1936, the British mathematician Alan Turing proved that a digital computer, which at the time existed only as a theoretical machine, could be programmed to perform the function of any other information-processing device. And that's what we're seeing today. The Internet, an immeasurably powerful computing system, is subsuming most of our other intellectual technologies. It's becoming our map and our clock, our printing press and our typewriter, our calculator and our telephone, and our radio and TV.

When the Net absorbs a medium, that medium is re-created in the Net's image. It injects the medium's content with hyperlinks, blinking ads, and other digital gewgaws, and it surrounds the content with the content of all the other media it has absorbed. A new e-mail message, for instance, may announce its arrival as we're glancing over the latest headlines at a newspaper's site. The result is to scatter our attention and diffuse our concentration.

The Net's influence doesn't end at the edges of a computer screen, either. As people's minds become attuned to the crazy quilt of Internet media, traditional media have to adapt to the audience's new expectations. Television programs add text crawls and pop-up ads, and magazines and newspapers shorten their articles, introduce capsule summaries, and crowd their pages with easy-to-browse info-snippets. When, in March of this year, *The New York Times* decided to devote the second and third pages of every edition to article abstracts, its design director, Tom Bodkin, explained that the "shortcuts" would give harried readers a quick "taste" of the day's news, sparing them the "less efficient" method of actually turning the pages and reading the articles. Old media have little choice but to play by the new-media rules.

Never has a communications system played so many roles in our lives—or exerted such broad influence over our thoughts—as the Internet does today. Yet, for all that's been written about the Net, there's been little consideration of how, exactly, it's reprogramming us. The Net's intellectual ethic remains obscure.

About the same time that Nietzsche started using his typewriter, an earnest young man named Frederick Winslow Taylor carried a stopwatch into the Midvale Steel plant in Philadelphia and began a historic series of experiments aimed at improving the efficiency of the plant's machinists. With the approval of Midvale's owners, he recruited a group of factory hands, set them to work on various metalworking machines, and recorded and timed their every movement as well as the operations of the machines. By breaking down every job into a sequence of small, discrete steps and then testing different ways of performing each one, Taylor created a set of precise instructions—an "algorithm," we might say today—for how each worker should work. Midvale's employees grumbled about the strict new regime, claiming that it turned them into little more than automatons, but the factory's productivity soared.

More than a hundred years after the invention of the steam engine, the Industrial Revolution had at last found its philosophy and its philosopher. Taylor's tight industrial choreography—his "system," as he liked to call it—was embraced by manufacturers throughout the country and, in time, around the world. Seeking maximum speed, maximum efficiency, and maximum output, factory owners used time-and-motion studies to organize their work and configure the jobs of their workers. The goal, as Taylor defined it in his celebrated 1911 treatise, *The Principles of Scientific Management*, was to identify and adopt, for every job, the "one best method" of work and thereby to effect "the gradual substitution of science for rule of thumb throughout the mechanic arts." Once his system was applied to all acts of manual labor, Taylor assured his followers, it would bring about a restructuring not only of industry but of society, creating a utopia of perfect efficiency. "In the past the man has been first," he declared; "in the future the system must be first."

Taylor's system is still very much with us; it remains the ethic of industrial manufacturing. And now, thanks to the growing power that computer engineers and software coders wield over our intellectual lives, Taylor's ethic is beginning to govern the realm of the mind as well. The Internet is a machine designed for the efficient and automated collection, transmission, and manipulation of information, and its legions of programmers are intent on finding the "one best method"—the perfect algorithm—to carry out every mental movement of what we've come to describe as "knowledge work."

Google's headquarters, in Mountain View, California—the Googleplex—is the Internet's high church, and the religion practiced inside its walls is Taylorism. Google, says its chief executive, Eric Schmidt, is "a company that's founded around the science of measurement," and it is striving to "systematize everything" it does. Drawing on the terabytes of behavioral data it collects through its search engine and other sites, it carries out thousands of experiments a day, according to the *Harvard Business Review*, and it uses the results to refine the algorithms that increasingly control how people find information and extract meaning from it. What Taylor did for the work of the hand, Google is doing for the work of the mind.

The company has declared that its mission is "to organize the world's information and make it universally accessible and useful." It seeks to develop "the perfect search engine," which it defines as something that "understands exactly what you mean and gives you back exactly what you want." In Google's view, information is a kind of commodity, a utilitarian resource that can be mined and processed with industrial efficiency. The more pieces of information we can "access" and the faster we can extract their gist, the more productive we become as thinkers.

Where does it end? Sergey Brin and Larry Page, the gifted young men who founded Google while pursuing doctoral degrees in computer science at Stanford, speak frequently of their desire to turn their search engine into an artificial intelligence, a HAL-like machine that might be connected directly to our brains. "The ultimate search engine is something as smart as people—or smarter," Page said in a speech a few years back. "For us, working on search is a way to work on artificial intelligence." In a 2004 interview with *Newsweek*, Brin said, "Certainly if you had all the world's information directly attached to your brain, or an artificial brain that was smarter than your brain, you'd be better off." Last year, Page told a convention of scientists that Google is "really trying to build artificial intelligence and to do it on a large scale."

Such an ambition is a natural one, even an admirable one, for a pair of math whizzes with vast quantities of cash at their disposal and a small army of computer scientists in their employ. A fundamentally scientific enterprise, Google is motivated by a desire to use technology, in Eric Schmidt's words, "to solve problems that have never been solved before," and artificial intelligence is the hardest problem out there. Why wouldn't Brin and Page want to be the ones to crack it?

Still, their easy assumption that we'd all "be better off" if our brains were supplemented, or even replaced, by an artificial intelligence is unsettling. It suggests a belief that intelligence is the output of a mechanical process, a series of discrete steps that can be isolated, measured, and optimized. In Google's world, the world we enter when we go online, there's little place for the fuzziness of contemplation. Ambiguity is not an opening for insight but a bug to be fixed. The human brain is just an outdated computer that needs a faster processor and a bigger hard drive.

The idea that our minds should operate as high-speed data-processing machines is not only built into the workings of the Internet, it is the network's reigning business model as well. The faster we surf across the Web—the more links we click and pages we view—the more opportunities Google and other companies gain to collect information about us and to feed us advertisements. Most of the proprietors of the commercial Internet have a financial stake in collecting the crumbs of data we leave behind as we flit from link to link—the more crumbs, the better. The last thing these companies want is to encourage leisurely reading or slow, concentrated thought. It's in their economic interest to drive us to distraction.

Maybe I'm just a worrywart. Just as there's a tendency to glorify technological progress, there's a countertendency to expect the worst of every new tool or machine. In Plato's *Phaedrus*, Socrates bemoaned the development of writing. He feared that, as people came to rely on the written word as a substitute for the knowledge they used to carry inside their heads, they would, in the words of one of the dialogue's characters, "cease to exercise their memory and become forgetful." And because they would be able to "receive a quantity of information without proper instruction," they would "be thought very knowledgeable when they are for the most part quite ignorant." They would be "filled with the conceit of wisdom instead of real wisdom." Socrates wasn't wrong—the new technology did often have the effects he feared—but he was shortsighted. He couldn't foresee the many ways that writing and reading would serve to spread information, spur fresh ideas, and expand human knowledge (if not wisdom).

The arrival of Gutenberg's printing press, in the 15th century, set off another round of teeth gnashing. The Italian humanist Hieronimo Squarciafico worried that the easy availability of books would lead to intellectual laziness, making men "less studious" and weakening their minds. Others argued that cheaply printed books and broadsheets would undermine religious authority, demean the work of scholars and scribes, and spread sedition and debauchery. As New York University professor Clay Shirky notes, "Most of the arguments made against the printing press were correct, even prescient." But, again, the doomsayers were unable to imagine the myriad blessings that the printed word would deliver.

So, yes, you should be skeptical of my skepticism. Perhaps those who dismiss critics of the Internet as Luddites or nostalgists will be proved correct, and from our hyperactive, data-stoked minds will spring a golden age of intellectual discovery and universal wisdom. Then again, the Net isn't the alphabet, and although it may replace the printing press, it produces something altogether different. The kind of deep reading that a sequence of printed pages promotes is valuable not just for the knowledge we acquire from the author's words but for the intellectual vibrations those words set off within our own minds. In the quiet spaces opened up by the sustained, undistracted reading of a book, or by any other act of contemplation, for that matter, we make our own associations, draw our own inferences and analogies, foster our own ideas. Deep reading, as Maryanne Wolf argues, is indistinguishable from deep thinking.

If we lose those quiet spaces, or fill them up with "content," we will sacrifice something important not only in our selves but in our culture. In a recent essay, the playwright Richard Foreman eloquently described what's at stake:

I come from a tradition of Western culture, in which the ideal (my ideal) was the complex, dense and "cathedral-like" structure of the highly educated and articulate personality—a man or woman who carried inside themselves a personally constructed and unique version of the entire heritage of the West. [But now] I see within us all (myself included) the replacement of complex inner density with a new kind of self—evolving under the pressure of information overload and the technology of the "instantly available."

As we are drained of our "inner repertory of dense cultural inheritance," Foreman concluded, we risk turning into "'pancake people'—spread wide and thin as we connect with that vast network of information accessed by the mere touch of a button."

I'm haunted by that scene in *2001*. What makes it so poignant, and so weird, is the computer's emotional response to the disassembly of its mind: its despair as one circuit after another goes dark, its childlike pleading with the astronaut—"I can feel it. I can feel it. I'm afraid"—and its final reversion to what can only be called a state of innocence. HAL's outpouring of feeling contrasts with the emotionlessness that characterizes the human figures in the film, who go about their business with an almost robotic efficiency. Their thoughts and actions feel scripted, as if they're following the steps of an algorithm. In the world of *2001*, people have become so machinelike that the most human character turns out to be a machine. That's the essence of Kubrick's dark prophecy: as we come to rely on computers to mediate our understanding of the world, it is our own intelligence that flattens into artificial intelligence.

Indian Education

SHERMAN ALEXIE

INDIAN EDUCATION

Alexie attended the tribal school on the Spokane reservation through the seventh grade, when he decided to seek a better education at an off-reservation all-white high school. As this year-by-year account of his schooling makes clear, he was not firmly at home in either setting. The essay first appeared in Alexie's *The Lone Ranger* and *Tonto Fistfight in Heaven*.

FIRST GRADE

My hair was too short and my US Government glasses were horn-rimmed, ugly, and all that first winter in school, the other Indian boys chased me from one comer of the playground to the other. They pushed me down, buried me in the snow until I couldn't breathe, thought I'd never breathe again.

They stole my glasses and threw them over my head, around my out-stretched hands, just beyond my reach, until someone tripped me and sent me falling again, facedown in the snow.

I was always falling down; my Indian name was Junior Falls Down. Sometimes it was Bloody Nose or Steal-His-Lunch. Once, it was Cries-Like-a-White-Boy, even though none of us had seen a white boy cry.

Then it was a Friday morning recess and Frenchy SiJohn threw snowballs at me while the rest of the Indian boys tortured some other top-yogh-yaught kid, another weakling. But Frenchy was confident enough to torment me all by himself, and most days I would have let him.

But the little warrior in me roared to life that day and knocked Frenchy to the ground, held his head against the snow, and punched him so hard that my knuckles and the snow made symmetrical bruises on his face. He almost looked like he was wearing war paint.

But he wasn't the warrior. I was. And I chanted *It's a good day to die, it's a good day to die,* all the way down to the principal's office.

SECOND GRADE

Betty Towle, missionary teacher, redheaded and so ugly that no one ever had a puppy crush on her, made me stay in for recess fourteen days straight.

"Tell me you're sorry," she said.

"Sorry for what?" I asked.

"Everything," she said and made me stand straight for fifteen minutes, eagle-armed with books in each hand. One was a math book; the other was English. But all I learned was that gravity can be painful.

For Halloween I drew a picture of her riding a broom with a scrawny cat on the back. She said that her God would never forgive me for that.

Once, she gave the class a spelling test but set me aside and gave me a test designed for junior high students. When I spelled all the words right, she crumpled up the paper and made me eat it.

"You'll learn respect," she said.

She sent a letter home with me that told my parents to either cut my braids or keep me home from class. My parents came in the next day and dragged their braids across Betty Towle's desk.

"Indians, indians, indians." She said it without capitalization. She called me "indian, indian, indian."

And I said, *Yes, I am. I am Indian. Indian, I am.*

THIRD GRADE

My traditional Native American art career began and ended with my very first portrait: *Stick Indian Taking a Piss in My Backyard.*

As I circulated the original print around the classroom, Mrs. Schluter intercepted and confiscated my art.

Censorship, I might cry now. *Freedom of expression,* I would write in editorials to the tribal newspaper.

In third grade, though, I stood alone in the corner, faced the wall, and waited for the punishment to end.

I'm still waiting.

FOURTH GRADE

"You should be a doctor when you grow up," Mr. Schluter told me, even though his wife, the third grade teacher, thought I was crazy beyond my years. My eyes always looked like I had just hit-and-run someone.

"Guilty," she said. "You always look guilty."

"Why should I be a doctor?" I asked Mr. Schluter.

"So you can come back and help the tribe. So you can heal people."

That was the year my father drank a gallon of vodka a day and the same year that my mother started two hundred different quilts but never finished any. They sat in separate, dark places in our HUD[1] house and wept savagely.

I ran home after school, heard their Indian tears, and looked in the mirror. *Doctor Victor,* I called myself, invented an education, talked to my reflection. *Doctor Victor to the emergency room.*

FIFTH GRADE

I picked up a basketball for the first time and made my first shot. No. I missed my first shot, missed the basket completely, and the ball landed in the dirt and sawdust, sat there just like I had sat there only minutes before.

But it felt good, that ball in my hands, all those possibilities and angles. It was mathematics, geometry. It was beautiful.

At that same moment, my cousin Steven Ford sniffed rubber cement from a paper bag and leaned back on the merry-go-round. His ears rang, his mouth was dry, and everyone seemed so far away.

But it felt good, that buzz in his head, all those colors and noises. It was chemistry, biology. It was beautiful.

Oh, do you remember those sweet, almost innocent choices that the Indian boys were forced to make?

SIXTH GRADE

Randy, the new Indian kid from the white town of Springdale, got into a fight an hour after he first walked into the reservation school.

Stevie Flett called him out, called him a squawman, called him a pussy, and called him a punk.

---

1. Housing and Urban Development, a US government department—Eds.

Randy and Stevie, and the rest of the Indian boys, walked out into the playground.

"Throw the first punch," Stevie said as they squared off.

"No," Randy said.

"Throw the first punch," Stevie said again.

"No," Randy said again.

"Throw the first punch!" Stevie said for the third time, and Randy reared back and pitched a knuckle fastball that broke Stevie's nose.

We all stood there in silence, in awe.

That was Randy, my soon-to-be first and best friend, who taught me the most valuable lesson about living in the white world: *Always throw the first punch.*

SEVENTH GRADE

I leaned through the basement window of the HUD house and kissed the white girl who would later be raped by her foster-parent father, who was also white. They both lived on the reservation, though, and when the headlines and stories filled the papers later, not one word was made of their color.

Just Indians being Indians, someone must have said somewhere and they were wrong.

But on the day I leaned through the basement window of the HUD house and kissed the white girl, I felt the good-byes I was saying to my entire tribe. I held my lips tight against her lips, a dry, clumsy, and ultimately stupid kiss.

But I was saying good-bye to my tribe, to all the Indian girls and women I might have loved, to all the Indian men who might have called me cousin, even brother.

I kissed that white girl and when I opened my eyes, she was gone from the reservation, and when I opened my eyes, I was gone from the reservation, living in a farm town where a beautiful white girl asked my name.

"Junior Polatkin," I said, and she laughed.

After that, no one spoke to me for another five hundred years.

EIGHTH GRADE

At the farm town junior high, in the boys' bathroom, I could hear voices from the girls' bathroom, nervous whispers of anorexia and bulimia. I could hear the white girls' forced vomiting, a sound so familiar and natural to me after years of listening to my father's hangovers.

"Give me your lunch if you're just going to throw it up," I said to one of those girls once.

I sat back and watched them grow skinny from self-pity.

Back on the reservation, my mother stood in line to get us commodities. We carried them home, happy to have food, and opened the canned beef that even the dogs wouldn't eat.

But we ate it day after day and grew skinny from self-pity.

There is more than one way to starve.

NINTH GRADE

At the farm town high school dance, after a basketball game in an over-heated gym where I had scored twenty-seven points and pulled down thirteen rebounds, I passed out during a slow song.

As my white friends revived me and prepared to take me to the emergency room where doctors would later diagnose my diabetes, the Chicano teacher ran up to us.

"Hey," he said. "What's that boy been drinking? I know all about these Indian kids. They start drinking real young."

Sharing dark skin doesn't necessarily make two men brothers.

TENTH GRADE

I passed the written test easily and nearly flunked the driving, but still received my Washington State driver's license on the same day that Wally Jim killed himself by driving his car into a pine tree.

No traces of alcohol in his blood, good job, wife and two kids.

"Why'd he do it?" asked a white Washington State trooper.

All the Indians shrugged their shoulders, looked down at the ground.

"Don't know," we all said, but when we look in the mirror, see the history of our tribe in our eyes, taste failure in the tap water, and shake with old tears, we understand completely.

Believe me, everything looks like a noose if you stare at it long enough.

ELEVENTH GRADE

Last night I missed two free throws which would have won the game against the best team in the state. The farm town high school I play for is nicknamed the "Indians," and I'm probably the only actual Indian ever to play for a team with such a mascot.

This morning I pick up the sports page and read the headline: INDIANS LOSE AGAIN.

Go ahead and tell me none of this is supposed to hurt me very much.

TWELFTH GRADE

I walk down the aisle, valedictorian of this farm town high school, and my cap doesn't fit because I've grown my hair longer than it's ever been. Later, I stand as the school-board chairman recites my awards, accomplishments, and scholarships.

I try to remain stoic for the photographers as I look toward the future.

Back home on the reservation, my former classmates graduate: a few can't read, one or two are just given attendance diplomas, most look forward to the parties. The bright students are shaken, frightened, because they don't know what comes next.

They smile for the photographer as they look back toward tradition.

The tribal newspaper runs my photograph and the photograph of my former classmates side by side.

POSTSCRIPT: CLASS REUNION

Victor said, "Why should we organize a reservation high school reunion? My graduating class has a reunion every weekend at the Powwow Tavern."

Coming to an Awareness of Language

MALCOLM X

I've never been one for inaction. Everything I've ever felt strongly about, I've done something about. I guess that's why, unable to do anything else, I soon began writing to people I had known in the hustling world, such as Sammy the Pimp, John Hughes, the gambling house owner, the thief Jumpsteady, and several dope peddlers. I wrote them all about Allah and Islam and Mr. Elijah Muhammad. I had no idea where most of them lived. I addressed their letters in care of the Harlem or Roxbury bars and clubs where I'd known them.

I never got a single reply. The average hustler and criminal was too uneducated to write a letter. I have known many slick, sharp-looking hustlers, who would have you think they had an interest in Wall Street; privately, they would get someone else to read a letter if they received one. Besides, neither would I have replied to anyone writing me something as wild as "the white man is the devil."

What certainly went on the Harlem and Roxbury wires was that Detroit Red was going crazy in stir, or else he was trying some hype to shake up the warden's office.

During the years that I stayed in the Norfolk Prison Colony, never did any official directly say anything to me about those letters, although, of course, they all passed through the prison censorship. I'm sure, however, they monitored what I wrote to add to the files which every state and federal prison keeps on the conversion of Negro inmates by the teachings of Mr. Elijah Muhammad.

But at that time, I felt that the real reason was that the white man knew that he was the devil.

Later on, I even wrote to the Mayor of Boston, to the Governor of Massachusetts, and to Harry S. Truman. They never answered; they probably never even saw my letters. I handscratched to them how the white man's society was responsible for the black man's condition in this wilderness of North America.

It was because of my letters that I happened to stumble upon starting to acquire some kind of a homemade education.

I became increasingly frustrated at not being able to express what I wanted to convey in letters that I wrote, especially those to Mr. Elijah Muhammad. In the street, I had been the most articulate hustler out there—I had commanded attention when I said something. But now, trying to write simple English, I not only wasn't articulate, I wasn't even functional. How would I sound writing in slang, the way I would say it, something such as, "Look, daddy, let me pull your coat about a cat, Elijah Muhammad—"

Many who today hear me somewhere in person, or on television, or those who read something I've said, will think I went to school far beyond the eighth grade. This impression is due entirely to my prison studies.

It had really begun back in the Charlestown Prison, when Bimbi first made me feel envy of his stock of knowledge. Bimbi had always taken charge of any conversation he was in, and I had tried to emulate him. But every book I picked up had few sentences which didn't contain anywhere from one to nearly all of the words that might as well have been in Chinese. When I just skipped those words, of course, I really ended up with little idea of what the book said. So I had come to the Norfolk Prison Colony still going through only book-reading motions. Pretty soon, I would have quit even these motions, unless I had received the motivation that I did.

I saw that the best thing I could do was get hold of a dictionary—to study, to learn some words. I was lucky enough to reason also that I should try to improve my penmanship. It was sad. I couldn't even write in a straight line. It was both ideas together that moved me to request a dictionary along with some tablets and pencils from the Norfolk Prison Colony school.

I spent two days just riffling uncertainly through the dictionary's pages. I'd never realized so many words existed! I didn't know which words I needed to learn. Finally, just to start some kind of action, I began copying.

In my slow, painstaking, ragged handwriting, I copied into my tablet everything printed on that first page, down to the punctuation marks.

I believe it took me a day. Then, aloud, I read back, to myself, everything I'd written on the tablet. Over and over, aloud, to myself, I read my own handwriting.

I woke up the next morning, thinking about those words—immensely proud to realize that not only had I written so much at one time, but I'd written words that I never knew were in the world. Moreover, with a little effort, I also could remember what many of these words meant. I reviewed the words whose meanings I didn't remember. Funny thing, from the dictionary first page right now, that "aardvark" springs to my mind. The dictionary had a picture of it, a long-tailed, long-eared, burrowing African mammal, which lives off termites caught by sticking out its tongue as an anteater does for ants.

I was so fascinated that I went on—I copied the dictionary's next page. And the same experience came when I studied that. With every succeeding page, I also learned of people and places and events from history. Actually the dictionary is like a miniature encyclopedia. Finally the dictionary's A section had filled a whole tablet—and I went on into the B's. That was the way I started copying what eventually became the entire dictionary. It went a lot faster after so much practice helped me to pick up handwriting speed. Between what I wrote in my tablet, and writing letters, during the rest of my time in prison I would guess I wrote a million words.

I suppose it was inevitable that as my word-base broadened, I could for the first time pick up a book and read and now begin to understand what the book was saying. Anyone who has read a great deal can imagine the new world that opened. Let me tell you something: from then until I left that prison, in every free moment I had, if I was not reading in the library, I was reading on my bunk. You couldn't have gotten me out of books with a wedge. Between Mr. Muhammad's teachings, my correspondence, my visitors . . . and my reading of books, months passed without my even thinking about being imprisoned. In fact, up to then, I never had been so truly free in my life.

Explaining White Privilege to a Broke White Person

GINA CROSLEY-CORCORAN

Years ago some feminist on the Internet told me I was "privileged."

"THE F&CK!?!?" I said.

I came from the kind of poor that people don't want to believe still exists in this country. Have you ever spent a frigid northern-Illinois winter without heat or running water? I have. At 12 years old were you making ramen noodles in a coffee maker with water you fetched from a public bathroom? I was. Have you ever lived in a camper year-round and used a random relative's apartment as your mailing address? We did. Did you attend so many different elementary schools that you can only remember a quarter of their names? Welcome to my childhood.

This is actually a much nicer trailer setup than the one I grew up in.

So when that feminist told me I had "white privilege," I told her that my white skin didn't do shit to prevent me from experiencing poverty. Then, like any good, educated feminist would, she directed me to Peggy McIntosh's now-famous 1988 piece "White Privilege: Unpacking the Invisible Knapsack."

After one reads McIntosh's powerful essay, it's impossible to deny that being born with white skin in America affords people certain unearned privileges in life that people of other skin colors simply are not afforded. For example:

"I can turn on the television or open to the front page of the paper and see people of my race widely represented."

"When I am told about our national heritage or about 'civilization,' I am shown that people of my color made it what it is."

"If a traffic cop pulls me over or if the IRS audits my tax return, I can be sure I haven't been singled out because of my race."

"I can if I wish arrange to be in the company of people of my race most of the time."

If you read through the rest of the list, you can see how white people and people of color experience the world in very different ways. But listen: This is not said to make white people feel guilty about their privilege. It's not your fault that you were born with white skin and experience these privileges. But whether you realize it or not, you *do* benefit from it, and it *is* your fault if you don't maintain awareness of that fact.

I do understand that McIntosh's essay may rub some people the wrong way. There are several points on the list that I felt spoke more to the author's status as a middle-class person than to her status as a white person. For example:

"If I should need to move, I can be pretty sure of renting or purchasing housing in an area, which I can afford and in which I would want to live."

"I can be pretty sure that my neighbors in such a location will be neutral or pleasant to me."

"I can go shopping alone most of the time, pretty well assured that I will not be followed or harassed."

"If I want to, I can be pretty sure of finding a publisher for this piece on white privilege."

And there are so many more points in the essay where the word "class" could be substituted for the word "race," which would ultimately paint a very different picture. That is why I had such a hard time identifying with this essay for so long. When I first wrote about white privilege years ago, I demanded to know why this white woman felt that my experiences were the same as hers when, no, my family most certainly could not rent housing "in an area which we could afford and want to live," and no, I couldn't go shopping without fear in our low-income neighborhoods.

The idea that any ol' white person can find a publisher for a piece is most certainly a symptom of class privilege. Having come from a family of people who didn't even graduate from high school, who knew not a single academic or intellectual person, it would never occur to me to assume that I could be published. It is absolutely a freak anomaly that I'm in graduate school, considering that not one person on either side of my family has a college degree. And it took me until my 30s to ever believe that someone from my stock could achieve such a thing. Poverty colors nearly everything about your perspective on opportunities for advancement in life. Middle-class, educated people assume that anyone can achieve their goals if they work hard enough. Folks steeped in poverty rarely see a life past working at the gas station, making the rent on their trailer, and self-medicating with cigarettes and prescription drugs until they die of a heart attack. (I've just described one whole side of my family and the life I assumed I'd be living before I lucked out of it.)

I, maybe more than most people, can completely understand why broke white folks get pissed when the word "privilege" is thrown around. As a child I was constantly discriminated against because of my poverty, and those wounds still run very deep. But luckily my college education introduced me to a more nuanced concept of privilege: the term "intersectionality." The concept of intersectionality recognizes that people can be privileged in some ways and definitely not privileged in others. There are many different types of privilege, not just skin-color privilege, that impact the way people can move through the world or are discriminated against. These are all things you are born into, not things you earned, that afford you opportunities that others may not have. For example:

▶ **Citizenship:** Simply being born in this country affords you certain privileges that non-citizens will never access.

▶ **Class:** Being born into a financially stable family can help guarantee your health, happiness, safety, education, intelligence, and future opportunities.

▶ **Sexual orientation:** If you were born straight, every state in this country affords you privileges that non-straight folks have to fight the Supreme Court for.

▶ **Sex:** If you were born male, you can assume that you can walk through a parking garage without worrying that you'll be raped and then have to deal with a defense attorney blaming it on what you were wearing.

▶ **Ability:** If you were born able-bodied, you probably don't have to plan your life around handicap access, braille, or other special needs.

▶ **Gender identity:** If you were born cisgender (that is, your gender identity matches the sex you were assigned at birth), you don't have to worry that using the restroom or locker room will invoke public outrage.

As you can see, belonging to one or more category of privilege, especially being a straight, white, middle-class, able-bodied male, can be like winning a lottery you didn't even know you were playing. But this is not to imply that any form of privilege is exactly the same as another, or that people lacking in one area of privilege understand what it's like to be lacking in other areas. Race discrimination is not equal to sex discrimination and so forth.

And listen: Recognizing privilege doesn't mean suffering guilt or shame for your lot in life. Nobody's saying that straight, white, middle-class, able-bodied males are all a bunch of assholes who don't work hard for what they have. Recognizing privilege simply means being aware that some people have to work much harder just to experience the things you take for granted (if they ever can experience them at all).

I know now that I *am* privileged in many ways. I am privileged as a natural-born white citizen. I am privileged as a cisgender woman. I am privileged as an able-bodied person. I am privileged that my first language is also our national language, and that I was born with an intellect and ambition that pulled me out of the poverty that I was otherwise destined for. I was privileged to be able to marry my way "up" by partnering with a privileged, middle-class, educated male who fully expected me to earn a college degree.

There are a million ways I experience privilege, and some that I certainly don't. But thankfully, intersectionality allows us to examine these varying dimensions and degrees of discrimination while raising awareness of the results of multiple systems of oppression at work.

Tell me: Are you a white person who's felt uncomfortable with the term "white privilege"? Does a more nuanced approach help you see your own privilege more clearly?

Marie Kondo and the Privilege of Clutter

ARIELLE BERNSTEIN

At every wedding I've been to this past year, the event space has been decorated with family portraits—black-and-white photos of grandmothers and grandfathers, pictures of parents with giant smiles and '70s hairstyles. Meanwhile, the bride and groom wear family relics and heirlooms: jewelry passed from mother to daughter, cufflinks and ties passed from father to son.

As a child I used to cry when looking at those kinds of photos and mementos. But it wasn't until this past summer when I was planning my own wedding that I understood just why these kinds of items inspired so many complicated feelings. When my now-husband asked if we wanted to make a slideshow of our family photos for our own wedding, I realized we barely had any. Both my grandmother and grandfather emigrated from Poland to Cuba in the years preceding the Holocaust: my grandmother by boat with her mother in 1930 when she was 8 years old, and my grandfather in 1937, at the age of 18. They fell in love with each other and the country that took them in, even as they grieved the family members who didn't make it out alive.

After Fidel Castro came to power in 1959, their lives changed once more. Their small store was closed for periods of time by the government (the boards covering their storefront were frequently graffitied with threatening swastikas, a sign that they may not have entirely escaped the frightening environment they tried to leave in Europe). As the revolution began, material comforts began to disappear. Eventually, their business and home were both shut down by the Cuban government and, in 1968, my grandparents, mother, and aunt came to the U.S., leaving everything but a few pieces of clothing behind.

In the U.S,. my grandparents and mother responded to the trauma they'd experienced by holding on to things. My grandfather was a collector who was prone to hoarding. He'd often find random trinkets on the street and bring them home, and he kept everything, from books to receipts to costume jewelry. My grandmother and my mother were more practical, saving and storing canned foods, socks, and pantyhose. In my home, we didn't throw out food or plastic bags, or clothing that was out of style but that still fit us. We saved everything.

Today, when my mother comes to visit she still brings bags full of useful items, from Goya beans to cans of tuna fish and coffee: things she knows will last us for months and months. It doesn't matter if I tell her we just went to the store, or that we have plenty of food, or that I don't need any more socks or underwear. A full pantry, a house stocked with usable objects, is the ultimate expression of love.

As a girl growing up in the U.S., I was often exhausted by this proliferation of items—by what seemed to me to be an old-world expression of maternal love. Like many who are privileged enough to not have to worry about having basic things, I tend to idolize the opposite—the empty spaces of yoga studios, the delightful feeling of sorting through a pile of stuff that I can discard. I'm not alone in appreciating the lightness and freedom of a minimalist lifestyle. The KonMari method, a popular practical philosophy for de-cluttering your home, has tapped into a major cultural zeitgeist.

Since the Japanese "professional organizer" Marie Kondo's *The Life-Changing Magic of Tidying Up* was released in 2014, it's become a *New York Times* bestseller and sold over 3 million copies. Kondo's tips on de-cluttering have been featured everywhere from *The Today Show* to *Real Simple* to *The Guardian*, and have inspired the follow-ups *Spark Joy*, an illustrated guide to tidying things up even more, and *Life-Changing Magic*, a journal where you can ruminate on the pleasures of owning only your most cherished personal belongings.

It doesn't matter if I tell her we just went to the store. A full pantry, a house stocked with usable objects, is the ultimate expression of love.

At its heart, the KonMari method is a quest for purity. To Kondo, living your life surrounded by unnecessary items is "undisciplined," while a well-tidied house filled with only the barest essentials is the ultimate sign of personal fulfillment. Kondo's method involves going through all the things you own to determine whether or not they inspire feelings of joy. If something doesn't immediately provoke a sense of happiness and contentment, you should get rid of it.

Kondo seems suspicious of the idea that our relationship with items might change over time. She instructs her readers to get rid of books we never finished, and clothes we only wore once or twice. She warns us not to give our precious things to our family and friends, unless they expressly ask for them. She's especially skeptical of items that have sentimental value. In her first book, *The Life-Changing Magic of Tidying Up*, Kondo says,

Just as the word implies, mementos are reminders of a time when these items gave us joy. The thought of disposing them sparks the fear that we'll lose those precious memories along with them. But you don't need to worry. Truly precious memories will never vanish even if you discard the objects associated with them … No matter how wonderful things used to be, we cannot live in the past. The joy and excitement we feel in the here and now are most important.

Throughout *Spark Joy*, Kondo includes adorable minimalist drawings of happily organized bathrooms, kitchens and closets. Sometimes she even includes drawings of anthropomorphized forest animals lovingly placing items into drawers using the KonMari method.

Kondo is unfailingly earnest in her assertion that the first step to having a joyful life is through mindful consideration of your possessions. Emotions throughout both of her books are presented as being as simple as her drawings. You either feel pure love for an object or you let it go. But beneath some of the self-help-inspired platitudes about how personally enriched you'll feel after you've discarded items you don't need, there's an underlying tone of judgment about the emotional well-being of those who submit to living in clutter. Those who live in KonMari homes are presented as being more disciplined: invulnerable to the throes of nostalgia, impervious to the temptation of looking back at something that provokes mixed feelings.

Though an article on Gwyneth Paltrow's wellness website *Goop* claims that American culture is the embodiment of excess, it's pretty clear to me why the KonMari Method has caught on in the U.S. A recurring emphasis on self-improvement and an obsession with restriction can be found in everything from diet trends (where we learn to cut calories in order to be smaller and less encumbered by literal weight), to the consumer culture fixation with replacing old things that no longer provide joy with new, "improved" things that will.

For affluent Americans who've never wanted for anything, Kondo sells an elegant fantasy of paring back and scaling down at a time when simplicity is a hot trend. The tiny-house movement, for example, urges consumers to eschew McMansion-style houses for the adorably twee simplicity of a 250-square-foot home.

If our life is made from the objects we collect over time, then surely our very sense of who we are is dependent upon the things we carry.

Of course, in order to feel comfortable throwing out all your old socks and handbags, you have to feel pretty confident that you can easily get new ones. Embracing a minimalist lifestyle is an act of trust. For a refugee, that trust has not yet been earned. The idea that going through items cheerfully evaluating whether or not objects inspire happiness is fraught for a family like mine, for whom cherished items have historically been taken away. For my grandparents, the question wasn't whether an item sparked joy, but whether it was necessary for their survival. In America, that obsession transformed into a love for all items, whether or not they were valuable in a financial or emotional sense. If our life is made from the objects we collect over time, then surely our very sense of who we are is dependent upon the things we carry.

It's particularly ironic that the KonMari Method has taken hold now, during a major refugee crisis, when the news constantly shows scenes of people fleeing their homes and everything they have. A *Vice* article, "All the Stuff Syrian Refugees Leave Behind During Their Journey to Europe" shows discarded things ranging from trash to toys to ticket stubs. Each item looks lonely and lost: like evidence of a life left behind. For a project titled "The Most Important Thing," the photographer Brian Sokol asks refugees to show him the most important thing they kept from the place they left behind. The items they proffer range from the necessary (crutches), to the practical (a sewing machine), to the deeply sentimental (photographs of someone deeply loved, treasured instruments, family pets).

Against this backdrop, Kondo's advice to live in the moment and discard the things you don't need seems to ignore some important truths about what it means to be human. It's easy to see the items we own as oppressive when we can so easily buy new ones. That we can only guess at the things we'll need in the future and that we don't always know how deeply we love something until it's gone.

In this way, I was built for the KonMari method in a way my mother never was. I grew up in a middle-class American home. While we were never wealthy, we also never truly wanted for material things. As an adolescent, I would tell my mother that I was an American, and that, as an American, I didn't have to be loyal to anything or anyone if I didn't want to. I'd throw away the last dregs of shampoo or toothpaste, which my mom would painstakingly rescue from the trash before scolding me for being so wasteful. I'd happily throw out or donate clothing I didn't want anymore.

My quick disposal of things always made my mother irreparably sad. She mourned the loss of my prom dress (which I gave to a friend) and the pots and pans she gave me for college (which I left in the group house I lived in), and she looked horrified when I once dumped a bunch of letters from friends and family in the trash. For me, being able to dispose of things has always been one of the ways I learned to identify as an American—a way to try and separate myself from the weight of growing up in a home where the important things that defined my family had long been lost.

It's easy to see the items we own as oppressive when we can so easily buy new ones.

To my mother, the KonMari method isn't joyful; it's cold. "Americans love throwing things away," she tells me, "And yet they are fascinated by the way that Cubans have maintained their houses, their cars. Yes, growing up we took great pleasure in preserving things. But we also didn't really have a choice."

Today, of course, my mother has plenty of choices, but throwing things away still makes her anxious. Now that my grandparents have both passed away, my mother still struggles to decide what to do with all that stuff. It's very painful for her, and my father's encouragement that she sift through everything, organize it in some kind of clearly delineated way, often falls on deaf ears.

A few months ago, when I was visiting home, my father asked if I would help go through some of the items. Now that he and my mom are older and my brother and I are grown, they've both expressed a desire to downsize. In the car, my dad recommended starting with my childhood bedroom, which looks exactly as it did when I was 14 years old, pink and purple, filled with childhood books and stuffed animals, half-filled journals, and never worn shoes. At first I was enthusiastic about the project. "We can give a lot of those things to charity," I said.

But at home, I sat in front of my bookshelf and did exactly what Kondo cautions most against: I started my project of decluttering by going through the things that mattered most to me: the books I loved when I was a child; the CDs made by dear friends and stacked high in no particular order; the college textbooks I never remembered to return. Objects imbued with memories of a person I once was, and a person that part of me always will be.

I didn't want to give any of it up.

Kondo says that we can appreciate the objects we used to love deeply just by saying goodbye to them. But for families that have experienced giving their dearest possessions up unwillingly, "putting things in order" is never going to be as simple as throwing things away. Everything they manage to hold onto matters deeply. Everything is confirmation they survived.

Toys

French toys: one could not find a better illustration of the fact that the adult Frenchman sees the child as another self. All the toys one commonly sees are essentially a microcosm of the adult world; they are all reduced copies of human objects, as if in the eyes of the public the child was, all told, nothing but a smaller man, a homunculus to whom must be supplied objects of his own size.

Invented forms are very rare: a few sets of blocks, which appeal to the spirit of do-it-yourself, are the only ones which offer dynamic forms. As for the others, French toys *always mean something*, and this something is always entirely socialized, constituted by the myths or the techniques of modern adult life: the Army, Broadcasting, the Post Office, Medicine (miniature instrument-cases, operating theaters for dolls), School, Hair-Styling (driers for permanent-waving), the Air Force (Parachutists), Transport (trains, Citroens, Vedettes, Vespas, petrol-stations), Science (Martian toys).

The fact that French toys *literally* prefigure the world of adult functions obviously cannot but prepare the child to accept them all, by constituting for him, even before he can think about it, the alibi of a Nature which has at all times created soldiers, postmen and Vespas. Toys here reveal the list of all the things the adult does not find unusual: war, bureaucracy, ugliness, Martians, etc. It is not so much, in fact, the imitation which is the sign of an abdication, as its literalness: French toys are like a Jivaro head, in which one recognizes, shrunken to the size of an apple, the wrinkles and hair of an adult. There exist, for instance, dolls which urinate; they have an oesophagus, one gives them a bottle, they wet their nappies; soon, no doubt, milk will turn to water in their stomachs. This is meant to prepare the little girl for the causality of house-keeping, to 'condition' her to her future role as mother. However, faced with this world of faithful and complicated objects, the child can only identify himself as owner, as user, never as creator; he does not invent the world, he uses it: there are, prepared for him, actions without adventure, without wonder, without joy. He is turned into a little stay-at-home householder who does not even have to invent the mainsprings of adult causality; they are supplied to him ready-made: he has only to help himself, he is never allowed to discover anything from start to finish. The merest set of blocks, provided it is not too refined, implies a very different learning of the world: then, the child does not in any way create meaningful objects, it matters little to him whether they have an adult name; the actions he performs are not those of a user but those of a demiurge. He creates forms which walk, which roll, he creates life, not property: objects now act by themselves, they are no longer an inert and complicated material in the palm of his hand. But such toys are rather rare: French toys are usually based on imitation, they are meant to produce children who are users, not creators.

The bourgeois status of toys can be recognized not only in their forms, which are all functional, but also in their substances. Current toys are made of a graceless material, the product of chemistry, not of nature. Many are now moulded from complicated mixtures; the plastic material of which they are made has an appearance at once gross and hygienic, it destroys all the pleasure, the sweetness, the humanity of touch. A sign which fills one with consternation is the gradual disappearance of wood, in spite of its being an ideal material because of its firmness and its softness, and the natural warmth of its touch. Wood removes, from all the forms which it supports, the wounding quality of angles which are too sharp, the chemical coldness of metal. When the child handles it and knocks it, it neither vibrates nor grates, it has a sound at once muffled and sharp. It is a familiar and poetic substance, which does not sever the child from close contact with the tree, the table, the floor. Wood does not wound or break down; it does not shatter, it wears out, it can last a long time, live with the child, alter little by little the relations between the object and the hand. If it dies, it is in dwindling, not in swelling out like those mechanical toys which disappear behind the hernia of a broken spring. Wood makes essential objects, objects for all time. Yet there hardly remain any of these wooden toys from the Vosges, these fretwork farms with their animals, which were only possible, it is true, in the days of the craftsman. Henceforth, toys are chemical in substance and color; their very material introduces one to a coenaesthesis of use, not pleasure. These toys die in fact very quickly, and once dead, they have no posthumous life for the child.

"I Just Called to Say I Love You"

Cell phones, sentimentality, and the decline of public space

JONATHAN FRANZEN

One of the great irritations of modern technology is that when some new development has made my life palpably worse and is continuing to find new and different ways to bedevil it, I'm still allowed to complain for only a year or two before the peddlers of coolness start telling me to get over it already Grampaw—this is just the way life is now.

I'm not opposed to technological developments. Digital voice mail and caller ID, which together destroyed the tyranny of the ringing telephone, seem to me two of the truly great inventions of the late 20th century. And how I love my BlackBerry, which lets me deal with lengthy, unwelcome e-mails in a few breathless telegraphic lines for which the recipient is nevertheless obliged to feel grateful, because I did it with my thumbs. And my noise-canceling headphones, on which I can blast frequency-shifted white noise ("pink noise") that drowns out even the most determined woofing of a neighbor's television set: I love them. And the whole wonderful world of DVD technology and high-definition screens, which have already spared me from so many sticky theater floors, so many rudely whispering cinema-goers, so many open-mouthed crunchers of popcorn: yes.

Privacy, to me, is not about keeping my personal life hidden from other people. It's about sparing me from the intrusion of other people's personal lives. And so, although my very favorite gadgets are actively privacy enhancing, I look kindly on pretty much any development that doesn't force me to interact with it. If you choose to spend an hour every day tinkering with your Facebook profile, or if you don't see any difference between reading Jane Austen on a Kindle and reading her on a printed page, or if you think Grand Theft Auto IV is the greatest Gesamtkunstwerk since Wagner, I'm very happy for you, as long as you keep it to yourself.

The developments I have a problem with are the insults that keep on insulting, the injuries of yesteryear that keep on giving pain. Airport TV, for example: it seems to be actively watched by about one traveler in ten (unless there's football on) while creating an active nuisance for the other nine. Year after year, in airport after airport, a small but apparently permanent diminution in the quality of the average traveler's life. Or, another example, the planned obsolescence of great software and its replacement by bad software. I'm still unable to accept that the best word-processing program ever written, WordPerfect 5.0 for DOS, won't even run on any computer I can buy now. Oh, sure, in theory you can still run it in

Windows' little DOS-emulating window, but the tininess and graphical crudeness of that emulator are like a deliberate insult on Microsoft's part to those of us who would prefer not to use a feature-heavy behemoth. WordPerfect 5.0 was hopelessly primitive for desktop publishing but unsurpassable for writers who wanted only to write. Elegant, bug-free, negligible in size, it was bludgeoned out of existence by the obese, intrusive, monopolistic, crash-prone Word. If I hadn't been collecting old 386s and 486s in my office closet, I wouldn't be able to use WordPerfect at all by now. And already I'm down to my last old 486. And yet people have the nerve to be annoyed with me if I won't send them texts in a format intelligible to all-powerful Word. We live in a Word world now, Grampaw. Time to take your GOI pill.

But these are mere annoyances. The technological development that has done lasting harm of real social significance–the development that, despite the continuing harm it does, you risk ridicule if you publicly complain about today–is the cell phone.

Just 10 years ago, New York City (where I live) still abounded with collectively maintained public spaces in which citizens demonstrated respect for their community by not inflicting their banal bedroom lives on it. The world 10 years ago was not yet fully conquered by yak. It was still possible to see the use of Nokias as an ostentation or an affectation of the affluent. Or, more generously, as an affliction or a disability or a crutch. There was unfolding, after all, in New York in the late 1990s, a seamless citywide transition from nicotine culture to cellular culture. One day the lump in the shirt pocket was Marlboros, the next day it was Motorola. One day the vulnerably unaccompanied pretty girl was occupying her hands and mouth and attention with a cigarette, the next day she was occupying them with a very important conversation with a person who wasn't you. One day a crowd gathered around the first kid on the playground with a pack of Kools, the next day around the first kid with a color screen. One day travelers were clicking lighters the second they were off an airplane, the next day they were speed-dialing. Pack-a-day habits became hundred-dollar monthly Verizon bills. Smoke pollution became sonic pollution. Although the irritant changed overnight, the suffering of a self-restrained majority at the hands of a compulsive minority, in restaurants and airports and other public spaces, remained eerily constant. Back in 1998, not long after I'd quit cigarettes, I would sit on the subway and watch other riders nervously folding and unfolding phones, or nibbling on the teatlike antennae that all the phones then had, or just quietly clutching their devices like a mother's hand, and I would feel something close to sorry for them. It still seemed to me an open question how far the trend would go: whether New York truly wanted to become a city of phone addicts sleepwalking down the sidewalks in icky little clouds of private life, or whether the notion of a more restrained public self might somehow prevail.

Needless to say, there wasn't any contest. The cell phone wasn't one of those modern developments, like Ritalin or oversized umbrellas, for which significant pockets of civilian resistance hearteningly persist. Its triumph was swift and total. Its abuses were lamented and bitched about in essays and columns and letters to various editors, and then lamented and bitched about more trenchantly when the abuses seemed only to be getting worse, but that was the end of it. The complaints had been registered, some small token adjustments had been made (the "quiet car" on Amtrak trains; discreet little signs poignantly pleading for restraint in restaurants and gyms), and cellular technology was then free to continue doing its damage without fear of further criticism, because further criticism would be unfresh and uncool. Grampaw.

But just because the problem is familiar to us now doesn't mean steam stops issuing from the ears of drivers trapped behind a guy chatting on his phone in a passing lane and staying perfectly abreast of a vehicle in the slow lane. And yet: everything in our commercial culture tells the chatty driver that he is in the right and tells everybody else that we are in the wrong–that we are failing to get with the attractively priced program of freedom and mobility and unlimited minutes. Commercial culture tells us that if we're sore with the chatty driver it must be because we're not having as good a time as he is. What is wrong with us, anyway? Why can't we lighten up a little and take out our own phones, with our own Friends and Family plans, and start having a better time ourselves, right there in the passing lane?

Socially retarded people don't suddenly start acting more adult when social critics are peer-pressured into silence. They only get ruder. One currently worsening national plague is the shopper who remains engrossed in a call throughout a transaction with a checkout clerk. The typical combination in my own neighborhood, in Manhattan, involves a young white woman, recently graduated from someplace expensive, and a local black or Hispanic woman of roughly the same age but fewer advantages. It is, of course, a liberal vanity to expect your checkout clerk to interact with you or to appreciate the scrupulousness of your determination to interact with her. Given the repetitive and low-paying nature of her job, she's allowed to treat you with boredom or indifference; at worst, it's unprofessional of her. But this does not relieve you of your own moral obligation to acknowledge her existence as a person. And while it's true that some clerks don't seem to mind being ignored, a notably large percentage do become visibly irritated or angered or saddened when a customer is unable to tear herself off her phone for even two seconds of direct interaction. Needless to say, the offender herself, like the chatty freeway driver, is blissfully unaware of pissing anybody off. In my experience, the longer the line behind her, the more likely it is she'll pay for her $1.98 purchase with a credit card. And not the tap-and-go microchip kind of credit card, either, but the wait-for-the-printed-receipt-and-then-(only then)-with-zombiesh-clumsiness-begin-shifting-the-cell-phone-from-one-ear-to-the-other-and-awkwardly-pin-the-phone-with-ear-to-shoulder-while-signing-the-receipt-and-continuing-to-express-doubt-about-whether-she-really-feels-like-meeting-up-with-that-Morgan-Stanley-guy-Zachary-at-the-Etats-Unis-wine-bar-again-tonight kind of credit card.

There is, to be sure, one positive social consequence of these worsening misbehaviors. The abstract notion of civilized public spaces, as rare resources worth defending, may be all but dead, but there's still consolation to be found in the momentary ad hoc microcommunities of fellow sufferers that bad behaviors create. To look out your car window and see the steam coming out of another driver's ears, or to meet the eyes of a pissed-off checkout clerk and to shake your head along with her: it makes you feel a little less alone.

Which is why, of all the worsening varieties of bad cell-phone behavior, the one that most deeply irritates me is the one that seems, because it is ostensibly victimless, to irritate nobody else. I'm talking about the habit, uncommon 10 years ago, now ubiquitous, of ending cell-phone conversations by braying the words "LOVE YOU!" Or, even more oppressive and grating: "I LOVE YOU!" It makes me want to go and live in China, where I don't understand the language. It makes me want to scream.

The cellular component of my irritation is straightforward. I simply do not, while buying socks at the Gap, or standing in a ticket line and pursuing my private thoughts, or trying to read a novel on a plane that's being boarded, want to be imaginatively drawn into the sticky world of some nearby human being's home life. The very essence of the cell phone's hideousness, as a social phenomenon–the bad news that stays bad news–is that it enables and encourages the inflicting of the personal and individual on the public and communal. And there is no higher-caliber utterance than "I love you"–nothing worse that an individual can inflict on a communal public space. Even "Fuck you, dickhead" is less invasive, since it's the kind of thing that angry people do sometimes shout in public, and it can just as easily be directed at a stranger.

My friend Elisabeth assures me that the new national plague of love yous is a good thing: a healthy reaction against the repressed family dynamics of our Protestant childhoods some decades ago. What could be wrong, Elisabeth asks, with telling your mother that you love her, or with hearing from her that she loves you? What if one of you dies before you can speak again? Isn't it nice that we can say these things to each other so freely now?

I do here admit the possibility that, compared with everyone else on the airport concourse, I am an extraordinarily cold and unloving person; that the sudden overwhelming sensation of loving somebody (a friend, a spouse, a parent, a sibling), which to me is such an important and signal sensation that I'm at pains not to wear out the phrase that best expresses it, is for other people so common and routine and easily achieved that it can be reëxperienced and reëxpressed many times in a single day without significant loss of power.

It's also possible, however, that too-frequent habitual repetition empties phrases of their meaning. Joni Mitchell, in the last verse of "Both Sides Now," referenced the solemn amazement of saying I love you "right out loud": of giving vocal birth to such intensity of feeling. Stevie Wonder, in lyrics written 17 years later, sings of calling somebody up on an ordinary afternoon simply to say "I love you," and being Stevie Wonder (who probably really is a more loving person than I am), he half succeeds in making me believe in his sincerity–at least until the last line of the chorus, where he finds it necessary to add: "And I mean it from the bottom of my heart." No such avowal is thinkable for the person who really does mean something from the bottom of his heart.

And, just so, when I'm buying those socks at the Gap and the mom in line behind me shouts "I love you!" into her little phone, I am powerless not to feel that something is being performed; overperformed; publicly performed; defiantly inflicted. Yes, a lot of domestic things get shouted in public which really aren't intended for public consumption; yes, people get carried away. But the phrase "I love you" is too important and loaded, and its use as a sign-off too self-conscious, for me to believe I'm being made to hear it accidentally. If the mother's declaration of love had genuine, private emotional weight, wouldn't she take at least a little care to guard it from public hearing? If she truly meant what she was saying, from the bottom of her heart, wouldn't she have to say it quietly? Overhearing her, as a stranger, I have the feeling of being made party to an aggressive assertion of entitlement. At a minimum, the person is saying to me and to everyone else present: "My emotions and my family are more important to me than your social comfort." And also, often enough, I suspect: "I want you all to know that unlike many people, including my cold bastard of a father, I am the kind of person who always tells my loved ones that I love them."

Or am I, in my admittedly now rather lunatic-sounding irritation, simply projecting all this?

The cell phone came of age on September 11, 2001. Imprinted that day on our collective consciousness was the image of cell phones as conduits of intimacy for the desperate. In every too-loud I love you that I hear nowadays, as in the more general national orgy of connectedness–the imperative for parents and children to connect by phone once or twice or five or ten times daily–it's difficult not to hear an echo of those terrible, entirely appropriate, heartbreaking I love yous uttered on the four doomed planes and in the two doomed towers. And it's precisely this echo, the fact that it's an echo, the sentimentality of it, that so irritates me.

My own experience of 9/11 was anomalous for the lack of television in it. At nine in the morning, I got a phone call from my book editor, who, from his office window, had just seen the second plane hit the towers. I did immediately go to the nearest TV, in the conference room of the real-estate office downstairs from my apartment, and watch with a group of agents as first one tower and then the other went down. But then my girlfriend came home and we spent the rest of the day listening to the radio, checking the Internet, reassuring our families, and watching from our roof and from the middle of Lexington Avenue (which was filled with pedestrians streaming uptown) as the dust and smoke at the bottom of Manhattan diffused into a sickening pall. In the evening, we walked down to 42nd Street and met up with an out-of-town friend and found an unremarkable Italian restaurant in the West 40s which happened to be serving dinner. Every table was packed with people drinking heavily; the mood was wartime. I got another brief glimpse of a TV screen, this one showing the face of George W. Bush, as we were departing through the restaurant's bar. "He looks like a scared mouse," somebody said. Sitting on a 6 train at Grand Central, waiting for it to move, we watched a New York commuter angrily complain to a conductor about the lack of express service to the Bronx.

Three nights later, from 11:00 p.m. to nearly 3:00 a.m., I sat in a frigid room at ABC News from which I could see my fellow New Yorker David Halberstam and speak by video link to Maya Angelou and a couple of other out-of-town writers while we waited to offer Ted Koppel a literary perspective on Tuesday morning's attacks. The wait was not short. Footage of the attacks and the ensuing collapses and fires was shown again and again, interspersed with long segments on the emotional toll on ordinary citizens and their impressionable children. Every once in a while, one or two of us writers would have 60 seconds to say something writerly before the coverage reverted to more carnage and wrenching interviews with friends and family of the dead and the missing. I spoke four times in three and a half hours. The second time, I was asked to confirm widespread reports that Tuesday's attacks had profoundly changed the personality of New Yorkers. I could not confirm these reports. I said that the faces I had seen were somber, not angry, and I described seeing people shopping in the stores in my neighborhood on Wednesday afternoon, buying fall clothes. Ted Koppel, in his response, made clear that I'd failed at the task I'd been waiting half the night to perform. With a frown, he said that his own impression was very different: that the attacks had indeed profoundly changed the personality of New York City.

Naturally, I assumed that I was speaking truth and Koppel merely retransmitting received opinion. But Koppel had been watching TV and I had not. I didn't understand that the worst damage to the country was being done not by the pathogen but by the immune system's massive overresponse to it, because I didn't have a TV. I was mentally comparing Tuesday's death toll with other tallies of violent death–3,000 Americans killed in traffic accidents in the 30 days preceding September 11–because, not seeing the images, I thought the numbers mattered. I was devoting energy to imagining, or resisting imagining, the horror of sitting in a window seat while your plane came in low along the West Side Highway, or of being trapped on the 95th floor and hearing the steel structure below you begin to groan and rumble, while the rest of the country was experiencing actual real-time trauma by watching the same footage over and over. And so I was not in need of–was, for a while, not even aware of–the national televised group therapy session, the vast techno-hugathon, that unfolded in the following days and weeks and months in response to the trauma of exposure to televised images.

What I could see was the sudden, mysterious, disastrous sentimentalization of American public discourse. And just as I can't help blaming cellular technology when people pour parental or filial affection into their phones and rudeness onto every stranger within earshot, I can't help blaming media technology for the national foregrounding of the personal. Unlike in, say, 1941, when the United States responded to a terrible attack with collective resolve and discipline and sacrifice, in 2001 we had terrific visuals. We had amateur footage and could break it down frame by frame. We had screens to bring the violence raw into every bedroom in the country, and voice mail to record the desperate final calls of the doomed, and late-model psychology to explicate and heal our trauma. But as for what the attacks actually signified, and what a sensible response to them might look like, attitudes varied. This was the wonderful thing about digital technology: No more hurtful censoring of anybody's feelings! Everybody entitled to express his or her own opinion! Whether or not Saddam Hussein had personally bought plane tickets for the hijackers therefore remained open to lively debate. What everybody agreed to agree on, instead, was that the families of 9/11's victims had a right to approve or veto plans for the memorial at Ground Zero. And everybody could share in the pain experienced by the families of the fallen cops and firefighters. And everybody agreed that irony was dead. The bad, empty irony of the '90s was simply "no longer possible" post-9/11; we'd stepped forward into a new age of sincerity.

On the plus side, Americans in 2001 were a lot better at saying "I love you" to their children than their fathers or grandfathers had been. But competing economically? Pulling together as a nation? Defeating our enemies? Forming strong international alliances? Perhaps a bit of a minus side there.

My parents met two years after Pearl Harbor, in the fall of 1943, and within a few months they were exchanging cards and letters. My father worked for the Great Northern Railway and was often on the road, in small towns, inspecting or repairing bridges, while my mother stayed in Minneapolis and worked as a receptionist. Of the letters from him to her in my possession, the oldest is from Valentine's Day 1944. He was in Fairview, Montana, and my mother had sent him a Valentine's card in the style of all her cards in the year leading up to their marriage: sweetly drawn babies or toddlers or baby animals voicing sweet sentiments. The front of her valentine (which my father likewise saved) shows a pigtailed little girl and a blushing little boy standing beside each other with their eyes bashfully averted and their hands tucked bashfully behind their backs.

I wish I were a little rock,

'Cause then when I grew older,
Maybe I would find some day
I was a little "boulder."

Inside the card is a drawing of the same two kids, but holding hands now, with my mother's cursive signature ("Irene") at the feet of the little girl. A second verse reads:

And that would really help a lot
It sure would suit me fine,
For I'd be "bould" enough to say,
"Please be my Valentine."

My father's letter in response was postmarked Fairview, Montana, February 14.

Tuesday Evening

Dear Irene,

I'm sorry to have disappointed you on Valentine's Day; I did remember but after not being able to get one at the drugstore, I felt a little foolish about asking at the grocery or hardware store. I'm sure they have heard about Valentine's Day out here. Your card fit the situation out here perfectly and I'm not sure if it were intentional or accidental, but I guess I did tell about our rock troubles. Today we ran out of rock so I'm wishing for little rocks, big rocks or any kind of rocks as there is nothing we can do until we get some. There is little enough for me to do when the contractor is working and now there is nothing at all. Today I hiked out to the bridge where we are working just to kill time and get a little exercise; it's about four miles which is far enough with a sharp wind blowing. Unless we get rock on the freight in the morning, I'm going to sit right here and read philosophy; it hardly seems right that I should get paid for putting in that kind of day. About the only other pastime around here is to sit in the hotel lobby and take in the town gossip, and the old timers who haunt the place can sure put it out. You would get a kick out of it because there is sure a broad cross section of life represented here–from the local doctor down to the town drunk. And the last is probably the most interesting; I heard that he taught at the University of N.D. at one time, and he seems really to be quite an intelligent person, even when drunk. Normally the talk is pretty rough, about like Steinbeck must have used for a pattern, but this evening there came in a great big woman who made herself right at home. It all sort of makes me realize how sheltered a life we city people live. I grew up in a small town and feel quite at home here but I somehow now seem to view things differently. You will hear more of this.

I hope to get back to St. Paul on Saturday night but cannot tell for certain now. I'll call you when I get in.

With all my love,

Earl

My father had recently turned 29. It's impossible to know how my mother, in her innocence and optimism, received his letter at the time, but in general, considering the woman I grew up knowing, I can say that it was absolutely not the sort of letter she would have wanted from her romantic interest. Her valentine's cutely punning conceit taken literally as a reference to *track ballast*? And she, who spent her whole life shuddering free of the hotel bar where her father had worked as a bartender, *getting a kick out of* hearing "rough talk" from the *town drunk*? Where were the endearments? Where were the dreamy discussions of love? It was obvious that my father still had a lot to learn about her.

To me, though, his letter seems full of love. Love for my mother, certainly: he's tried to get her a valentine, he's read her card carefully, he wishes she were with him, he has ideas he wants to share with her, he's sending all his love, he'll call her as soon as he's back. But love, too, for the larger world: for the varieties of people in it, for small towns and big cities, for philosophy and literature, for hard work and fair pay, for conversation, for thinking, for long walks in a sharp wind, for carefully chosen words and perfect spelling. The letter reminds me of the many things I loved in my father, his decency, his intelligence, his unexpected humor, his curiosity, his conscientiousness, his reserve and dignity. Only when I place it alongside the valentine from my mother, with its big-eyed babies and preoccupation with pure sentiment, does my focus shift to the decades of mutual disappointment that followed my parents' first few years of half-seeing bliss.

Late in life, my mother complained to me that my father had never told her that he loved her. And it may literally be true that he never spoke the big three words to her–I certainly never heard him do it. But it's definitely not true that he never wrote the words. One reason it took me years to summon the courage to read their old correspondence is that the first letter of my father's that I glanced at, after my mother died, began with an endearment ("Irenie") that I had never heard him utter in the 35 years I knew him, and it ended with a declaration ("I love you, Irene") that was more than I could stand to see. It sounded nothing like him, and so I buried all the letters in a trunk in my brother's attic. More recently, when I retrieved the letters and managed to read through them all, I discovered that my father had in fact declared his love dozens of times, using the big three words, both before and after he married my mother. But maybe, even then, he'd been incapable of saying the words out loud, and maybe this was why, in my mother's memory, he'd never "said" them at all. It's also possible that his written declarations had sounded as strange and untrue to his character in the 1940s as they now sound to me, and that my mother, in her complaints, was remembering a deeper truth now concealed by his seemingly affectionate words. It's possible that, in guilty response to the onslaught of sentiment he was getting from her notes to him ("I love you with all my heart," "With oh so much love," etc.), he'd felt obliged to perform romantic love in return, or to try to perform it, the way he'd tried (sort of) to buy a valentine in Fairview, Montana.

"Both Sides Now," in the Judy Collins version, was the first pop song that ever stuck in my head. It was getting heavy radio play when I was eight or nine, and its reference to declaring love "right out loud," combined with the crush I had on Judy Collins's voice, helped to ensure that for me the primary import of "I love you" was sexual. I did eventually live through the '70s and become capable, in rare accesses of emotion, of telling my brothers and many of my best male friends that I loved them. But throughout grade school and junior high, the words had only one meaning for me. "I love you" was the phrase I wanted to see scrawled on a note from the cutest girl in the class or to hear whispered in the woods on a school picnic. It happened only a couple of times, in those years, that a girl I liked actually said or wrote this to me. But when it did happen, it came as a shot of pure adrenaline. Even after I got to college and started reading Wallace Stevens and found him making fun, in "Le Monocle de Mon Oncle," of indiscriminately love-seeking people like me–

If sex were all, then every trembling hand

Could make us squeak, like dolls, the wished-for words–

–those wished-for words continued to signify the opening of a mouth, the offering of a body, the promise of intoxicating intimacy.

And so it was highly awkward that the person I constantly heard these words from was my mother. She was the only woman in a house of males, and she lived with such an excess of unrequitable feeling that she couldn't help reaching for romantic expressions of it. The cards and endearments that she bestowed on me were identical in spirit to the ones she'd once bestowed on my father. Long before I was born, her effusions had come to seem intolerably babyish to my father. To me, though, they weren't nearly babyish enough. I went to elaborate lengths to avoid reciprocating them. I survived many stretches of my childhood, the long weeks in which the two of us were alone in the house together, by clinging to crucial distinctions in intensity between the phrases "I love you"; "I love you, too"; and "Love you." The one thing that was vital was never, ever to say "I love you" or "I love you, Mom." The least painful alternative was a muttered, essentially inaudible "Love you." But "I love you, too," if pronounced rapidly enough and with enough emphasis on the "too," which implied rote responsiveness, could carry me through many an awkward moment. I don't remember that she ever specifically called me out on my mumbling or gave me a hard time if (as sometimes happened) I was incapable of responding with anything more than an evasive grunt. But she also never told me that saying "I love you" was simply something she enjoyed doing because her heart was full of feeling, and that I shouldn't feel I had to say "I love you" in return every time. And so, to this day, when I'm assaulted by the shouting of "I love you" into a cell phone, I hear coercion.

My father, despite writing letters filled with life and curiosity, saw nothing wrong with consigning my mother to four decades of cooking and cleaning at home while he was enjoying his agency out in the world of men. It seems to be the rule, in both the small world of marriage and the big world of American life, that those without agency have sentimentality and vice versa. The various post-9/11 hysterias, both the plague of I love yous and the widespread fear and hatred of the ragheads, were hysterias of the powerless and overwhelmed. If my mother had had greater scope for accomplishment, she might have tailored her sentiments more realistically to their objects.

Cold or repressed or sexist though my father may appear by contemporary standards, I'm grateful that he never told me, in so many words, that he loved me. My father loved privacy, which is to say: he respected the public sphere. He believed in restraint and protocol and reason, because without them, he believed, it was impossible for a society to debate and make decisions in its best interest. It might have been nice, especially for me, if he'd learned how to be more demonstrative with my mother. But every time I hear one of those brayed parental cellular I love yous nowadays, I feel lucky to have had the dad I did. He loved his kids more than anything. And to know that he felt it and couldn't say it; to know that he could trust me to know he felt it and never expect him to say it: this was the very core and substance of the love I felt for him. A love that I in turn was careful never to declare out loud to him.

And yet: this was the easy part. Between me and the place where my dad is now–i.e., dead–nothing but silence can be transmitted. Nobody has more privacy than the dead. My dad and I aren't saying a whole lot less to each other now than we did in many a year when he was alive. The person I find myself actively missing–mentally arguing with, wanting to show stuff to, wishing to see in my apartment, making fun of, feeling remorse about–is my mother. The part of me that's angered by cellular intrusions comes from my father. The part of me that loves my BlackBerry and wants to lighten up and join the world comes from my mother. She was the more modern of the two of them, and although he, not she, was the one with agency, she ended up on the winning side. If she were still alive and still living in St. Louis, and if you happened to be sitting next to me in Lambert Airport, waiting for a New York-bound flight, you might have to suffer through hearing me tell her that I love her. I would keep my voice down, though.

The Meaning of Serena Williams

On tennis and black excellence

CLAUDIA RANKINE

There is no more exuberant winner than Serena Williams. She leaps into the air, she laughs, she grins, she pumps her fist, she points her index finger to the sky, signaling she's No. 1. Her joy is palpable. It brings me to my feet, and I grin right back at her, as if I've won something, too. Perhaps I have.

There is a belief among some African-Americans that to defeat racism, they have to work harder, be smarter, be *better*. Only after they give 150 percent will white Americans recognize black excellence for what it is. But of course, once recognized, black excellence is then supposed to perform with good manners and forgiveness in the face of any racist slights or attacks. Black excellence is not supposed to be emotional as it pulls itself together to win after questionable calls. And in winning, it's not supposed to swagger, to leap and pump its fist, to state boldly, in the words of Kanye West, "That's what it is, black excellence, baby."

Imagine you have won 21 Grand Slam singles titles, with only four losses in your 25 appearances in the finals. Imagine that you've achieved two "Serena Slams" (four consecutive Slams in a row), the first more than 10 years ago and the second this year. A win at this year's U.S. Open would be your fifth and your first calendar-year Grand Slam—a feat last achieved by Steffi Graf in 1988, when you were just 6 years old. This win would also break your tie for the most U.S. Open titles in the Open era, surpassing the legendary Chris Evert, who herself has called you "a phenomenon that once every hundred years comes around." Imagine that you're the player John McEnroe recently described as "the greatest player, I think, that ever lived." Imagine that, despite all this, there were so many bad calls against you, you were given as one reason video replay needed to be used on the courts. Imagine that you have to contend with critiques of your body that perpetuate racist notions that black women are hypermasculine and unattractive. Imagine being asked to comment at a news conference before a tournament because the president of the Russian Tennis Federation, Shamil Tarpischev, has described you and your sister as "brothers" who are "scary" to look at. Imagine.

The word "win" finds its roots in both joy and grace. Serena's grace comes because she won't be forced into stillness; she won't accept those racist projections onto her body without speaking back; she won't go gently into the white light of victory. Her excellence doesn't mask the struggle it takes to achieve each win. For black people, there is an unspoken script that demands the humble absorption of racist assaults, no matter the scale, because whites need to believe that it's no big deal. But Serena refuses to keep to that script. Somehow, along the way, she made a decision to be excellent while still being Serena. She would feel what she feels in front of everyone, in response to anyone. At Wimbledon this year, for example, in a match against the home favorite Heather Watson, Serena, interrupted during play by the deafening support of Watson, wagged her index finger at the crowd and said, "Don't try me." She will tell an audience or an official that they are disrespectful or unjust, whether she says, simply, "No, no, no" or something much more forceful, as happened at the U.S. Open in 2009, when she told the lineswoman, "I swear to God I am [expletive] going to take this [expletive] ball and shove it down your [expletive] throat." And in doing so, we actually see her. She shows us her joy, her humor and, yes, her rage. She gives us the whole range of what it is to be human, and there are those who can't bear it, who can't tolerate the humanity of an ordinary extraordinary person.

In the essay "Everybody's Protest Novel," James Baldwin wrote, "our humanity is our burden, our life; we need not battle for it; we need only to do what is infinitely more difficult—that is, accept it." To accept the self, its humanity, is to discard the white racist gaze. Serena has freed herself from it. But that doesn't mean she won't be emotional or hurt by challenges to her humanity. It doesn't mean she won't battle for the right to be excellent. There is nothing wrong with Serena, but surely there is something wrong with the expectation that she be "good" while she is achieving greatness. Why should Serena not respond to racism? In whose world should it be answered with good manners? The notable difference between black excellence and white excellence is white excellence is achieved without having to battle racism. Imagine.

Two years ago, recovering from cancer and to celebrate my 50th birthday, I flew from LAX to J.F.K. during Serena's semifinal match at the U.S. Open with the hope of seeing her play in the final. I had just passed through a year when so much was out of my control, and Serena epitomized not so much winning as the pure drive to win. I couldn't quite shake the feeling (I still can't quite shake it) that my body's frailty, not the cancer but the depth of my exhaustion, had been brought on in part by the constant onslaught of racism, whether something as terrible as the killing of Trayvon Martin or something as mundane as the guy who let the door slam in my face. The daily grind of being rendered invisible, or being attacked, whether physically or verbally, for being visible, wears a body down. Serena's strength and focus in the face of the realities we shared oddly consoled me.

That Sunday in Arthur Ashe Stadium at the women's final, though the crowd generally seemed pro-Serena, the man seated next to me was cheering for the formidable tall blonde Victoria Azarenka. I asked him if he was American. "Yes," he said.

"We're at the U.S. Open. Why are you cheering for the player from Belarus?" I asked.

"Oh, I just want the match to be competitive," he said.

After Serena lost the second set, at the opening of the third, I turned to him again, and asked him, no doubt in my own frustration, why he was still cheering for Azarenka. He didn't answer, as was his prerogative. By the time it was clear that Serena was likely to win, his seat had been vacated. I had to admit to myself that in those moments I needed her to win, not just in the pure sense of a fan supporting her player, but to prove something that could never be proven, because if black excellence could cure us of anything, black people—or rather this black person—would be free from needing Serena to win.

"You don't understand me," Serena Williams said with a hint of impatience in her voice. "I'm just about winning." She and I were facing each other on a sofa in her West Palm Beach home this July. She looked at me with wariness as if to say, Not you, too. I wanted to talk about the tennis records that she is presently positioned either to tie or to break and had tried more than once to steer the conversation toward them. But she was clear: "It's not about getting 22 Grand Slams," she insisted. Before winning a calendar-year Grand Slam and matching Steffi Graf's record of 22 Slams, Serena would have to win seven matches and defend her U.S. Open title; *those* were the victories that she was thinking about.

She was wearing an enviable pink jumpsuit with palm trees stamped all over it as if to reflect the trees surrounding her estate. It was a badass outfit, one only someone of her height and figure could rock. She explained to me that she learned not to look ahead too much by looking ahead. As she approached 18 Grand Slam wins in 2014, she said, "I went too crazy. I felt I had to even up with Chris Evert and Martina Navratilova." Instead, she didn't make it past the fourth round at the Australian Open, the second at the French Open or the third at Wimbledon. She tried to change her tactics and focused on getting only to the quarterfinals of the U.S. Open. Make it to the second week and see what happens, she thought. "I started thinking like that, and then I got to 19. Actually I got to 21 just like that, so I'm not thinking about 22." She raised her water bottle to her lips, looking at me over its edge, as if to give me time to think of a different line of questioning.

Three years ago she partnered with the French tennis coach Patrick Mouratoglou, and I've wondered if his coaching has been an antidote to negotiating American racism, a dynamic that informed the coaching of her father, Richard Williams. He didn't want its presence to prevent her and Venus from winning. In his autobiography, "Black and White: The Way I See It," he describes toughening the girls' "skin" by bringing "busloads of kids from the local schools into Compton to surround the courts while Venus and Serena practiced. I had the kids call them every curse word in the English language, including 'Nigger,'" he writes. "I paid them to do it and told them to 'do their worst.'" His focus on racism meant that the sisters were engaged in two battles on and off the court. That level of vigilance, I know from my own life, can drain you. It's easier to shut up and pretend it's not happening, as the bitterness and stress build up.

Mouratoglou shifted Serena's focus to records (even if, as she prepares for a Slam, she says she can't allow herself to think about them). Perhaps it's not surprising that she broke her boycott against Indian Wells, where the audience notoriously booed her with racial epithets in 2001, during their partnership. Serena's decisions now seem directed toward building her legacy. Mouratoglou has insisted that she can get to 24 Grand Slams, which is the most won by a single player—Margaret Court —to date. Serena laughed as she recalled one of her earliest conversations with Mouratoglou. She told him: "I'm cool. I want to play tennis. I hate to lose. I want to win. But I don't have numbers in my head." He wouldn't allow that. "Now we are getting numbers in your head," he told her.

I asked how winning felt for her. I was imagining winning as a free space, one where the unconscious racist shenanigans of umpires, or the narratives about her body, her "unnatural" power, her perceived crassness no longer mattered. Unless racism destroyed the moment of winning so completely, as it did at Indian Wells, I thought it had to be the rare space free of all the stresses of black life. But Serena made it clear that she doesn't desire to dissociate from her history and her culture. She understands that even when she's focused only on winning, she is still representing. "I play for me," Serena told me, "but I also play and represent something much greater than me. I embrace that. I love that. I want that. So ultimately, when I am out there on the court, I am playing for me."

Her next possible victory is at the U.S. Open, the major where she has been involved in the most drama— everything from outrageous line calls to probations and fines. Serena admitted to losing her cool in the face of some of what has gone down there. In 2011, for example, a chair umpire, Eva Asderaki, ruled against Serena for yelling "Come on" before a point was completed, and as Serena described it to me, she "clutched her pearls" and told Asderaki not to look at her. But she said in recent years she finally felt embraced by the crowd. "No more incidents?" I asked. Before she could answer, we both laughed, because of course it's not wholly in her control. Then suddenly Serena stopped. "I don't want any incidents there," she said. "But I'm always going to be myself. If anything happens, I'm always going to be myself, true to myself."

I'm counting on it, I thought. Because just as important to me as her victories is her willingness to be an emotionally complete person while also being black. She wins, yes, but she also loses it. She jokes around, gets angry, is frustrated or joyous, and on and on. She is fearlessly on the side of Serena, in a culture that that has responded to living while black with death.

This July, the London School of Marketing (L.S.M.) released its list of the most marketable sports stars, which included only two women in its Top 20: Maria Sharapova and Serena Williams. They were ranked 12th and 20th. Despite decisively trailing Serena on the tennis court (Serena leads in their head-to-head matchups 18-2, and has 21 majors and 247 weeks at No. 1 to Sharapova's five majors and 21 weeks at number 1), Sharapova has a financial advantage off the court. This month Forbes listed her as the highest-paid female athlete, worth more than $29 million to Serena's $24 million.

When I asked Chris Evert about the L.S.M. list, she said, "I think the corporate world still loves the good-looking blond girls." It's a preference Evert benefited from in her own illustrious career. I suggested that this had to do with race. Serena, on occasion, has herself been a blonde. But of course, for millions of consumers, possibly not the right kind of blonde. "Maria was very aware of business and becoming a businesswoman at a much younger stage," Evert told me, adding, "She works hard." She also suggested that any demonstration of corporate preference is about a certain "type" of look or image, not whiteness in general. When I asked Evert what she made of Eugenie Bouchard, the tall, blond Canadian who has yet to really distinguish herself in the sport, being named the world's most marketable athlete by the British magazine *SportsPro* this spring, she said, with a laugh, "Well, there you have it." I took her statement to be perhaps a moment of agreement that Serena probably could not work her way to Sharapova's spot on Forbes's list.

"If they want to market someone who is white and blond, that's their choice," Serena told me when I asked her about her ranking. Her impatience had returned, but I wasn't sure if it was with me, the list or both. "I have a lot of partners who are very happy to work with me." JPMorgan Chase, Wilson Sporting Goods, Pepsi and Nike are among the partners she was referring to. "I can't sit here and say I should be higher on the list because I have won more." As for Sharapova, her nonrival rival, Serena was diplomatic: "I'm happy for her, because she worked hard, too. There is enough at the table for everyone."

There is another, perhaps more important, discussion to be had about what it means to be chosen by global corporations. It has to do with who is worthy, who is desirable, who is associated with the good life. As long as the white imagination markets itself by equating whiteness and blondness with aspirational living, stereotypes will remain fixed in place. Even though Serena is the best, even though she wins more Slams than anyone else, she is only superficially allowed to embody that in our culture, at least the marketable one.

But Serena was less interested in the ramifications involved in being chosen, since she had no power in this arena, and more interested in understanding her role in relation to those who came before her: "We have to be thankful, and we also have to be positive about it so the next black person can be No. 1 on that list," she told me. "Maybe it was not meant to be me. Maybe it's meant to be the next person to be amazing, and I'm just opening the door. Zina Garrison, Althea Gibson, Arthur Ashe and Venus opened so many doors for me. I'm just opening the next door for the next person."

I was moved by Serena's positioning herself in relation to other African-Americans. A crucial component of white privilege is the idea that your accomplishments can be, have been, achieved on your own. The private clubs that housed the tennis courts remained closed to minorities well into the second half of the 20th century. Serena reminded me that in addition to being a phenomenon, she has come out of a long line of African-Americans who battled for the right to be excellent in such a space that attached its value to its whiteness and worked overtime to keep it segregated.

Serena's excellence comes with the ability to imagine herself achieving a new kind of history for all of us. As long as she remains healthy, she will most likely tie and eventually pass Graf's 22 majors, regardless of what happens at the U.S. Open this year. I want Serena to win, but I know better than to think her winning can end something she didn't start. But Serena is providing a new script, one in which winning doesn't carry the burden of curing racism, in which we win just to win—knowing that it is simply her excellence, baby.

Correction: September 13, 2015

An article on Aug. 30 about Serena Williams misidentified the tennis official she confronted at the U.S. Open in 2009 after she was called for a foot fault. The official was a lineswoman, not a chair umpire.

Violent Media Is Good for Kids

GERARD JONES

At 13 I was alone and afraid. Taught by my well-meaning, progressive, English-teacher parents that violence was wrong, that rage was something to be overcome and cooperation was always better than conflict, I suffocated my deepest fears and desires under a nice-boy persona. Placed in a small, experimental school that was wrong for me, afraid to join my peers in their bumptious rush into adolescent boyhood, I withdrew into passivity and loneliness. My parents, not trusting the violent world of the late 1960s, built a wall between me and the crudest elements of American pop culture.

Then the Incredible Hulk smashed through it.

One of my mother's students convinced her that Marvel Comics, despite their apparent juvenility and violence, were in fact devoted to lofty messages of pacifism and tolerance. My mother borrowed some, thinking they'd be good for me. And so they were. But not because they preached lofty messages of benevolence. They were good for me because they were juvenile. And violent.

The character who caught me, and freed me, was the Hulk: overgendered and undersocialized, half-naked and half-witted, raging against a frightened world that misunderstood and persecuted him. Suddenly I had a fantasy self to carry my stifled rage and buried desire for power. I had a fantasy self who was a self: unafraid of his desires and the world's disapproval, unhesitating and effective in action. "Puny boy follow Hulk!" roared my fantasy self, and I followed.

I followed him to new friends—other sensitive geeks chasing their own inner brutes—and I followed him to the arrogant, self-exposing, self-assertive, superheroic decision to become a writer. Eventually, I left him behind, followed more sophisticated heroes, and finally my own lead along a twisting path to a career and an identity. In my 30s, I found myself writing action movies and comic books. I wrote some Hulk stories, and met the geek-geniuses who created him. I saw my own creations turned into action figures, cartoons, and computer games. I talked to the kids who read my stories. Across generations, genders, and ethnicities I kept seeing the same story: people pulling themselves out of emotional traps by immersing themselves in violent stories. People integrating the scariest, most fervently denied fragments of their psyches into fuller senses of selfhood through fantasies of superhuman combat and destruction.

I have watched my son living the same story—transforming himself into a bloodthirsty dinosaur to embolden himself for the plunge into preschool, a Power Ranger to muscle through a social competition in kindergarten. In the first grade, his friends started climbing a tree at school. But he was afraid: of falling, of the centipedes crawling on the trunk, of sharp branches, of his friends' derision. I took my cue from his own fantasies and read him old Tarzan comics, rich in combat and bright with flashing knives. For two weeks he lived in them. Then he put them aside. And he climbed the tree.

But all the while, especially in the wake of the recent burst of school shootings, I heard pop psychologists insisting that violent stories are harmful to kids, heard teachers begging parents to keep their kids away from "junk culture," heard a guilt-stricken friend with a son who loved Pokémon lament, "I've turned into the bad mom who lets her kid eat sugary cereal and watch cartoons!"

That's when I started the research.

"Fear, greed, power-hunger, rage: these are aspects of our selves that we try not to experience in our lives but often want, even need, to experience vicariously through stories of others," writes Melanie Moore, Ph.D., a psychologist who works with urban teens. "Children need violent entertainment in order to explore the inescapable feelings that they've been taught to deny, and to reintegrate those feelings into a more whole, more complex, more resilient selfhood."

Moore consults to public schools and local governments, and is also raising a daughter. For the past three years she and I have been studying the ways in which children use violent stories to meet their emotional and developmental needs -- and the ways in which adults can help them use those stories healthily. With her help I developed Power Play, a program for helping young people improve their self-knowledge and sense of potency through heroic, combative storytelling.

We've found that every aspect of even the trashiest pop-culture story can have its own developmental function. Pretending to have superhuman powers helps children conquer the feelings of powerlessness that inevitably come with being so young and small. The dual-identity concept at the heart of many superhero stories helps kids negotiate the conflicts between the inner self and the public self as they work through the early stages of socialization. Identification with a rebellious, even destructive, hero helps children learn to push back against a modern culture that cultivates fear and teaches dependency.

At its most fundamental level, what we call "creative violence" -- head-bonking cartoons, bloody videogames, playground karate, toy guns -- gives children a tool to master their rage. Children will feel rage. Even the sweetest and most civilized of them, even those whose parents read the better class of literary magazines, will feel rage. The world is uncontrollable and incomprehensible; mastering it is a terrifying, enraging task. Rage can be an energizing emotion, a shot of courage to push us to resist greater threats, take more control, than we ever thought we could. But rage is also the emotion our culture distrusts the most. Most of us are taught early on to fear our own. Through immersion in imaginary combat and identification with a violent protagonist, children engage the rage they've stifled, come to fear it less, and become more capable of utilizing it against life's challenges.

I knew one little girl who went around exploding with fantasies so violent that other moms would draw her mother aside to whisper, "I think you should know something about Emily...." Her parents were separating, and she was small, an only child, a tomboy at an age when her classmates were dividing sharply along gender lines. On the playground she acted out "Sailor Moon" fights, and in the classroom she wrote stories about people being stabbed with knives. The more adults tried to control her stories, the more she acted out the roles of her angry heroes: breaking rules, testing limits, roaring threats.

Then her mother and I started helping her tell her stories. She wrote them, performed them, drew them like comics: sometimes bloody, sometimes tender, always blending the images of pop culture with her own most private fantasies. She came out of it just as fiery and strong, but more self-controlled and socially competent: a leader among her peers, the one student in her class who could truly pull boys and girls together.

I worked with an older girl, a middle-class "nice girl," who held herself together through a chaotic family situation and a tumultuous adolescence with gangsta rap. In the mythologized street violence of Ice T, the rage and strutting of his music and lyrics, she found a theater of the mind in which she could be powerful, ruthless, invulnerable. She avoided the heavy drug use that sank many of her peers, and flowered in college as a writer and political activist.

I'm not going to argue that violent entertainment is harmless. I think it has helped inspire some people to real-life violence. I am going to argue that it's helped hundreds of people for every one it's hurt, and that it can help far more if we learn to use it well. I am going to argue that our fear of "youth violence" isn't well-founded on reality, and that the fear can do more harm than the reality. We act as though our highest priority is to prevent our children from growing up into murderous thugs -- but modern kids are far more likely to grow up too passive, too distrustful of themselves, too easily manipulated.

We send the message to our children in a hundred ways that their craving for imaginary gun battles and symbolic killings is wrong, or at least dangerous. Even when we don't call for censorship or forbid "Mortal Kombat," we moan to other parents within our kids' earshot about the "awful violence" in the entertainment they love. We tell our kids that it isn't nice to play-fight, or we steer them from some monstrous action figure to a pro-social doll. Even in the most progressive households, where we make such a point of letting children feel what they feel, we rush to substitute an enlightened discussion for the raw material of rageful fantasy. In the process, we risk confusing them about their natural aggression in the same way the Victorians confused their children about their sexuality. When we try to protect our children from their own feelings and fantasies, we shelter them not against violence but against power and selfhood.

Inside Major League Baseball's Dominican Sweatshop System

IAN GORDONMARCH

The baseball men started coming around when Yewri Guillén was 15. Like thousands of other boys in the Dominican Republic, he had been waiting for them for years, training on the sparse patch of grass and dirt across the road from the small concrete-and-wood house he shared with his mother, father, and two sisters in La Canela, a hamlet 45 minutes southwest of Santo Domingo. By the time the American scouts took notice, he had grown into a 5-foot-10, 165-pound, switch-hitting shortstop with quick hands and a laser arm. In 2009, at the age of 16, he signed for $30,000 with the Washington Nationals. The first thing he'd do with his bonus, he told his parents, was buy them a car and build them a new house.

But soon after Guillén's signing, Major League Baseball put his plans on hold. The league, having grown more vigilant about identity fraud, suspended him for a year, alleging that he'd lied about his date of birth on paperwork to boost his potential value to scouts. Guillén's family got a lawyer to fight the suspension, and in the meantime he lived and trained without pay at the Nationals' academy in Boca Chica, the epicenter of MLB's training facilities in the country. There, he was notoriously hard on himself. Johnny DiPuglia, the Nationals' international scouting director, said Guillén would even take himself out of games after making small mistakes like missing a sign from the third-base coach. "He had no education, none at all," DiPuglia told me. "I didn't think he had any teeth because he never smiled. And he always had watery eyes—there was always sadness in his eyes."

DiPuglia made it his mission to cheer up the teenager, "to open up his heart." He wouldn't let Guillén pass without giving him a hug and a smile, and little by little, DiPuglia said, Guillén started to loosen up, becoming a better teammate and a happier kid. Later, when other talent brokers approached Guillén claiming that they could get him a better deal with a different team, Guillén turned them away because he felt that he owed it to the Nationals for sticking with him. After MLB finally authorized his contract at the beginning of 2011, the Nationals told him they'd be sending him to play for their rookie league team in Florida. He was to leave in mid-April.

When the headaches first came on, they were barely bad enough to mention. On April 1, Guillén headed home to La Canela to get his travel documents in order. His family brought him to a clinic in nearby San Cristóbal. When he returned to the academy and missed a couple of games, DiPuglia called him out—in the Dominican Republic, nobody rides the bench because of a headache. When the pain got worse, DiPuglia sent Guillén to the trainer's room, where he was given some tea and an aspirin.

The next day, on April 6, the Nationals sent Guillén back to La Canela. He had a slight fever when he left the academy. On April 7, Michael Morla, a longtime local trainer who also acted as Guillén's agent, was at the field in La Canela when he saw Guillén, a damp towel wrapped around his head, lurching toward the community's health post, adjacent to the field. Morla approached Guillén's family, urging them to take him to Santo Domingo for care: "The boy is bad!"

Guillén's aunt and uncle rushed him to the Clínica Abreu, the capital's best private hospital. But because his contract hadn't been finalized he didn't have health insurance, and he was refused treatment when his family couldn't come up with the $1,300 admission fee. His aunt and uncle moved him to a more affordable Cuban-Dominican clinic nearby, where he was admitted on April 8. The doctors diagnosed bacterial meningitis. Guillén later had surgery to drain brain fluid, but the disease had progressed too far. On April 15, the day he was to leave for the United States, Yewri Guillén died.

The tragedy was a blip on the sports world's radar, a blurb on ESPN's Spanish-language crawl. The handful of news reports hit all the same notes: MLB said that the team followed appropriate protocols and did all that it could; the Nationals vowed to promptly vaccinate all the players at their academy; everyone from the team's medical director to the general manager expressed sorrow about the death.

"A 16-year-old doesn't know how to play baseball," Red Sox star David Ortiz told me. "I don't care what they say."

Here's what those stories left out: There wasn't a certified athletic trainer, let alone a doctor, to evaluate Guillén at the Nationals' academy, a spartan training camp with cinder-block dorms. No one from the team accompanied him to Santo Domingo or intervened when he couldn't get into the Clínica Abreu. (The club didn't cover the costs of his treatment until after he was admitted to the Cuban-Dominican clinic.) And following Guillén's death, the club required his parents to sign a release before handing over his signing bonus and life insurance money—a document also stating that they would never sue the team or its employees.

Guillén's death is the worst-case scenario in a recruiting system that treats young Dominicans as second-class prospects, paying them far less than young Americans and sometimes denying them benefits that are standard in the US minor leagues, such as health insurance and professionally trained medical staff. MLB regulations allow teams to troll for talent on the cheap in the Dominican Republic: Unlike American kids, who must have completed high school to sign, Dominicans can be signed as young as 16, when their bodies and their skills are far less developed.

"A 16-year-old doesn't know how to play baseball," the Boston Red Sox's David Ortiz, an eight-time All-Star who grew up in Santo Domingo, told me. "I don't care what they say. When I signed at 16, I didn't know what the fuck I was doing."

Teams are not eager to talk about the disparity between MLB's domestic and foreign rookie leagues, as I would learn firsthand when looking into Guillén's death in his native country. Nor is it much of a concern to locals: The sport is ubiquitous and beloved, and given the Dominican Republic's 40 percent poverty rate, the allure of the big leagues is powerful. Ortiz said Americans don't understand the pressure on Dominican teenagers, including in some cases to lie about their age. "The thing that made me mad about the whole situation is that people want to look at us like we are criminals," he said. "I would like to get in their face and ask them, if that was their only way out, what would they do?"

The legions of teens swinging bats and diving for ground balls each year on Dominican fields must negotiate a system with little in the way of support or a safety net. Whereas Major League Baseball requires all 189 minor league teams in the United States to have certified athletic trainers and "all reasonable medical supplies," no such requirement exists at the Dominican academies. Nearly two years after Guillén's death, *Mother Jones* found that 21 of MLB's 30 teams lack certified trainers in the Dominican Republic, including the Nationals.

Rafael Pérez, head of Dominican operations for Major League Baseball, said his office's role is to provide services to the clubs, not wag a regulatory finger at them: "Sometimes people have a negative reaction when things are imposed," he said. That's why the Nationals faced no sanctions, even though one of their players died of an entirely treatable illness. They had followed the rules, but those rules don't require the teams to do very much. Pérez insisted that the league has aimed to improve facilities and standards in recent years, albeit on a voluntary basis: "Some clubs are having a harder time than others. But they all have great intentions."

The reality is that a stark double standard persists, said Arturo Marcano, a Venezuelan-born lawyer who a decade ago coauthored a book on corruption and youth exploitation in MLB's Dominican operations. League officials recognize that the system is flawed and that it should be improved, he said. "They always say, 'We're working on it,' or, 'Things are getting better.' But in the end, it's the same response they've been giving since 2002."

Since then, Latin American players have become an ever more important part of the game. At the start of the 2012 season, players born in Latin American countries made up 42 percent of minor leaguers and 24 percent of major leaguers. They accounted for 6 of MLB's 25 highest earners, and like superstar Albert Pujols, who signed a 10-year, $240 million contract in December 2011, more than half of the Latin American players came from the Dominican Republic, the most from any country outside the United States.

And yet, if 2006 is any indication, of the hundreds of Dominican prospects at the academies each year (along with Venezuelans and other Latin Americans also training there), less than half will ever leave the island to play even in the minor leagues, let alone in the big show, where under 3 percent will eventually step up to the plate. More than three-quarters will drop out of baseball in four years. Americans in the rookie leagues also face long odds, of course, but nearly 70 percent of them will advance at least one minor league level, and they are more than four times as likely to crack a major league roster. They are also far better paid at the outset: The average signing bonus for American players drafted in 2011 was $232,000; for international players, it was approximately half that.

Everyone participating in the system—from the CEOs of major league franchises all the way down to the often sketchy local talent brokers in the Dominican Republic known as *buscones*—has a say. Except for the kids. "The objective in Latin America is to sign talent, but do so in an affordable way," Marcano said. "But there isn't anyone who speaks for the players, who are giving up their childhood in search of a dream that few realize."

Baseball first came to the Dominican Republic in the late 1800s, most likely brought to the island by Cuban immigrants. Although several teams formed and began playing tournaments by the early 1900s, it wasn't until Ozzie Virgil debuted for the New York Giants in 1956 that a Dominican made it to the American major leagues. Several accomplished players followed, including Hall of Fame pitcher Juan Marichal, but the first real wave came after Toronto Blue Jays scout Epy Guerrero started the first academy in 1973, turning a house and a cheap plot of land into a rudimentary training camp. A decade later, the Los Angeles Dodgers, recognizing a potentially rich vein of talent, created a template for the contemporary baseball academy called Campo Las Palmas. But most teams were content to play the odds, parachuting in to look for big-time talent at bargain basement prices. As former Colorado Rockies executive Dick Balderson once explained, "Instead of signing four American guys at $25,000 each, you sign 20 Dominican guys for $5,000 each."

Conditions at some academies were substandard and even dangerous. When the Nationals' DiPuglia was starting out with the St. Louis Cardinals in the mid-1990s, his players slept eight to a room and navigated a field full of rocks and the occasional goat. In his book, *Stealing Lives*, Marcano told the story of a player named Alexi Quiroz and his path through the Chicago Cubs' Dominican academy, a place the ballplayers referred to as "Vietnam." There, 19 teenage boys shared one bathroom without running water, a drunk coach allegedly threatened them with a gun, and, after Quiroz separated his shoulder playing shortstop one day, he was treated by a street doctor who stomped on the joint to pop it back into place, ending his career.

As American teams began paying more attention to Dominican prospects in the early aughts, more and more ex-players and wannabes started working as buscones, scouting and training teens even before they had turned 16. They had flashy nicknames like Cachaza or Aroboy, and their training methods and negotiating tactics led to rising bonuses for their players—typically along with a hefty 30 percent cut for their efforts. Some buscones gained a reputation as ruthless operators willing to do anything—forge player birth certificates, bribe investigators—to boost their take.

By 2009, following several high-profile identity fraud cases and bonus-skimming scandals, MLB dispatched executive Sandy Alderson (now the general manager of the New York Mets) to take stock of operations in the country. His report called for restructuring the league's Dominican office, improving identity investigations, regulating the buscones, and generally curtailing corruption.

But his recommendations were only advisory, and critics maintain that little has changed since. One big shift did go into effect in 2012: Major League Baseball restricted teams to a $2.9 million international free-agent budget, in part to blunt the power of buscones by driving down signing bonuses. The bonuses had hit a high point the prior year, when the Texas Rangers signed 16-year-old Dominican outfielder Nomar Mazara to a record $4.95 million deal, but since have begun to drop and will remain suppressed under the cap. A few teams, such as the Pittsburgh Pirates and San Diego Padres, have chosen to invest in better facilities and training programs, but they remain in the minority.

The Nationals, meanwhile, have been tight-lipped about their operation since Yewri Guillén died. (MLB later said Guillén had died of a sinus-related infection, not meningitis, but league officials declined to provide *Mother Jones* with any documentation confirming such a diagnosis.) And access to the team's academy proved challenging. Shortly after I arrived in the Dominican Republic in January 2012 and scheduled a tour of the Nationals' facilities, I received an email from team administrator Fausto Severino retracting the invitation: The visit was "not going to be possible for the moment."

"The only player I've had who could throw harder than this kid was Yewri Guillén. He was tremendous."

I headed over to the academy anyway. My cab driver drove out of downtown Boca Chica on a street that quickly gave way to a trash-lined dirt track. After a few bumpy minutes, the road dead-ended in front of the entrance, which had a large Nationals logo painted on the wall. A security guard sat near the metal gate, chitchatting with a couple of players, an empty batting cage behind them.

Eventually the guard stood up and waved me in. With its smallish concrete dorms, the facility was humble compared to the country's high-end academies, including the $6 million Pirates complex I'd visited a few days before. But it wasn't unpleasant, either; palm trees lined two well-manicured fields beyond the gravel driveway.

The guard suggested there was a kind of family atmosphere to the place, mentioning how some players who'd made it to the minor leagues came back in the offseason to work out. He seemed happy to talk, so I asked him if he knew the player who died.

"Ah, yes," he said, his voice dropping a little. "Yewri, he got sick, went home, and passed away. So sad."

I asked if he thought the team did right by Guillén's parents.

"They collected money," he said. "But what's that to a family that lost a child?"

DiPuglia would tell me later that he saw the settlement deal as fair. "We pushed it through," he said, noting that the team's owners were under no contractual obligation to give Guillén's family the $30,000 bonus or the $50,000 insurance payout. "I think they did the right thing, the humane thing."

Or was it just the relatively small cost of doing business? To hear veteran buscón Astin Jacobo Jr. tell it, locals are well aware that they've gotten the short end of the deal for a long time—even as some aggressively pursue their own stake in the recruiting game. Prior to checking out the Nationals' academy, I'd gone to meet with Jacobo in a resort town near his home base in San Pedro de Macorís, the legendary "cradle of shortstops" that has produced the likes of Alfonso Soriano and Robinson Canó.

As we sat down at a beachfront restaurant for a round of beers, it was hard to miss the costume ring Jacobo was sporting, a long-maned golden lion with faux-diamond eyes. First, he insisted that he wasn't a buscón, because that label implies someone who makes money without working, and he *definitely* works hard for his cut. Then he got right to the point about the market for raw talent. "It's not a secret to anybody that we were being taken advantage of for the last 50 years," he said, smiling. "The kind of players that we signed, for the kind of money that we sold those players, I mean, it's amazing."

Jacobo, who grew up in the Bronx, knows the history of the business. Long before emigrating to the United States, his father, Astin Jacobo Sr., was one of the first successful proto-buscones in the Dominican Republic, operating as a de facto broker for players who lived in the sugarcane mill towns around San Pedro de Macorís in the 1960s and '70s. Many of them, like Astin Sr. himself, were *cocolos*, or dark-skinned immigrants from the English-speaking West Indies. If an MLB scout back then suggested to Astin Sr. or his contemporaries that a 19-year-old wasn't worth signing, more often than not the kid would have a birth certificate in hand the next day showing he was 16. Even the tiny-sounding sums paid to prospects then exceeded the wildest dreams of most Dominicans. And like his son years later, Astin Sr. would get his slice.

As the table filled up with emptied Presidente Lights, Jacobo stepped up his criticism of Major League Baseball, which he said is only interested in reform insofar as it reduces teams' financial risk. He ticked off a list of wealthy Dominican stars who've made untold sums for their clubs and the league—and who were signed for next to nothing back in the day: "Sammy Sosa: $3,500. Miguel Tejada: $2,000. Vladimir Guerrero: $1,800. Trust me, if it was still like that, MLB would never talk about it."

Jacobo claimed that he and others ushered in higher signing bonuses by developing private academies for Dominicans as young as 13 years old. The idea was to better prepare players for showcases, which then helped buscones push for more money from major league teams come negotiation time. To those who charge that buscones take too big of a cut, Jacobo said that on average he spends $10,000 on each player he trains, housing, feeding, and even clothing them until they sign. "And if he's a very special player? You might end up spending $30,000 on a guy who is not your son."

After putting in all that work, he added, he'd be damned if anyone, MLB or otherwise, was going to limit how much he earns. "I have to tell you this," Jacobo said, the sun dipping behind the seaside shops. "We don't care what price they want to put on our players. They're our players. It's going to come down to how much I want to sell them for."

La Canela isn't so much a town as a smattering of houses off a winding two-lane coastal road, a way station between the Gatorade bottling plant in Haina and the Padres' $8 million academy in Najayo. The day I visited, the field where Yewri Guillén once played was filled with romping preteens shagging fly balls and taking turns swinging a cracked aluminum bat. Guillén's former mentor Michael Morla surveyed the scene from behind the first-base dugout, reflecting on the 50-plus players he'd signed to pro contracts since starting his own training program here 15 years ago. Scouts had been showing up frequently to watch Morla's latest star, Fernery Ozuna, another strong-armed, line-drive-smacking prospect.

"The only player I've had who could throw harder than this kid was Yewri," he said. "Guillén was tremendous. Tremendous."

Morla still wasn't sure how to reconcile Guillén's death. If MLB hadn't dallied so long with its identity investigation, he said, maybe Guillén would've been in the United States a year earlier. If the Nationals had sent him to a physician instead of back home to impoverished La Canela, maybe the infection would've been treated successfully.

He pointed me across the road, where several men were sitting in plastic chairs in front of a bright white house with curving iron bars and the letters "Y" and "G" on the facade. I introduced myself to Carlos Guillén, Yewri's father, a chocolate-skinned man with short-cropped silver hair and a raspy voice. His initial answers to questions about his dead son came out in staccato bursts. *He started playing when he was a kid. He played here. Yeah, I played. I was a pitcher. The scouts called him a prospect. Everyone said he would go far.*

I asked him about his son's illness. "He was sick there in the academy," he said. "And then they sent him here sick."

As he recounted the nightmare, his brother, Bienvenido Ortiz, interjected, saying he was the one who'd introduced his nephew to the game. "The only way for a boy to get millions right now in this country, without being an engineer, is baseball," Ortiz said. When Guillén fell ill, he said, he was the one who called around to get his nephew into a hospital and paid for him to be admitted. And when Guillén died, he said, he was the one who wanted to sue the Nationals.

"I told him," Ortiz continued, motioning toward his brother. "'Read the contract. A few strange things are going to show up in there.'"

Ortiz showed me the agreement Guillén's parents signed a month after the funeral, a notarized document that I photographed before handing it back. Exactly when and how Guillén became ill remains unclear to this day. But in 2011, in return for Guillén's $30,000 signing bonus, his parents agreed to the following terms:

(1) that Guillén died of bacterial meningitis, but that he'd contracted it outside of the facility and therefore it had nothing to do with the Nationals;
(2) that the team gave Guillén the appropriate treatment when he got sick;
(3) that they would never sue the team or its employees for the death of their son.

"They came here to screw us over," Ortiz said, his voice rising. "We didn't want problems—we just wanted things to be resolved."

Carlos Guillén looked off at the ball field across the street. It was empty; the kids had all gone home for lunch. Guillén's mother, Sandra Perdomo, later told me that despite the settlement she felt that the Nationals had forgotten about her son. Team officials always used to talk about how they were one big family, she said, "but then what happens? A month and a half after he died, I never heard from them again."

MLB's Rafael Pérez maintains that the league and the Nationals did everything they could. Pérez worked for the Mets at the time, and upon hearing the news, he said, he reviewed his own team's emergency plan. The Guillén tragedy, he said, raised teams' awareness: "I think we all understand that it could've happened any other place." But when pressed about his team's plan for dealing with medical emergencies at the time, or changes to those procedures since, he said, "I cannot go into the details of that. Just put it this way: I think great things came out."

After leaving the Guillén home, it was a short cab ride from La Canela to the tiny Iglesia San Antonio, perched on a small hill just off the road in Nigua. I scanned the church's graveyard, an overgrown, uneven plot filled with aboveground vaults. It took 20 minutes and a phone call back to La Canela to locate Yewri Guillén's final resting place, but eventually I found it, off to the far right.

The Nationals' DiPuglia, shaken by the tragedy, told me that shortly after Guillén's death he'd felt like he needed to come here to the grave, to ask for forgiveness. He hadn't meant to be so hard on the kid, coming down on him for missing a few games because of a stupid headache. "He was like a son," DiPuglia said, pain in his voice. "A second son."

The lower half of the vault was painted a bright sky blue, but the top half was plain concrete, rebar poking out at the corners. A dirty candleholder sat in front of a whitewashed cross, where the teen's first name was misspelled: YEWRY N. GUILLEN P. It was a hushed place in midafternoon, far removed from the busy ball field just minutes away.

Consider the Lobster

For 56 years, the Maine Lobster Festival has been drawing crowds with the promise of sun, fun, and fine food. One visitor would argue that the celebration involves a whole lot more.

DAVID FOSTER WALLACE

The enormous, pungent, and extremely well marketed Maine Lobster Festival is held every late July in the state's midcoast region, meaning the western side of Penobscot Bay, the nerve stem of Maine's lobster industry. What's called the midcoast runs from Owl's Head and Thomaston in the south to Belfast in the north. (Actually, it might extend all the way up to Bucksport, but we were never able to get farther north than Belfast on Route 1, whose summer traffic is, as you can imagine, unimaginable.) The region's two main communities are Camden, with its very old money and yachty harbor and five-star restaurants and phenomenal B&Bs, and Rockland, a serious old fishing town that hosts the Festival every summer in historic Harbor Park, right along the water.[1]

Tourism and lobster are the midcoast region's two main industries, and they're both warm-weather enterprises, and the Maine Lobster Festival represents less an intersection of the industries than a deliberate collision, joyful and lucrative and loud. The assigned subject of this article is the 56th Annual MLF, July 30 to August 3, 2003, whose official theme was "Lighthouses, Laughter, and Lobster." Total paid attendance was over 80,000, due partly to a national CNN spot in June during which a Senior Editor of a certain other epicurean magazine hailed the MLF as one of the best food-themed festivals in the world. 2003 Festival highlights: concerts by Lee Ann Womack and Orleans, annual Maine Sea Goddess beauty pageant, Saturday's big parade, Sunday's William G. Atwood Memorial Crate Race, annual Amateur Cooking Competition, carnival rides and midway attractions and food booths, and the MLF's Main Eating Tent, where something over 25,000 pounds of fresh-caught Maine lobster is consumed after preparation in the World's Largest Lobster Cooker near the grounds' north entrance. Also available are lobster rolls, lobster turnovers, lobster sauté, Down East lobster salad, lobster bisque, lobster ravioli, and deep-fried lobster dumplings. Lobster Thermidor is obtainable at a sit-down restaurant called The Black Pearl on Harbor Park's northwest wharf. A large all-pine booth sponsored by the Maine Lobster Promotion Council has free pamphlets with recipes, eating tips, and Lobster Fun Facts. The winner of Friday's Amateur Cooking Competition prepares Saffron Lobster Ramekins, the recipe for which is available for public downloading at www.mainelobsterfestival.com. There are lobster T-shirts and lobster bobblehead dolls and inflatable lobster pool toys and clamp-on lobster hats with big scarlet claws that wobble on springs. Your assigned correspondent saw it all, accompanied by one girlfriend and both his own parents—one of which parents was actually born and raised in Maine, albeit in the extreme northern inland part, which is potato country and a world away from the touristic midcoast.[2]

For practical purposes, everyone knows what a lobster is. As usual, though, there's much more to know than most of us care about—it's all a matter of what your interests are. Taxonomically speaking, a lobster is a marine crustacean of the family Homaridae, characterized by five pairs of jointed legs, the first pair terminating in large pincerish claws used for subduing prey. Like many other species of benthic carnivore, lobsters are both hunters and scavengers. They have stalked eyes, gills on their legs, and antennae. There are dozens of different kinds worldwide, of which the relevant species here is the Maine lobster, *Homarus americanus.* The name "lobster" comes from the Old English *loppestre,* which is thought to be a corrupt form of the Latin word for locust combined with the Old English *loppe,* which meant spider.

Moreover, a crustacean is an aquatic arthropod of the class Crustacea, which comprises crabs, shrimp, barnacles, lobsters, and freshwater crayfish. All this is right there in the encyclopedia. And an arthropod is an invertebrate member of the phylum Arthropoda, which phylum covers insects, spiders, crustaceans, and centipedes/millipedes, all of whose main commonality, besides the absence of a centralized brain-spine assembly, is a chitinous exoskeleton composed of segments, to which appendages are articulated in pairs.

The point is that lobsters are basically giant sea-insects.[3] Like most arthropods, they date from the Jurassic period, biologically so much older than mammalia that they might as well be from another planet. And they are—particularly in their natural brown-green state, brandishing their claws like weapons and with thick antennae awhip—not nice to look at. And it's true that they are garbagemen of the sea, eaters of dead stuff,[4] although they'll also eat some live shellfish, certain kinds of injured fish, and sometimes each other And it's true that they are garbagemen of the sea, eaters of dead stuff,[4] although they'll also eat some live shellfish, certain kinds of injured fish, and sometimes each other.

But they are themselves good eating. Or so we think now. Up until sometime in the 1800s, though, lobster was literally low-class food, eaten only by the poor and institutionalized. Even in the harsh penal environment of early America, some colonies had laws against feeding lobsters to inmates more than once a week because it was thought to be cruel and unusual, like making people eat rats. One reason for their low status was how plentiful lobsters were in old New England. "Unbelievable abundance" is how one source describes the situation, including accounts of Plymouth pilgrims wading out and capturing all they wanted by hand, and of early Boston's seashore being littered with lobsters after hard storms—these latter were treated as a smelly nuisance and ground up for fertilizer. There is also the fact that premodern lobster was often cooked dead and then preserved, usually packed in salt or crude hermetic containers. Maine's earliest lobster industry was based around a dozen such seaside canneries in the 1840s, from which lobster was shipped as far away as California, in demand only because it was cheap and high in protein, basically chewable fuel.

Now, of course, lobster is posh, a delicacy, only a step or two down from caviar. The meat is richer and more substantial than most fish, its taste subtle compared to the marine-gaminess of mussels and clams.

In the U.S. pop-food imagination, lobster is now the seafood analog to steak, with which it's so often twinned as Surf 'n' Turf on the really expensive part of the chain steak house menu.

In fact, one obvious project of the MLF, and of its omnipresently sponsorial Maine Lobster Promotion Council, is to counter the idea that lobster is unusually luxe or rich or unhealthy or expensive, suitable only for effete palates or the occasional blow-the-diet treat. It is emphasized over and over in presentations and pamphlets at the Festival that Maine lobster meat has fewer calories, less cholesterol, and less saturated fat than chicken.[5] And in the Main Eating Tent, you can get a "quarter" (industry shorthand for a 1-pound lobster), a 4-ounce cup of melted butter, a bag of chips, and a soft roll w/ butter-pat for around $12.00, which is only slightly more expensive than supper at McDonald's.

Be apprised, though, that the Main Eating Tent's suppers come in Styrofoam trays, and the soft drinks are iceless and flat, and the coffee is convenience-store coffee in yet more Styrofoam, and the utensils are plastic (there are none of the special long skinny forks for pushing out the tail meat, though a few savvy diners bring their own). Nor do they give you near enough napkins, considering how messy lobster is to eat, especially when you're squeezed onto benches alongside children of various ages and vastly different levels of fine-motor development—not to mention the people who've somehow smuggled in their own beer in enormous aisle-blocking coolers, or who all of a sudden produce their own plastic tablecloths and try to spread them over large portions of tables to try to reserve them (the tables) for their little groups. And so on. Any one example is no more than a petty inconvenience, of course, but the MLF turns out to be full of irksome little downers like this—see for instance the Main Stage's headliner shows, where it turns out that you have to pay $20 extra for a folding chair if you want to sit down; or the North Tent's mad scramble for the NyQuil-cup-size samples of finalists' entries handed out after the Cooking Competition; or the much-touted Maine Sea Goddess pageant finals, which turn out to be excruciatingly long and to consist mainly of endless thanks and tributes to local sponsors. What the Maine Lobster Festival really is is a midlevel county fair with a culinary hook, and in this respect it's not unlike Tidewater crab festivals, Midwest corn festivals, Texas chili festivals, etc., and shares with these venues the core paradox of all teeming commercial demotic events: It's not for everyone.[6] Nothing against the aforementioned euphoric Senior Editor, but I'd be surprised if she'd spent much time here in Harbor Park, watching people slap canal-zone mosquitoes as they eat deep-fried Twinkies and watch Professor Paddywhack, on six-foot stilts in a raincoat with plastic lobsters protruding from all directions on springs, terrify their children.

Lobster is essentially a summer food. This is because we now prefer our lobsters fresh, which means they have to be recently caught, which for both tactical and economic reasons takes place at depths of less than 25 fathoms. Lobsters tend to be hungriest and most active (i.e., most trappable) at summer water temperatures of 45–50°F. In the autumn, some Maine lobsters migrate out into deeper water, either for warmth or to avoid the heavy waves that pound New England's coast all winter. Some burrow into the bottom. They might hibernate; nobody's sure. Summer is also lobsters' molting season—specifically early-to mid-July. Chitinous arthropods grow by molting, rather the way people have to buy bigger clothes as they age and gain weight. Since lobsters can live to be over 100, they can also get to be quite large, as in 20 pounds or more—though truly senior lobsters are rare now, because New England's waters are so heavily trapped.[7] Anyway, hence the culinary distinction between hard- and soft-shell lobsters, the latter sometimes a.k.a. shedders. A soft-shell lobster is one that has recently molted. In midcoast restaurants, the summer menu often offers both kinds, with shedders being slightly cheaper even though they're easier to dismantle and the meat is allegedly sweeter. The reason for the discount is that a molting lobster uses a layer of seawater for insulation while its new shell is hardening, so there's slightly less actual meat when you crack open a shedder, plus a redolent gout of water that gets all over everything and can sometimes jet out lemonlike and catch a tablemate right in the eye. If it's winter or you're buying lobster someplace far from New England, on the other hand, you can almost bet that the lobster is a hard-shell, which for obvious reasons travel better.

As an à la carte entrée, lobster can be baked, broiled, steamed, grilled, sautéed, stir-fried, or microwaved. The most common method, though, is boiling. If you're someone who enjoys having lobster at home, this is probably the way you do it, since boiling is so easy. You need a large kettle w/ cover, which you fill about half full with water (the standard advice is that you want 2.5 quarts of water per lobster). Seawater is optimal, or you can add two tbsp salt per quart from the tap. It also helps to know how much your lobsters weigh. You get the water boiling, put in the lobsters one at a time, cover the kettle, and bring it back up to a boil. Then you bank the heat and let the kettle simmer—ten minutes for the first pound of lobster, then three minutes for each pound after that. (This is assuming you've got hard-shell lobsters, which, again, if you don't live between Boston and Halifax, is probably what you've got. For shedders, you're supposed to subtract three minutes from the total.) The reason the kettle's lobsters turn scarlet is that boiling somehow suppresses every pigment in their chitin but one. If you want an easy test of whether the lobsters are done, you try pulling on one of their antennae—if it comes out of the head with minimal effort, you're ready to eat.

A detail so obvious that most recipes don't even bother to mention it is that each lobster is supposed to be alive when you put it in the kettle. This is part of lobster's modern appeal: It's the freshest food there is. There's no decomposition between harvesting and eating. And not only do lobsters require no cleaning or dressing or plucking (though the mechanics of actually eating them are a different matter), but they're relatively easy for vendors to keep alive. They come up alive in the traps, are placed in containers of seawater, and can, so long as the water's aerated and the animals' claws are pegged or banded to keep them from tearing one another up under the stresses of captivity,[8] survive right up until they're boiled. Most of us have been in supermarkets or restaurants that feature tanks of live lobster, from which you can pick out your supper while it watches you point. And part of the overall spectacle of the Maine Lobster Festival is that you can see actual lobstermen's vessels docking at the wharves along the northeast grounds and unloading freshly caught product, which is transferred by hand or cart 100 yards to the great clear tanks stacked up around the Festival's cooker—which is, as mentioned, billed as the World's Largest Lobster Cooker and can process over 100 lobsters at a time for the Main Eating Tent.

So then here is a question that's all but unavoidable at the World's Largest Lobster Cooker, and may arise in kitchens across the U.S.: Is it all right to boil a sentient creature alive just for our gustatory pleasure? A related set of concerns: Is the previous question irksomely PC or sentimental? What does "all right" even mean in this context? Is it all just a matter of individual choice?

As you may or may not know, a certain well-known group called People for the Ethical Treatment of Animals thinks that the morality of lobster-boiling is not just a matter of individual conscience. In fact, one of the very first things we hear about the MLF …well, to set the scene: We're coming in by cab from the almost indescribably odd and rustic Knox County Airport[9] very late on the night before the Festival opens, sharing the cab with a wealthy political consultant who lives on Vinalhaven Island in the bay half the year (he's headed for the island ferry in Rockland). The consultant and cabdriver are responding to informal journalistic probes about how people who live in the midcoast region actually view the MLF, as in is the Festival just a big-dollar tourist thing or is it something local residents look forward to attending, take genuine civic pride in, etc. The cabdriver—who's in his seventies, one of apparently a whole platoon of retirees the cab company puts on to help with the summer rush, and wears a U.S.-flag lapel pin, and drives in what can only be called a very deliberate way—assures us that locals do endorse and enjoy the MLF, although he himself hasn't gone in years, and now come to think of it no one he and his wife know has, either. However, the demilocal consultant's been to recent Festivals a couple times (one gets the impression it was at his wife's behest), of which his most vivid impression was that "you have to line up for an ungodly long time to get your lobsters, and meanwhile there are all these ex–flower children coming up and down along the line handing out pamphlets that say the lobsters die in terrible pain and you shouldn't eat them."

And it turns out that the post-hippies of the consultant's recollection were activists from PETA. There were no PETA people in obvious view at the 2003 MLF,[10] but they've been conspicuous at many of the recent Festivals. Since at least the mid-1990s, articles in everything from *The Camden Herald* to *The New York Times* have described PETA urging boycotts of the MLF, often deploying celebrity spokespeople like Mary Tyler Moore for open letters and ads saying stuff like "Lobsters are extraordinarily sensitive" and "To me, eating a lobster is out of the question." More concrete is the oral testimony of Dick, our florid and extremely gregarious rental-car guy, to the effect that PETA's been around so much in recent years that a kind of brittlely tolerant homeostasis now obtains between the activists and the Festival's locals, e.g.: "We had some incidents a couple years ago. One lady took most of her clothes off and painted herself like a lobster, almost got herself arrested. But for the most part they're let alone. [Rapid series of small ambiguous laughs, which with Dick happens a lot.] They do their thing and we do our thing."

This whole interchange takes place on Route 1, 30 July, during a four-mile, 50-minute ride from the airport[11] to the dealership to sign car-rental papers. Several irreproducible segues down the road from the PETA anecdotes, Dick—whose son-in-law happens to be a professional lobsterman and one of the Main Eating Tent's regular suppliers—articulates what he and his family feel is the crucial mitigating factor in the whole morality-of-boiling-lobsters-alive issue: "There's a part of the brain in people and animals that lets us feel pain, and lobsters' brains don't have this part."

Besides the fact that it's incorrect in about 11 different ways, the main reason Dick's statement is interesting is that its thesis is more or less echoed by the Festival's own pronouncement on lobsters and pain, which is part of a Test Your Lobster IQ quiz that appears in the 2003 MLF program courtesy of the Maine Lobster Promotion Council: "The nervous system of a lobster is very simple, and is in fact most similar to the nervous system of the grasshopper. It is decentralized with no brain. There is no cerebral cortex, which in humans is the area of the brain that gives the experience of pain."

Though it sounds more sophisticated, a lot of the neurology in this latter claim is still either false or fuzzy. The human cerebral cortex is the brain-part that deals with higher faculties like reason, metaphysical self-awareness, language, etc. Pain reception is known to be part of a much older and more primitive system of nociceptors and prostaglandins that are managed by the brain stem and thalamus.[12] On the other hand, it is true that the cerebral cortex is involved in what's variously called suffering, distress, or the emotional experience of pain—i.e., experiencing painful stimuli as unpleasant, very unpleasant, unbearable, and so on.

Before we go any further, let's acknowledge that the questions of whether and how different kinds of animals feel pain, and of whether and why it might be justifiable to inflict pain on them in order to eat them, turn out to be extremely complex and difficult. And comparative neuroanatomy is only part of the problem. Since pain is a totally subjective mental experience, we do not have direct access to anyone or anything's pain but our own; and even just the principles by which we can infer that others experience pain and have a legitimate interest in not feeling pain involve hard-core philosophy—metaphysics, epistemology, value theory, ethics. The fact that even the most highly evolved nonhuman mammals can't use language to communicate with us about their subjective mental experience is only the first layer of additional complication in trying to extend our reasoning about pain and morality to animals. And everything gets progressively more abstract and convoluted as we move farther and farther out from the higher-type mammals into cattle and swine and dogs and cats and rodents, and then birds and fish, and finally invertebrates like lobsters.

The more important point here, though, is that the whole animal-cruelty-and-eating issue is not just complex, it's also uncomfortable. It is, at any rate, uncomfortable for me, and for just about everyone I know who enjoys a variety of foods and yet does not want to see herself as cruel or unfeeling. As far as I can tell, my own main way of dealing with this conflict has been to avoid thinking about the whole unpleasant thing. I should add that it appears to me unlikely that many readers of *Gourmet* wish to think hard about it, either, or to be queried about the morality of their eating habits in the pages of a culinary monthly. Since, however, the assigned subject of this article is what it was like to attend the 2003 MLF, and thus to spend several days in the midst of a great mass of Americans all eating lobster, and thus to be more or less impelled to think hard about lobster and the experience of buying and eating lobster, it turns out that there is no honest way to avoid certain moral questions.

There are several reasons for this. For one thing, it's not just that lobsters get boiled alive, it's that you do it yourself—or at least it's done specifically for you, on-site.[13] As mentioned, the World's Largest Lobster Cooker, which is highlighted as an attraction in the Festival's program, is right out there on the MLF's north grounds for everyone to see. Try to imagine a Nebraska Beef Festival[14] at which part of the festivities is watching trucks pull up and the live cattle get driven down the ramp and slaughtered right there on the World's Largest Killing Floor or something—there's no way.

The intimacy of the whole thing is maximized at home, which of course is where most lobster gets prepared and eaten (although note already the semiconscious euphemism "prepared," which in the case of lobsters really means killing them right there in our kitchens). The basic scenario is that we come in from the store and make our little preparations like getting the kettle filled and boiling, and then we lift the lobsters out of the bag or whatever retail container they came home in …whereupon some uncomfortable things start to happen. However stuporous the lobster is from the trip home, for instance, it tends to come alarmingly to life when placed in boiling water. If you're tilting it from a container into the steaming kettle, the lobster will sometimes try to cling to the container's sides or even to hook its claws over the kettle's rim like a person trying to keep from going over the edge of a roof. And worse is when the lobster's fully immersed. Even if you cover the kettle and turn away, you can usually hear the cover rattling and clanking as the lobster tries to push it off. Or the creature's claws scraping the sides of the kettle as it thrashes around. The lobster, in other words, behaves very much as you or I would behave if we were plunged into boiling water (with the obvious exception of screaming).[15] A blunter way to say this is that the lobster acts as if it's in terrible pain, causing some cooks to leave the kitchen altogether and to take one of those little lightweight plastic oven timers with them into another room and wait until the whole process is over.

There happen to be two main criteria that most ethicists agree on for determining whether a living creature has the capacity to suffer and so has genuine interests that it may or may not be our moral duty to consider.[16] One is how much of the neurological hardware required for pain-experience the animal comes equipped with—nociceptors, prostaglandins, neuronal opioid receptors, etc. The other criterion is whether the animal demonstrates behavior associated with pain. And it takes a lot of intellectual gymnastics and behaviorist hairsplitting not to see struggling, thrashing, and lid-clattering as just such pain-behavior. According to marine zoologists, it usually takes lobsters between 35 and 45 seconds to die in boiling water. (No source I could find talked about how long it takes them to die in superheated steam; one rather hopes it's faster.)

There are, of course, other fairly common ways to kill your lobster on-site and so achieve maximum freshness. Some cooks' practice is to drive a sharp heavy knife point-first into a spot just above the midpoint between the lobster's eyestalks (more or less where the Third Eye is in human foreheads). This is alleged either to kill the lobster instantly or to render it insensate—and is said at least to eliminate the cowardice involved in throwing a creature into boiling water and then fleeing the room. As far as I can tell from talking to proponents of the knife-in-the-head method, the idea is that it's more violent but ultimately more merciful, plus that a willingness to exert personal agency and accept responsibility for stabbing the lobster's head honors the lobster somehow and entitles one to eat it. (There's often a vague sort of Native American spirituality-of-the-hunt flavor to pro-knife arguments.) But the problem with the knife method is basic biology: Lobsters' nervous systems operate off not one but several ganglia, a.k.a. nerve bundles, which are sort of wired in series and distributed all along the lobster's underside, from stem to stern. And disabling only the frontal ganglion does not normally result in quick death or unconsciousness. Another alternative is to put the lobster in cold salt water and then very slowly bring it up to a full boil. Cooks who advocate this method are going mostly on the analogy to a frog, which can supposedly be kept from jumping out of a boiling pot by heating the water incrementally. In order to save a lot of research-summarizing, I'll simply assure you that the analogy between frogs and lobsters turns out not to hold.

Ultimately, the only certain virtues of the home-lobotomy and slow-heating methods are comparative, because there are even worse/crueler ways people prepare lobster. Time-thrifty cooks sometimes microwave them alive (usually after poking several extra vent holes in the carapace, which is a precaution most shellfish-microwavers learn about the hard way). Live dismemberment, on the other hand, is big in Europe: Some chefs cut the lobster in half before cooking; others like to tear off the claws and tail and toss only these parts in the pot.

And there's more unhappy news respecting suffering-criterion number one. Lobsters don't have much in the way of eyesight or hearing, but they do have an exquisite tactile sense, one facilitated by hundreds of thousands of tiny hairs that protrude through their carapace. "Thus," in the words of T.M. Prudden's industry classic *About Lobster,* "it is that although encased in what seems a solid, impenetrable armor, the lobster can receive stimuli and impressions from without as readily as if it possessed a soft and delicate skin." And lobsters do have nociceptors,[17] as well as invertebrate versions of the prostaglandins and major neurotransmitters via which our own brains register pain.

Lobsters do not, on the other hand, appear to have the equipment for making or absorbing natural opioids like endorphins and enkephalins, which are what more advanced nervous systems use to try to handle intense pain. From this fact, though, one could conclude either that lobsters are maybe even *more* vulnerable to pain, since they lack mammalian nervous systems' built-in analgesia, or, instead, that the absence of natural opioids implies an absence of the really intense pain-sensations that natural opioids are designed to mitigate. I for one can detect a marked upswing in mood as I contemplate this latter possibility: It could be that their lack of endorphin/enkephalin hardware means that lobsters' raw subjective experience of pain is so radically different from mammals' that it may not even deserve the term *pain.* Perhaps lobsters are more like those frontal-lobotomy patients one reads about who report experiencing pain in a totally different way than you and I. These patients evidently do feel physical pain, neurologically speaking, but don't dislike it—though neither do they like it; it's more that they feel it but don't feel anything *about* it— the point being that the pain is not distressing to them or something they want to get away from. Maybe lobsters, who are also without frontal lobes, are detached from the neurological-registration-of-injury- or-hazard we call pain in just the same way. There is, after all, a difference between (1) pain as a purely neurological event, and (2) actual suffering, which seems crucially to involve an emotional component, an awareness of pain as unpleasant, as something to fear/dislike/want to avoid.

Still, after all the abstract intellection, there remain the facts of the frantically clanking lid, the pathetic clinging to the edge of the pot. Standing at the stove, it is hard to deny in any meaningful way that this is a living creature experiencing pain and wishing to avoid/escape the painful experience. To my lay mind, the lobster's behavior in the kettle appears to be the expression of a *preference;* and it may well be that an ability to form preferences is the decisive criterion for real suffering.[18] The logic of this (preference p suffering) relation may be easiest to see in the negative case. If you cut certain kinds of worms in half, the halves will often keep crawling around and going about their vermiform business as if nothing had happened. When we assert, based on their post-op behavior, that these worms appear not to be suffering, what we're really saying is that there's no sign that the worms know anything bad has happened or would *prefer* not to have gotten cut in half.

Lobsters, however, are known to exhibit preferences. Experiments have shown that they can detect changes of only a degree or two in water temperature; one reason for their complex migratory cycles (which can often cover 100-plus miles a year) is to pursue the temperatures they like best.[19] And, as mentioned, they're bottom-dwellers and do not like bright light: If a tank of food lobsters is out in the sunlight or a store's fluorescence, the lobsters will always congregate in whatever part is darkest. Fairly solitary in the ocean, they also clearly dislike the crowding that's part of their captivity in tanks, since (as also mentioned) one reason why lobsters' claws are banded on capture is to keep them from attacking one another under the stress of close-quarter storage.

In any event, at the Festival, standing by the bubbling tanks outside the World's Largest Lobster Cooker, watching the fresh-caught lobsters pile over one another, wave their hobbled claws impotently, huddle in the rear corners, or scrabble frantically back from the glass as you approach, it is difficult not to sense that they're unhappy, or frightened, even if it's some rudimentary version of these feelings . . . and, again, why does rudimentariness even enter into it? Why is a primitive, inarticulate form of suffering less urgent or uncomfortable for the person who's helping to inflict it by paying for the food it results in? I'm not trying to give you a PETA-like screed here—at least I don't think so. I'm trying, rather, to work out and articulate some of the troubling questions that arise amid all the laughter and saltation and community pride of the Maine Lobster Festival. The truth is that if you, the Festival attendee, permit yourself to think that lobsters can suffer and would rather not, the MLF can begin to take on aspects of something like a Roman circus or medieval torture-fest.

Does that comparison seem a bit much? If so, exactly why? Or what about this one: Is it not possible that future generations will regard our own present agribusiness and eating practices in much the same way we now view Nero's entertainments or Aztec sacrifices? My own immediate reaction is that such a comparison is hysterical, extreme—and yet the reason it seems extreme to me appears to be that I believe animals are less morally important than human beings;[20] and when it comes to defending such a belief, even to myself, I have to acknowledge that (a) I have an obvious selfish interest in this belief, since I like to eat certain kinds of animals and want to be able to keep doing it, and (b) I have not succeeded in working out any sort of personal ethical system in which the belief is truly defensible instead of just selfishly convenient.

Given this article's venue and my own lack of culinary sophistication, I'm curious about whether the reader can identify with any of these reactions and acknowledgments and discomforts. I am also concerned not to come off as shrill or preachy when what I really am is confused. Given the (possible) moral status and (very possible) physical suffering of the animals involved, what ethical convictions do gourmets evolve that allow them not just to eat but to savor and enjoy flesh-based viands (since of course refined *enjoyment*, rather than just ingestion, is the whole point of gastronomy)? And for those gourmets who'll have no truck with convictions or rationales and who regard stuff like the previous paragraph as just so much pointless navel-gazing, what makes it feel okay, inside, to dismiss the whole issue out of hand? That is, is their refusal to think about any of this the product of actual thought, or is it just that they don't want to think about it? Do they ever think about their reluctance to think about it? After all, isn't being extra aware and attentive and thoughtful about one's food and its overall context part of what distinguishes a real gourmet? Or is all the gourmet's extra attention and sensibility just supposed to be aesthetic, gustatory?

These last couple queries, though, while sincere, obviously involve much larger and more abstract questions about the connections (if any) between aesthetics and morality, and these questions lead straightaway into such deep and treacherous waters that it's probably best to stop the public discussion right here. There are limits to what even interested persons can ask of each other.

ENDNOTES

1. There's a comprehensive native apothegm: "Camden by the sea, Rockland by the smell."
2. N.B. All personally connected parties have made it clear from the start that they do not want to be talked about in this article.
3. Midcoasters' native term for a lobster is, in fact, "bug," as in "Come around on Sunday and we'll cook up some bugs."
4. Factoid: Lobster traps are usually baited with dead herring.
5. Of course, the common practice of dipping the lobster meat in melted butter torpedoes all these happy fat-specs, which none of the Council's promotional stuff ever mentions, any more than potato-industry PR talks about sour cream and bacon bits.
6. In truth, there's a great deal to be said about the differences between working-class Rockland and the heavily populist flavor of its Festival versus comfortable and elitist Camden with its expensive view and shops given entirely over to $200 sweaters and great rows of Victorian homes converted to upscale B&Bs. And about these differences as two sides of the great coin that is U.S. tourism. Very little of which will be said here, except to amplify the above-mentioned paradox and to reveal your assigned correspondent's own preferences. I confess that I have never understood why so many people's idea of a fun vacation is to don flip-flops and sunglasses and crawl through maddening traffic to loud hot crowded tourist venues in order to sample a "local flavor" that is by definition ruined by the presence of tourists. This may (as my Festival companions keep pointing out) all be a matter of personality and hardwired taste: The fact that I just do not like tourist venues means that I'll never understand their appeal and so am probably not the one to talk about it (the supposed appeal). But, since this note will almost surely not survive magazine-editing anyway, here goes:

   As I see it, it probably really is good for the soul to be a tourist, even if it's only once in a while. Not good for the soul in a refreshing or enlivening way, though, but rather in a grim, steely-eyed, let's-look-honestly-at-the-facts-and-find-some-way-to-deal-with-them way. My personal experience has not been that traveling around the country is broadening or relaxing, or that radical changes in place and context have a salutary effect, but rather that intranational tourism is radically constricting, and humbling in the hardest way—hostile to my fantasy of being a real individual, of living somehow outside and above it all. (Coming up is the part that my companions find especially unhappy and repellent, a sure way to spoil the fun of vacation travel:) To be a mass tourist, for me, is to become a pure late-date American: alien, ignorant, greedy for something you cannot ever have, disappointed in a way you can never admit. It is to spoil, by way of sheer ontology, the very unspoiledness you are there to experience. It is to impose yourself on places that in all noneconomic ways would be better, realer, without you. It is, in lines and gridlock and transaction after transaction, to confront a dimension of yourself that is as inescapable as it is painful: As a tourist, you become economically significant but existentially loathsome, an insect on a dead thing.

7. Datum: In a good year, the U.S. industry produces around 80 million pounds of lobster, and Maine accounts for more than half that total.

8. N.B. Similar reasoning underlies the practice of what's termed "debeaking" broiler chickens and brood hens in modern factory farms. Maximum commercial efficiency requires that enormous poultry populations be confined in unnaturally close quarters, under which conditions many birds go crazy and peck one another to death. As a purely observational side-note, be apprised that debeaking is usually an automated process and that the chickens receive no anesthetic. It's not clear to me whether most gourmet readers know about debeaking, or about related practices like dehorning cattle in commercial feedlots, cropping swine's tails in factory hog farms to keep psychotically bored neighbors from chewing them off, and so forth. It so happens that your assigned correspondent knew almost nothing about standard meat-industry operations before starting work on this article.

9. The terminal used to be somebody's house, for example, and the lost-luggage-reporting room was clearly once a pantry.

10. It turned out that one Mr. William R. Rivas-Rivas, a high-ranking PETA official out of the group's Virginia headquarters, was indeed there this year, albeit solo, working the Festival's main and side entrances on Saturday, August 2, handing out pamphlets and adhesive stickers emblazoned with "Being Boiled Hurts," which is the tagline in most of PETA's published material about lobster. I learned that he'd been there only later, when speaking with Mr. Rivas-Rivas on the phone. I'm not sure how we missed seeing him *in situ* at the Festival, and I can't see much to do except apologize for the oversight—although it's also true that Saturday was the day of the big MLF parade through Rockland, which basic journalistic responsibility seemed to require going to (and which, with all due respect, meant that Saturday was maybe not the best day for PETA to work the Harbor Park grounds, especially if it was going to be just one person for one day, since a lot of diehard MLF partisans were off-site watching the parade (which, again with no offense intended, was in truth kind of cheesy and boring, consisting mostly of slow homemade floats and various midcoast people waving at one another, and with an extremely annoying man dressed as Blackbeard ranging up and down the length of the crowd saying "Arrr" over and over and brandishing a plastic sword at people, etc.; plus it rained)).

11. The short version regarding why we were back at the airport after already arriving the previous night involves lost luggage and a miscommunication about where and what the local National Car Rental franchise was—Dick came out personally to the airport and got us, out of no evident motive but kindness. (He also talked nonstop the entire way, with a very distinctive speaking style that can be described only as manically laconic; the truth is that I now know more about this man than I do about some members of my own family.)

12. To elaborate by way of example: The common experience of accidentally touching a hot stove and yanking your hand back before you're even aware that anything's going on is explained by the fact that many of the processes by which we detect and avoid painful stimuli do not involve the cortex. In the case of the hand and stove, the brain is bypassed altogether; all the important neurochemical action takes place in the spine.

13. Morality-wise, let's concede that this cuts both ways. Lobster-eating is at least not abetted by the system of corporate factory farms that produces most beef, pork, and chicken. Because, if nothing

else, of the way they're marketed and packaged for sale, we eat these latter meats without having to consider that they were once conscious, sentient creatures to whom horrible things were done. (N.B. PETA distributes a certain video—the title of which is being omitted as part of the elaborate editorial compromise by which this note appears at all—in which you can see just about everything meat--related you don't want to see or think about. (N.B.[2]Not that PETA's any sort of font of unspun truth. Like many partisans in complex moral disputes, the PETA people are -fanatics, and a lot of their rhetoric seems simplistic and self-righteous. Personally, though, I have to say that I found this unnamed video both credible and deeply upsetting.))

14. Is it significant that "lobster," "fish," and "chicken" are our culture's words for both the animal and the meat, whereas most mammals seem to require euphemisms like "beef" and "pork" that help us separate the meat we eat from the living creature the meat once was? Is this evidence that some kind of deep unease about eating higher animals is endemic enough to show up in English usage, but that the unease diminishes as we move out of the mammalian order? (And is "lamb"/"lamb" the counterexample that sinks the whole theory, or are there special, biblico-historical reasons for that equivalence?)

15. There's a relevant populist myth about the high-pitched whistling sound that sometimes issues from a pot of boiling lobster. The sound is really vented steam from the layer of seawater between the lobster's flesh and its carapace (this is why shedders whistle more than hard-shells), but the pop version has it that the sound is the lobster's rabbitlike death scream. Lobsters communicate via pheromones in their urine and don't have anything close to the vocal equipment for screaming, but the myth's very persistent—which might, once again, point to a low-level cultural unease about the boiling thing.

16. "Interests" basically means strong and legitimate preferences, which obviously require some degree of consciousness, responsiveness to stimuli, etc. See, for instance, the utilitarian philosopher Peter Singer, whose 1974 *Animal Liberation* is more or less the bible of the modern animal-rights movement: "It would be nonsense to say that it was not in the interests of a stone to be kicked along the road by a schoolboy. A stone does not have interests because it cannot suffer. Nothing that we can do to it could possibly make any difference to its welfare. A mouse, on the other hand, does have an interest in not being kicked along the road, because it will suffer if it is."

17. This is the neurological term for special pain receptors that are (according to Jane A. Smith and Kenneth M. Boyd's *Lives in the Balance*) "sensitive to potentially damaging extremes of temperature, to mechanical forces, and to chemical substances which are released when body tissues are damaged."

18. "Preference" is maybe roughly synonymous with "interest," but it is a better term for our purposes because it's less abstractly philosophical—"preference" seems more personal, and it's the whole idea of a living creature's personal experience that's at issue.

19. Of course, the most common sort of counterargument here would begin by objecting that "like best" is really just a metaphor, and a misleadingly anthropomorphic one at that. The counterarguer would posit that the lobster seeks to maintain a certain optimal ambient temperature out of nothing but unconscious instinct (with a similar explanation for the low-light affinities about to be mentioned in the main text). The thrust of such a counterargument will be that the lobster's thrashings and clankings in the kettle express not unpreferred pain but involuntary reflexes, like your leg shooting out when the doctor hits your knee. Be advised that there are professional scientists, including many

researchers who use animals in experiments, who hold to the view that nonhuman creatures have no real feelings at all, only "behaviors." Be further advised that this view has a long history that goes all the way back to Descartes, although its modern support comes mostly from behaviorist psychology.

To these what-look-like-pain-are-really-only-reflexes counterarguments, however, there happen to be all sorts of scientific and pro-animal-rights countercounterarguments. And then further attempted rebuttals and redirects, and so on. Suffice to say that both the scientific and the philosophical arguments on either side of the animal-suffering issue are involved, abstruse, technical, often informed by self-interest or ideology, and in the end so totally inconclusive that as a practical matter, in the kitchen or restaurant, it all still seems to come down to individual conscience, going with (no pun) your gut.

20. Meaning a *lot* less important, apparently, since the moral comparison here is not the value of one human's life vs. the value of one animal's life, but rather the value of one animal's life vs. the value of one human's taste for a particular kind of protein. Even the most diehard carniphile will acknowledge that it's possible to live and eat well without consuming animals.Sed que parciatiant od mo berfera tempore peresecus es magnam fuga. Nam inusaerspid eius ipsam est essin cum earchitate doloresti ate dem natatusaecus duntore aceat reruptae que verionseque sedissunt vit re re cus reprere, et, quiaecus nihilique re, in re occum, ad que premolores de vellati aessecatesti rem sinitiis aliquisimod min re odicium qui omnis eicilitasit eature et, ullectis eosamus es est, unt aute nulpa sima praeriatem et es doluptatur aliqui od que sa nonsequiam inctae volupta ne cone corestia si assequam vera nossi inctem ad mi, omnihicat magnam, omni corrovi tamenis erferibus aute cus eariora temodit, ommolor sum iur raturiatur sit quas ditatiu stotas iditiae nos ressim utempor roviduntur a sequis dolestibus eatem qui consequas commolorum dolo iunt, cus re reperem. Nam quas el et qui nim faccusdae recuptae conem ut ut fugia cumquo ipis es moles coreribus rempores mollacc ullaut alibust empelec earibus simincte latae eiumquiam, nonsequae volorro consedicae voloria venda preic tem nos molorioriti blationsenda dolorro tem repel is ni sitatest et erit eaqui officias dit, ommodis et a quibus del id quos seriaspe vellore il ipsum hitatis sequiam harcitatur?

Tem voluptas moditas ni autemos est labo. Ita voloreped ea sit ad que nis pro mil etur rerit offici dolupid uciisqu aeruptiamet repeliquam hil in perferiae volum a quo et harcient venis excera denet lamusandae. Et as nam quidit vitium simporiam accum doluptatur sinis aspidun dandis volupta quatis re volessunt acium ut laturit a volectiam essecti iscipitium et, sequam harchil lecaepe lliatus, omnis erum voluptatem in resto cumque officaectaes nectaquos quia doloreribea coribus sed modiore mporeprenis ipsum fuga. Et ommolup taerum rescia doluptus arum dolende rchilibus eiuntorum aut moles pre si ute eos nam a sedis explign iatem. Moluptatem quas anditiatis molorep ernatem qui quisquas qui offici dolupta tionseque rendaest aut quibus volest repelectus recea dunto des prero conestio bero ium dolorati vendipsam que acipsa dia incid maior maionsed quam con et quam escita sit, eos et harum volor alignih illuptur, ut acepedi doluptatem vella pel eiur seces sunt et adit, sitis nem adi dolorpo rendicitia dolor aliquibus.

Ficipsam, oditate sequate cestiam, ullaborehent eaqui aut atet odi consequi officillupta doluptia atusam que nos eum estrume sundit velenia pa nonest la velenit maionseque nobit latur?

Em venderfero est lautend itatur sequia venisim poribus sit alit prate volest exeressunt, conse sum eaqui nimpori tem in rerrunt.

Unt, od qui ipsamustiat dolute volupta quatinc ipsumque sit velia verum reriaecae. Icipsapit am sediame liciamusae imi, opti tessin repel et ommolut labo. Nam aut de prerfer estoriant volupta tatent.

Explaut anis alis et modisquo te quis mod earum et quodisim dolendi quidem et am nobit aut ut dolupta temquam quiscimendis que mollabo rruntorerit, ea doluptur moluptatur, od qui nost, que sequas eum eari natur? Ut rest occabo. Must quat et qui aditio et iur sitae nus coreperes maximin vernam quidit, nonesciis et volorerae nullupta doluptas ipsandae voloreiciae est hiliciis cullabo. Itas est odis esci cum, sent, ute vendam natur, sequi nonest, si volore ipitiate voluptatium faccatquos is intium qui blabori ostions ectiat quiam cones es nit aut liquidem quis eatecum reperchictas vid maio. Et dolorporem ipsaeperfero et ad quia conectotas dolorem. Itat.

Fic to odipsam el intibusandi cullatur molestibus, conecte nihilis ne voluptis et abor simo quatem aut exerumenitat offic tem volorit, odis velis non et ea que solupta tempor aliquo molorumque nos est, non pre cone sa nonsed quiam quatur?

Et et libus, sedi re culliqu atesedi nis expliquidel molest, tem eum rem faccuscia consed quiaepero con comnisquias quis evelit, comnitaquae voluptur aces maximosse none num fugia nihille sequis nonescit velignate non rerferum velluptassi veratem ne prehend icatibusanda comnient facillabo. Et unt acita et volut alitatat doluptatiis qui ut hilit veriaspedi incipsa perchit laborep erepellupta que pro volorer ectatus andelestione aut dunt que etur re non coris ea nonsequo eost, cullanist esequam volupta tionseq uosandist, nis apicipi deliqui tem facillaudant omnieniet aborunt, quam fuga. Ga. Ficipsa nonet opti omnis volore molorem volor si omnient inctium as doluptiae lam ipidunt unt odionse quatem re volectat.

Am et modignimus incipsa erum faceatet que ventium volorat ibusdam et quae. Os eiusam eostori bustorrum rem laborent optati rem ut inci il inctati que dem liquisit debisti orporerae occus et, ilignis sitatia dollor sustiunt essime suntis dolor sitat omnimus aut etur re vercit dolori sint ommo illore cus velluptatem fugitem alit et perum repta nobistin cumqui omni con peria quasperum fuga. Ut faceatur, consequ aturis est eum explique cullestore cor mi, imodita tiatem everum estotatur, simillu ptatent ex expe nonseri orumquam, a niti illest et aut facepud ignihil eatem faccatqui voloremporit autent quia comnist ruptaque duci dellorum conseque is illupta temolorrum quis adis iniati dolutaectur?

Aquis dolum fugiataerio. Ugiant il id est magnam, quos quia doluptur rem sereiunt quost doluptassunt ad quam aliquaepti anditibusae non nisquo berum alibustiae eos sit inusdame vides comnihil esti tem harum eicia plit aut moluptatem hictatem atus etum et etur, secatatiant, arum et ea quo magnis et qui bla con conseca borehentia quasintiam que maxim que suntur si qui ut aut restium, odis min ea vel ma provid quundae laciis vellitis dollabo resciunt ex eum quisque velesci psapit anto officto eos sandis rem quod maximperum quia serem que volecatem et et audanimil id et quatia qui sime simet, ut que voluptatur? At asitae labores accus enim aperro dolorum, aliscimus magnissunt pe omnimetur, qui aliquos dellaut est quatusa ndipsamusdae aut ani untin et, a veris seditaquia quodissunt hit, si consequ ideria as magnis et, ea inverciuntem explam net quianditam ius ratur solupta vid ut hit, andam quam quatatque quiatiaesti que et ad quae soluptae videnis eos sunt qui dit apidel is verro to beaquas de volore, optatus, cum faci occusa voluptas non corem cuptati busaperspe volupta tument, occum fuga. Ut placcatia se aut quas min rem vellore netur ra perionemque nonseque dolenia ipsum aut quibus et faccae diorio bearum, officid qui ipitam, auda suntus magnistium et quatia voluptur sinitat molenitem doluptam qui si num quam, cus et erovides se premper erempor apis aperovi tatur? Qui quaeserrumet officienia sunt omnis asinvel et plibus. Ihicient. Atiur am, quis aliteces et reribus quatur, omnihil labora sum explabo rehendae vitat officat inimpos simus, quiatur aspiciisquae experrum quati tore nesequas mod estia conectem re porehen duciam inctem vendis dolor ma et quatinu llatum vent eatur, corias aspic tem vernatiae. Eritatiatur sam et ex earchicit alitaturi blatem que am rehentemqui tem estemporeped ea vellaute sitat maximinctem

PART 3

Award-Winning Student Essays

Nicole Bowman
Anne Wheeler
College Writing 113-16
September 29, 2015

What a Nun Taught Me About Feminism

At 9:47 am on August 27th, 2015, the door to a new world of literacy was cracked open. It was the first day of my senior year in high school. I strolled into room 36 that morning sporting my senior blue tie dye and a smile that was far too big for my face. It was time for the Bay View Academy students to start their period B class. No other girl in Mercy Hall would be as happy as I was during those ninety minutes in our academic schedules. This was not just any class; this was Honors Literary Analysis with Sister Carol.

Sister Carol is not your run of the mill nun. She does not wear a habit or smack our knuckles with rulers. No, Sister Carol is a Sister of Mercy, the cool order of nuns. She is a kind, selfless, and intelligent teacher who was not afraid to touch upon controversial topics. With her profound voice, glasses, blonde pixie haircut, and fabulous sass, she ran the classroom like no one's business. Sister Carol incorporated major political and ethical themes and issues throughout our course's curriculum that challenged us not just as students, but as human beings. Her lessons and assignments made me ask myself what it means to be a woman in our world. Sister Carol's class made me the feminist I am today, and for that I am truly grateful.

I took a seat at an open desk. After some brief introductions and an overview of the syllabus, the first lesson began. "Literature is art, ladies." Sister Carol summed up the beautiful system of written words so simply. She continued with her lecture, "literature uses words to unleash creativity, self-expression, and emotion, much like any art piece." But how do we as readers tap into that? Sister Carol explained how writers use diction, syntax, tone, and imagery to paint their masterpieces.

This new vocabulary awakened the reader in me that always wanted more. We learned how writers do not choose their words willy-nilly. A writer thinks about what they want to say and that is the unique pattern of language they choose. No other person on this earth would write the same exact piece. We learned to listen and feel the atmosphere the writing gave us. Is it creepy and haunting? Motivational and uplifting? Humorous and entertaining? Boring and dull? We learned to be attentive to the images and figurative language the author provides. The writer is painting you a picture and it is necessary to look at it to understand the artwork.

Sister Carol equipped us with our annotation toolbox on the first day of class. That has been the greatest gift I have received in high school. I now had the ability to connect to a world that I thought I knew, but had no idea how truly amazing it really was. It was time to explore. We were going to be digging deep into literature and getting dirty with words.

Our very first assignment was to read and annotate an essay entitled, "Wholeness," written by Joan Chittister. We were to highlight vivid imagery, figures of speech, and note words or phrases that had meaning to us. I had never done something like this before. I never thought about what was behind the words, all my life I was only touching the surface. Now I was probing, picking, and pulling apart every syllable of an essay.

Using my fancy Notability App on my iPad, I underlined, highlighted, and made notes all over the pages. My screen became a rainbow of literary analysis. I was really tuning into the words, content, and the voice of Joan Chittister. Paying close attention to the figurative language and reason behind the writing made me feel Chittister's fiery spirit. She blended ecology, theology, feminism so beautifully into a new worldview. Her essay was focused on how humans have turned away from God, exploited all of mother earth's resources, and are treating women like "potted plants." She listed ten ideals that humanity has created and lives because we believe that "each plane of creation is higher than the last." Humanity has molded all of the earth's creation into a pyramid of power. Joan sarcastically states, "humans are superior to nature, and men – males – the crown, the pinnacle, the divine pride of creation, are superior to women." Underneath the top tiers of humanity are all of our resources. Men come to believe that "nature has no reason for existence except to serve human existence." The men suppress the power and importance of God, women, and nature all throughout time. If you think Chittister is making this up, please, open a history book.

Joan Chittister proposed a new worldview. One in which we see God, men, women, and the environment as one, a "concert of waves." She explains that, "Eco-feminism brings humanity to wholeness, wholeness to religion, and integrity to a science, which having proved that there is no one species on earth that is the only one that counts, does, in that instance, give the lie to the anthropocentric to the andocentric, and to the oppression and invisibility in the public arena of women as well." This woman quickly became my eco-feminism superhero.

"Wholeness" taught me that feminism is multidimensional. We have a big issue on our hands. Women are fighting the "crown of creation" for equality and autonomy, but what are we going to do with those once we get it? How are we going to tell the male species that their worldview is totally wrong and we need to fix it? We need to unleash the power of eco-feminism. Peace comes when we see all creation as extension of life. Every race, species, planet, body of water, needs to be treated with respect and love because we were all created by one God. There is one spirit that lives in all, all of earth is really one body. Treating women poorly is like punching yourself in stomach, your whole body is going to ache if you do not stop. A healthy body needs holistic love and care, and so does creation.

"Wholeness," was an excellent introduction to our very first unit in the course, "Women's Struggle for Self-Realization." We read and annotated a number or essays, short stories, plays, and a novel. These selections included *A Doll's House*, "Chrysanthemums," "Miss Brill," and "Eveline." Each story shouted feminism louder and louder as I became better at annotating and analyzing.

The independent reading selection for this unit was *Handmaid's Tale*, by Margaret Atwood. The novel is set in a fictional future when human reproduction becomes extremely difficult due to the high population of "sterile" men in America. The government takes control in the epidemic. Guards invade every home and take all the women away to prepare them for their mission in this new society, The Republic of Gilead. Each woman is given their own job: Martha, Aunt, or handmaid. The main character, Offred, is torn away from her husband and daughter to become the handmaid to "The Commander". The Republic of Gilead is a nation of no humanity, no love, and absolutely no autonomy.

As a handmaid, Offred is responsible for human reproduction in Gilead. One certain nights, she must participate in what is called, "the ceremony." During this event, Offred engages in sexual intercourse with The Commander while she lies down in his wife's lap. This is to symbolize that the two women are one. There is absolutely nothing pleasurable about "the ceremony." All three participants hate it. Atwood is trying to make a point through this very weird scene that women are nothing but containers in society. Their reason for being is solely biological, to conceive, carry, and give birth to a child so the human species does not become extinct.

Along with reading this complex novel and writing a paper, an entire class period was dedicated to discussing the novel in a seminar. Sister Carol initiated the seminar by asking us what we liked and did not like about the book. I assure you, no other girl in my class has ever read a novel similar to *Handmaid's Tale.* This made our very first independent reading seminar all the more awkward. The classroom fell silent. The novel had some very graphic sexual scenes, which was the big elephant in the room.

Sister Carol is not a conventional Catholic nun; she was completely comfortable with talking about sex. Ironically, a group of teenagers were the ones having trouble talking about such topics. She whipped out her incredible sass and started referring to sex as "tumbling." I love how Sister Carol used her spunky personality to break the ice. As the seminar progressed, we became more comfortable talking about the novel with our classmates. The conversation quickly escalated when we discussed our hatred for The Commander and our love for Nick, a Gilead guard. Themes such as feminism, autonomy, freedom, and the potential of women were examined and debated. We ended the conversation by talking about how this book is relevant in our society and the world today. My own opinion, which was shared by many of my classmates, was that women everywhere are being degraded to housewives, caregivers, and baby makers when we have so much more to offer. Both males and females are blind to the amazing abilities women have.

This seminar enhanced my literary understanding because I could talk intelligibly about my understandings of the novel and listen to the interpretations of others. "Women's Struggle for Self-Realization" allowed feminism to grab my hand and pull me into the pages. I danced along the lines of essays, plays, and books with a new understanding of what it is to read.

I grew in my literacy every day senior year. I was analyzing the words intensely, understanding complex themes clearly, making connection between my own life experiences and what I was reading, and feeling the writer's emotions more deeply. Before Sister Carol's class, literature was a square. Now it is a box. I never knew I could I pick it up, turn it over, open it up, and unpack what is inside.

CORAL REEF HEALTH   1

The Importance of Coral Reefs

Luke Wilcox

Professor Harrington

College Writing 1

CORAL REEF HEALTH   2

The Importance of Coral Reefs

As Jacques Cousteau, a French naval officer, explorer, conservationist, co-developer of the Aqua-Lung, and member of the Académie Française, humorously states, "The Sea, the great unifier, is man's only hope. Now, as never before, the old phrase has a literal meaning: we are all in the same boat." Coral reefs are becoming extinct at an accelerated rate in recent years. It is time for everyone to change their behaviors regarding the way we treat our oceans, so we can reverse the damage we have already caused. Humans are responsible for destroying the planet's oceans in so many ways. Drilling for oil and dumping toxic waste and radioactive chemicals into shores are just some of the ways that humans have been irresponsible and destructive to our oceans. Global warming, for example, has had a very detrimental effect on our ocean's marine life and coral reef structures. What can the implications of destructive human behaviors and global warming be on our planet's oceans, and how will that affect ocean life specifically coral reefs?

Background

Since the late 1970s, research biologists from all over the world have kept records of the health and maintenance of coral reefs. Localized anthropogenic activities such as channelization, removal of calcium carbonate, siltification due to farming or construction, and overfishing are responsible for reef destruction (Adey, 2000). However, on a global scale the most recent data shows that global warming is destroying the world's reefs at an unprecedented rate. Statistics suggest that the damage is only going to continue. The latest reports state that as much as 27 percent of

CORAL REEF HEALTH   3

monitored reef formations have been lost, and about 60 percent of the world's reefs are

at risk due to destructive, human-related activities (Cesar, 2003). By the 2030s, 90%

of reefs are estimated to be at risk from both human activities and climate change. In

October of 2016, the Great Barrier Reef, the world's largest reef encompassing over

2,900 individual reefs, and stretching for over 1,600 miles, was pronounced dead after

25 million years on this Earth.

Skepticism

Even with these facts, there is still a great deal of skepticism and doubt that

surrounds the idea of global warming. Certain individuals and corporations feel that

there is a lack of sufficient evidence to claim that humans are the main cause of ocean

acidification, coral bleaching, and global warming in general. One article written by

Milan Radovanovic states, "during the last few years more and more articles appear

in which the current temperature changes are tried to be explained by the Sun-Earth

connection". He also includes evidence to support his claim by citing an article of

his own in which he again states, "The first sentence in Steinhilber's paper, in the

Introduction is: "The Sun is the main driver of the Earth's climate"

(p. 18). Radovanovic does not deny the evidence that supports the claim that global

temperatures have risen due to an increase anthropogenic activity. He is stating that

scientific papers and the media should stop using the term 'global warming' and start

referring to the issue as 'climate change'. However some individuals believe that the

entire idea of global warming, or climate change, is a hoax. Their arguments state that

changes in the Earth's surface temperature has always occurred, and that the Earth

CORAL REEF HEALTH   4

is just in the stage of warmth which will be transitioning into a period of colder weather, like a cyclical pattern. Although the Earth does experience cyclical temperature variation, a study done by Climate Central measured the top ten hottest years on record and found that they have all occurred within the last 25 years (Climate, 2016). It is also worth noting that over the period of 1951 to 2010, greenhouse gases contributed to a global mean surface warming likely to be in the range of 0.5 °C to 1.3 °C (Radovanovic, 2014). Despite the information opposing anthropogenic centered climate change, it is worth noting that there is a consensus within the scientific community that the reduction of toxic gases in the atmosphere is something that should be continuously pursued.

Economics and Politics

Unfortunately, politicians and big businesses use money and the economy to rationalize their lack of support for our environment and environmental legislation. President-Elect Donald Trump's newly acquired political power mixed with his environmental beliefs provide a great example of this. It is already clear that President Trump's administration will be far friendlier to fossil fuel companies than it will be to the environment. According to an article by Desmog, Trump will be appointing a noted climate change denier, Myron Ebell, as the head of the EPA. Trump also plans to pull the United States out of the 'Paris Climate Agreement', a treaty which was signed by more than 180 countries last year with hopes to keep the world below 2° C of warming (Cousins, 2016). It is not only the United States that suffers from this type of economic-environment debate. Industrial countries around the world are reluctant

CORAL REEF HEALTH   5

to reduce the amount of CO_2 and other greenhouse gases that they produce because

mostly all factories run on the burning of coal powered plants. One article from the

Stern School of Business states, "One of the key challenges in mounting a global

response to it [global warming] is the seeming unwillingness of the fastest growing

economies such as China and India to sign a treaty that limits their emissions" (Dutta,

2012). Both China and India are leaders in technology and innovation. It is unfortunate

to see such world leaders neglect the environment by continuing to rely on fossil fuel

to power their industrial factories. Reducing coal powered factories would dramatically

affect the economies of China and India, which in turn would have an impact on the

rest of the world's economies. Making a switch to less anthropogenic energy sources

do not always have a negative economical effect.

The Benefits of Coral Reefs

Healthy coral reefs around the world for example, do actually effect the

economies of coastal cities a great deal. The Great Barrier Reef is a huge economic

force for Queensland, Australia. According to an article written by Sierra Club, more

than 70,000 jobs such as fisherman and dive operators rely on a healthy coral reef. In

fact, $5 billion of income a year is generated by The Great Barrier Reef alone (Spring,

2016). It is estimated that all the coral reefs across the globe generates approximately

$375 billion a year.

Revenue isn't the only benefit we get from healthy reefs. The sturdy structure

of coral reefs create a barrier against ocean storms, protecting shorelines from

hurricanes, flooding, and other natural disasters by helping to dissipate the waves' force against the coast (Megan, 2013). One statistic shows that coral reefs rival the tropical rainforests as the most diverse ecosystems on Earth. With a wide variety of plant, animal, and microbial life, coral reefs occupy less than 0.1% of the world's ocean surface, yet they provide a home for at least 25% of all marine species (Spalding, 1997). It is estimated that less than 10% of reef biodiversity is currently known by scientists. The chances of finding a new prescription drug in the sea, particularly in the coral reef structure, may be 300 to 400 times more likely than discovering a new drug on Earth's surface (Bruckner, 2002). Only a small fraction of known coral life has been tested for "active compounds". At the rate at which coral species are becoming extinct, the potential to discover new pharmaceutical drugs will unfortunately be lost (Adey, 2000). There are currently a plethora of pharmaceutical drugs that are developed from coral reefs. Secosteroids, which gives the coral protection from bacterial fungi, is used to treat asthma, arthritis and other inflammatory disorders. Bryozoan, which is found in the species *Bugula neritina,* contains the compound bryostatin 1. This substance is used in many drugs for its anti-cancer properties (Levins, 2016).

Despite the obvious benefits coral reefs provide everyone, there still seems to be a lackof effort and lack of attention to saving these incredible structures. The general public just doesn't know what role they can have to prevent ocean acidification and coral bleaching. One product that has a big effect on damaging reef health is sunscreen. Across the world each year, up to 14,000 tons of sunscreen lotions are discharged into the ocean, killing coral reefs around the globe. Sunscreen contains

CORAL REEF HEALTH   7

between 1% and 10% oxybenzone, which is a photo-toxicant that according to a study done by the EWG is ineffective and harmful (Cesar, 2003), yet it is found in almost every brand of sunscreen available. Oxybenzone is directly linked to the declining health of coral reefs, and yet sunscreen is bought and worn by virtually everyone who goes to the beach.

Conclusion

There is enough data to support the claim that global warming, ocean acidification, and coral bleaching have resulted mainly in part from the negligence of our society's destructive tendencies, and lack of response to scientists and other conservative biologist's warnings. Based on the information provided it is evident that coral reefs provide us with coastal protection, marine life diversity, economic growth, the potential to develop new medicines. The fact that coral reefs are being destroyed so rapidly begs the question, what would life without the reefs and ocean life be like, and how would our society be affected by such a loss of biodiversity? Is it too late to prevent such an unsettling future, and if not what is there that our society can still do to reverse the damage already done? These questions should not be exclusively for biologists and other scientists of similar fields. For our society to raise awareness and build support for coral reef protection there needs to be more media coverage and education about coral reef destruction.

References

Adey, W. H. (2000). *Coral Reef Ecosystems and Human Health: Biodiversity Counts! Ecosystem Health,* 6(4), 227–236.

CORAL REEF HEALTH 8

Bruckner, Andrew W. (2002). Life-saving products from coral reefs. *Issues in Science and Technology, 18*(3). Retrieved from www.issues.org.

Burnett, M. E., Wang, S. Q. (2011). Current sunscreen controversies: A critical review. *Photo dermatology, Photo immunology & Photo medicine. 27*(2), 58–67.

Centers for Disease Control (2008). Americans carry body burden of toxic sunscreen chemical. Environmental Working Group. Retrieved from www.ewg.org.

Cesar, H. J. S.; Burke, L.; Pet-Soede, L. (2003). The economics of worldwide coral reef degradation (PDF). *The Netherlands: Cesar Environmental Economics Consulting.*

Climate Central (2016). The 10 hottest years on record. Retrieved from www. climatecentral.org.

Cousins, Farron. (2016). Donald Trump's anti-environment agenda could tank US economy. *DeSmogBlog.* Retrieved from www.desmogblog.org.

Dutta, P. K., & Radner, R. (2012). Capital growth in a global warming model: will China and India sign a climate treaty? *Economic Theory, 49*(2).

K., Megan. (2013). The impact of ecosystems: Coral reefs are the medicine cabinets of the ocean. Ian Somerhalder Foundation. Retrieved from www.isfoundation.org.

Levins, Nicole. (2016). Oceans and coasts coral reefs: Nature's medicine cabinet. *Coral Reefs and Medicine, the Nature Conservancy.*

Radovanovic, M. M., Ducic, V., & Mukherjee, S. (2014). Climate changes instead of global warming. *Thermal Science, 18*(3).

CORAL REEF HEALTH   9

Shaun M. McCoshum, Alicia M. Schlarb and Kristen A. Baum. (2016). Journal:
     Hydrobiologia.

Spalding, M. D., Grenfell, A. M. (1997). New estimates of global and regional coral
     reef areas. *Coral Reefs*. 16 (4): 225–230.

Spring, Joe. 12 Dec. 2016, "The largest die-off of corals ever just happened on the
     Great Barrier Reef." Sierra Club. Sierra Magazine.

Greg Allen

Jody Santos

College Writing

7 March 2015

Disney: Sexist and Racist Since 1937

A family gathers together, pulls the hot, buttery popcorn out of the microwave and pours it into a bowl. They grab warm blankets and get cuddled up on the couch. The children's eyes are wide as ever as the father pops *Peter Pan* into the VCR. The family is in for a magical night of entertainment as the Disney production appears on the screen. However, what else is entering the minds of these children? When the viewer digs a little deeper, Disney becomes a monster. Its productions are absurdly racist and sexist across the board. Many criticized Disney for some of its racism and sexism, and some changes were made, but there is still an underlying element in each of its films. Many would argue that with the productions of *Pocahontas, Mulan, Princess and the Frog,* and more, Disney entered a post-racial and post-sexist era. However, so many of the stereotypes still exist—even in those films. Children that absorb these movies are affected by the images presented, and almost nothing has changed since some of the first Disney productions.

According to the documentary, *Mickey Mouse Monopoly*, in some of the earliest Disney movies like *Fantasia* (1940) and *Snow White and the Seven Dwarves* (1937), there is a very distinct image of females that is presented. The common traits include long, dashing eyelashes and very skinny waists. The bodies are highly

Allen 2

sexualized, and the behaviors of the females are extremely seductive. Overtime, however, nothing has changed. As the years carry on, the traits remain the same. These traits are seen in *Bambi* (1942), *The Jungle Book* (1967), *The Little Mermaid* (1989), *Beauty and the Beast* (1991), *Aladdin* (1992), *Pocahontas* (1995), *Hercules* (1997), *Frozen* (2013) and many more. One example of the seductiveness is seen in *Aladdin.* There is a scene in which Jasmine uses her body and seduces a man as a distraction for Aladdin to accomplish a task. This is dangerous for girls because it teaches them that they can use their bodies to get what they want. Perhaps the worst part is, the images do not even come close to resembling real females. As the images of females repeat themselves throughout the films, young girls get the idea that they should look just like the women in the movies. If a girl is normal, there is a high chance she becomes uncomfortable in her own skin because of the extremely beautiful and unrealistic females that are in the Disney films (*Mickey Mouse Monopoly*). Something else that has to do with body image is the evil person in Disney films. The "bad person" always seems to be unattractive. This is true in *Snow White and the Seven Dwarfs* where the witch is short, round, and has a very different face than Snow White or any "good person" in the movie. It is also seen in *The Little Mermaid*. Ursala is larger and has a blemish on her face. This idea is bad for girls because if a girl has a blemish or is a little larger, they receive the message that they aren't as good as a skinny girl with no blemishes.

However, the images do not just effect young girls. Males are highly affected by gender qualities in Disney movies as well. In most films, the men are brave,

Allen 3

adventurous, unemotional, and physically strong (Collier-Meek, 559). In *Tarzan,* for example, he is extremely strong and he is the hero who kills the leopard and protects Jane, the innocent and helpless female. In *Beauty and the Beast*, the beast is assertive and dominant over Belle. According to *Mickey Mouse Monopoly* and Dr. Carolyn Newburger, a psychologist at Harvard University, he screams at her, imprisons her, refuses to feed her, and throws her around like a rag doll. The beast is abusive and controlling, but in the end he still gets the beautiful girl. This is perhaps the most dangerous message because it shows that men can attain what they want by being in control and abusing a woman (*Mickey Mouse Monopoly*).

Another issue with gender and Disney is that no matter how independent or strong a woman may be, she still always needs to be rescued by a male character. The females are always the ones that seem to find trouble, and the males always come to the rescue. One example of this is seen in *The Hunchback of Notre Dame*. When the woman is tied to the pole and is about to be burned, the male comes swinging in on a rope to save her. When children see this they begin to play the roles. According to Allison Wilson in *Mickey Mouse Monopoly*, there were children playing on a playground and one girl was laying against a fence crying for help, and all the boys were going to rescue her (*Mickey Mouse Monopoly*).

Disney received a standing ovation after producing the movie *Pocahontas* because a Native American was added to the previously Caucasian-dominated princess series. However, the Native American culture is still depicted very unfairly. Throughout *Pocahontas,* the Natives are referred to on nearly every occasion as

Allen 4

"savages" by the Englishmen. It is a word that indicates uncivilized, animal-like people that have no right to live by their own standards. When children see this movie and see the way Native Americans are referred to, they get the idea shoved into their heads that Native Americans are not people, but animals that do not belong. There is a similar portrayal of this in *Peter Pan.* When the kids in the movie are introduced to the Native Americans, the Natives are sitting with their legs crossed, singing songs, running, jumping, and yelling while repeatedly hitting their hand against their mouth to create the stereotypical Native American sound. For many young viewers these films are the only time they have seen Native American people so their only perception is the untrue, savage behavior that is shown in the movies (*Mickey Mouse Monopoly*).

Another race that is neglected throughout Disney productions is the Latino race. In Disney films there are hardly any Latino characters, and when there are, they are animals, play a minor role, and fit the typical stereotypes of a Mexican or Latin person. Two examples of this are seen in *Oliver and Company* and in *Lady and the Tramp* with the chihuahuas. In these movies, the dogs do things that they aren't supposed to do. In *Oliver and Company,* Alonzo steals a car. The dogs also have heavy accents in the movies and they represent something that nobody wants. They are filthy, dirty "things" that nobody would even ponder wanting something to do with (*Mickey Mouse Monopoly*). African Americans are also highly oppressed in Disney films. They also always seem to be represented by animals. They are crows, or monkeys, or, in *The Lion King,* hyenas. There is also a very unfair, stereotypical representation of African Americans. In *Dumbo,* the crows have a slowed down, slurred speech. In

Allen 5

The Jungle Book, there are monkeys that sound and dance like a stereotypical black person. They sing a song about how they want to be like men, but they will never be able to accomplish that. *Tarzan,* which takes place in Africa, does not represent black people at all. Lastly, in *The Lion King,* the hyenas also sound like a stereotypical black person and the hyenas are the bad guys. They do bad things to Simba and try to hurt him. This representation is so glaring that one little boy was at a playground and he ran over to his mother and said, "Mommy, Mommy, it's the hyenas!" The mother looked up to see African American children playing on the swing set. However, she admitted that when she put her head down and just listened to the boys playing, they sounded exactly like the hyenas in *The Lion King.* This is dangerous for kids because when Latinos and African Americans are represented doing bad or illegal things in movies, Caucasian children become afraid of those races in real life. It is also dangerous to Latino and African American children because they see these images and believe that they should act in a similar manner (*Mickey Mouse Monopoly*).

In a study conducted by Sherri Burr, a law professor at the University of New Mexico, children were asked how often they saw their race on television and the roles that their race played. The results were shocking. 58 percent of children said that they saw white people having a lot of money. Only eight percent of minorities said they saw their races with a substantial amount of money. 71 percent of white children said they saw whites on television very often, where just 42 percent of African American children saw their race on television (Burr). Many people, like Neal Gabler of *The Los Angeles Times,* argue that as of the mid-2000s, this has come to an end. In 2009, the

Allen 6

Disney production, *The Princess and the Frog* was released, and the movie featured an African American princess. Gabler says, "Even before it opens later this week, Disney's new animated feature, 'The Princess and the Frog,' is already considered something of a cultural and animation landmark." The author goes on to argue that Walt Disney himself was the man who brought all the racism to Disney, but now that he has passed, we have entered a post-racial era (Gabler). However, Gabler's argument seems invalid as many other experts would argue that just because the movie features a black princess, it does not mean the film doesn't have its flaws. In a *The New York Times* article by Brooks Barnes, he states, "Disney obviously does not think a black man is worthy of the title 'prince'." He supports the quote by saying that the prince in the film has hair and features that are clearly non-black, and his skin is very fair (Barnes). Another interesting observation is that a black princess falls for a black prince. Of course Disney is not going to make an interracial relationship. There is one interracial relationship in Disney which is between Pocahontas and John Smith, but that movie is based off of a true story so Disney was forced to make the relationship. It is also untrue in the sense that Pocahontas actually married John Rolfe.

It is tough to argue that Disney is perhaps the greatest form of magical and fantasy-like entertainment for children and families. However, the underlying qualities of Disney's films are vicious. Children absorb the messages in the movies and get ideas and thoughts put into their brains about society that are not true. There has also been an extreme lack of progress for Disney over the years despite the criticism it has received. Even after the movie *The Princess and the Frog,* Disney went back to its old ways with the 2013 production of *Frozen*. In the film every character is white, the princesses are still skinny and abnormally beautiful, and they still need to be saved by males at different times throughout the movie. For example, when they are running away from the wolves, the male does all the work to escape the chasing animals. The males in the movie are still adventurous, physically strong, and unemotional—all characteristics of males in past films from decades ago. Disney is a corrupt company, and its films are still portraying the same negative messages to children. A change needs to be made if people in today's society want racism and sexism to end. Disney movies are the first thing that children see in life, and if the films are giving negative signals to those children, nothing in society is going to change.

Allen 8

Works Cited

Barnes, Brooks. "Her Prince Has Come. Critics, Too." *The New York Times* 29 May 2009: Web.

Burr, Sherry. "Television and Societal Effects: An Analysis of Media Images of African-Americans in Historical Context." Racism.org. Web. 1 Mar. 2015.

Collier-Meek, Mellissa, Descartes, Lara, England, Dawn. "Gender Role Portrayal and the Disney Princesses." Springer Science and Business Media, LLC. 10 February 2011. Web.

Gabler, Neal. "Walt Disney—Prince or Toad" *The Los Angeles Times* 22 November 2009: Web.

Picker, Miguel. *Mickey Mouse Monopoly.* 2001. Film.

Josh Shuman

Professor Lartigue

College Writing 1:00

Biases about Language

Throughout history people have tried to discriminate others based on how they speak. People use this to attack the speaker's arguments without actually proving them wrong. When people discriminate against others for how they speak there is an underlying reason which could be racism, misogyny, or many others. Some people who face this discrimination are people with different regional accents, people with nonnative accents, people with speech impediments, people who speak with an African American vernacular, and women who speak with up talk and vocal fry. Each of these ways of speaking carries different negative connotations. People with strong regional accents are often viewed as uneducated and too informal, while people with nonnative accents are viewed as lazy, stupid, and non-compliant. Speakers who have speech impediments are looked as less intelligent and forced to accommodate to the majority of those without speech impediments. Those who speak with an African American vernacular are believed to be stupid and uneducated. Women who speak with up talk and vocal fry are viewed as immature, stupid, and are not taken seriously. Since these people deviate from a neutral American accent, they get mistreated even though there is no link between how one speaks and their intellect. Additionally, discriminating against people for how they speak is wrong because how someone speaks depends on where they grew up, the way their parents speak, and physiological patterns.

A strong regional accent doesn't mean that someone is speaking incorrect English. Unfortunately, there are many people who think that those with different regional accents are uneducated and sound like fools. However, there is no link between how someone speaks and their intellect. Even if these people are more working class people and less educated it does not make them inferior to those who speak with an average American accent. In fact, Professor of Linguistics Dr. Dennis R. Preston asserts that this myth "runs deep, strong and true". Since people have a more neutral American accent are usually of higher status, they force others to comply with how they speak. Anyone who deviates is accused of speaking incorrect English. For example, many people view a southern accent as incorrect since they have a slower way of speaking, different pronunciations, and different slang. Dr. Preston found that even southerners believe their accent isn't correct English. They do enjoy their accent more as they show their regional pride ("They Speak Really Bad English down South and in New York City"). Interestingly enough, Saumya Viashampayan who writes for the *Wall Street Journal* cites a George Mason University study in which they found people believed that a British accent is more intelligent than a Southern accent (qtd. in "When an Accent Gets in the Way of a Job"). This sort of dividing can cause hatred for people one doesn't even know. It also causes people who have these heavier accents to be discriminated in society and the work place. This forces them to change the way they speak which can cause great psychological damage as they try to measure up to society's status quo.

Besides regional accents, those with nonnative accents of English face great obstacles daily based on how they speak. Raymond Hernandez shows in his article in

The New York Times how some people have dealt with this discrimination. Carmen Friedman emigrated from Colombia and still struggled with her accent even after 5 years in America. She was fed up and decided to take classes to get rid of her accent. Sadly, her accent was damaging and was hurting her image of herself she didn't "want to feel uncomfortable every time I say something" ("When an Accent Becomes an Issue; Immigrants turn to Speech Classes to Reduce Sting of Bias"). Unfortunately, there are numerous stories of people with nonnative accents facing bias. It has hurt them on job interviews and even in the workplace as Paul Foy of the *Insurance Journal* found that Filipino hospital workers won a case for being discriminated for having an accent and speaking in their language at any time during work ("More Workers Claiming Job Discrimination over Language, Accents"). Not all nonnative accents are treated the same way, though, argues associate professor at The Pennsylvania State University Patreese D. Ingram. Many times it is nonwhite people who face the discrimination. There aren't any records of people with various western European accents getting discriminated against. ("Are Accents One of the Last Acceptable Areas for Discrimination") This shows that the underlying bias is a form of racism and xenophobia. Most don't identify with these people so they expect them to talk differently. This can go even further and people can have the expectation that these people are less intelligent since they can't speak the same way. Consequently, the effects of this discrimination can be psychological, as proven by researchers Meifen Wei, Tsun-Yao Ku, and Kenneth T. Wang; they found there to be positive connections between perceived language discrimination and depression and anxiety. There were also negative connections for perceived language discrimination and life satisfaction and self-esteem ("A Development and Validation of the Perceived Language Discrimination Scale", 348–349). These people feel rejected by society which can cause major damage to their well-being. Companies will benefit with more diversity in the workplace as people exchange experiences and talk with people of different backgrounds; therefore it is in the best interest of both groups to stop the bias against them.

People with speech impediments face great obstacles just trying to communicate on a daily basis. Not to mention the lack of understanding that comes along with their impediment. A common speech impediment is stuttering while speaking. People who stutter usually inherit this and it takes many hours of speech therapy to fix it. Sometimes it can never be fixed since it is a physiological disability. People assume because someone stutters that they aren't intelligent or aren't confident in what they are saying. Reporter for the *New York Times* Richard Perez-Pena talks of the story of Philip Garber Jr. The story shows how teachers can discriminate against students with speech impediments by not allowing them to participate in class because they take up too much time. Two students in the class thought that he didn't take up too much time and his input benefitted the class (*Language Awareness* 517–520). This sends the class a message that they are there to listen to the teacher, not to participate and ask questions, resulting in the students worrying if they can respond quickly enough to the teacher to even ask questions. Additionally, the students with speaking disabilities feel as if their opinions aren't even wanted. They have to write down questions and ask after class. This could result in loss of motivation to participate at all.

A less severe impediment is the use of verbal pauses in one's speech like "uh". This is used in many people's speech. It is usually used while someone is thinking of what to say. While many people dislike these filler words, writer for *Slate* Michael Erard believes the uses of these pauses are important and shouldn't be expelled from speech. These pauses are present in other languages like French, German, and Japanese. Surprisingly, the trend to eliminate them only started in the early 20th century. Many people prefer people who speak with verbal pauses because it shows that it is a genuine response. Many studies have found that the verbal pause lets people know that something important is coming. The added emphasis helps listeners tune in (*Language Awareness,* 126-128). This development shows that there is a reason for these pauses and they actually are more beneficial than no pauses at all. The reasons against are coming from the higher class who believe the average speaker must be wrong since they are less educated.

An African American or black vernacular is often associated with being less intelligent and lazy. This sort of assumption has hurt many in the workplace and in school. Sociolinguist professor at North Carolina State University Walt Wolfram talks of the "linguistic inferiority principle" which says the accent of the socially lower class people will be viewed as inferior to other accents (Wolfram, 104). People argue that the use of multiple negatives in black vernacular is wrong since it doesn't logically make sense. However, logic doesn't apply to language and communication. These multiple negatives are also present in older English, French and Spanish so this shows that there is no basis of saying that this is an incorrect way to speak ("Myth 14: Double Negatives are Illogical"). There are many other cases of people trying to punch holes in this vernacular which are proven wrong. This sort of indoctrinated belief has been spread largely due to racial discrimination. Since African Americans have been in the lower social class in America since they arrived, the assumption that they speak incorrectly has stuck. Professor of legal analysis and writing and race and the law William Y. Chin has found that the bias against them in the classroom as well. The teachers believe this dialect is inappropriate for class and they are called on less because of it. The discrimination in the classroom spreads further as they get worse recommendations and put on slower learning tracks ("Linguistic Profiling In Education: How Accent Bias Denies Equal Educational Opportunities To Students Of Color"). This sort of bias can cause damage to the student's life as they try to progress in their education. If their education is hurt than their prospect for a job will hurt too. This causes a cycle that can be passed down if the students are constantly limited in their educational opportunities.

Women face great discrimination in the work environment if they speak with up talk or vocal fry. Up talk is when speakers bring their voice higher up at the end of the sentence, almost making everything sound like a question. Whereas, vocal fry is when the speaker begins to bring their voice down towards the end of the sentence causing their voice to crackle as it goes deeper with less emphasis on each word. Writer James Gorman talks of the various uses of up talk. He found that up talk is a sign that the speaker is not done speaking. Up talk is used to question the listener and keep them engaged in the conversation. Gorman talks about other uses of up talk as he cites linguist Cynthia Gorman. She did a study on college sorority members in Texas. She found that the use of it was to be more inclusive and connect people to the conversation (*Language Awareness,* 169-172). This shows up talk has a direct use and developed for better communication. Women who speak with up talk are accused of being overly feminine, submissive, and stupid. Vocal fry is another way women are discriminated for how they speak. This is a much deeper and creakier voice. Vocal fry is called too masculine and said to make the speaker sound disinterested. Journalist Jessica Grose was receiving complaints for her voice on a *Slate* podcast. She then hired a vocal coach to help her since she didn't want it to affect her job. This caused psychological distress too. She thought about her voice every time she spoke when before that she never even considered it ("From Upspeak to Vocal Fry: Are We 'Policing' Young Women's Voices?"). The policing of women's speech is not equal to the policing males. Jane Kelly of *UVA Today* found that there are highly distinguished males who use this vocal fry. Famous linguist Noam Chomsky and NPR podcast host Ira Glass both use a deep creaky voice ("What's In a Voice? The Debate Over 'Vocal Fry' And What It Means For Women"). This sort of discrimination shows there may be an underlying feeling of misogyny associated with the hatred for how women speak. The reasons for the discrimination could be the myth that women can't be speaking correctly since they aren't on top of society like men.

In conclusion, the discrimination of people based on how they speak is wrong and damaging to society. The discrimination has no factual evidence to back up that there is an incorrect way to speak English. Meaning their discrimination is usually founded on some other hatred of the person like misogyny or racism. As a result, the bias against these people can cause great psychological distress and hold them back in school and work. The more this discrimination is continued the more it will be accepted as right and passed down generations. Thus continuing the cycle of hatred towards people who behave differently.

Works Cited

Chin, William Y. "Linguistic Profiling in Education: how Accent Bias Denies Equal Educational Opportunities to Students of Color." *The Scholar* 12:335 (n.d.): 355–384. Web. 24 Nov. 2015.

Eschholz, Paul, Alfred Rosa, and Virginia Clark. *Language Awareness 11th edition.* New York: Bedford/St. Martin's, 2013. Print.

Foy, Paul. "More Workers Claiming Job Discrimination Over Language, Accents." *InsuranceJournal.com.* Wells Media Group, Inc. 4 Dec. 2012. Web. 24 Nov. 2014.

Grosse, Jessica, Penny Eckert, and Susan Sankin. "From Upspeak to Vocal Fry: Are We 'Policing' Young Women's Voices?" *NPR.org.* NPR. 23 July 2015. Web. 24 Nov. 2015.

Hernandez, Raymond. "When an Accent Becomes an Issue; Immigrants Turn to Speech Class to Reduce Sting of Bias." *NYTimes.com.* The New York Times Company. 2 March 1993. Web. 24 Nov. 2015.

Ingram, Patreese D. "Are Accents One of the Last Acceptable Areas for Discrimination?" *Commentary* 47.1 (2009): n. pag. *Journal of Extension.* Web. 24 Nov. 2015.

Kelly, Jane. "What's in a Voice? The Debate Over 'Vocal Fry' and What it Means for Women." *News.virginia.edu.* University of Virginia. 12 Aug. 2015. Web. 24 Nov. 2015.

Preston, Dennis R. "Do You Speak American?" *Language Prejudice.* PBS, 2005. Web. 24 Nov. 2015

Trudgill, Peter, Ray Harlow, Jean Aitchison, Anthony Lodge, Edward Carney, Lars-Gunnar Andersson, James Milroy, Michael Montgomery, Winifred Bauer, Howard Giles, Nancy Niedzielski, Lesley Milroy, Walt Wolfram, Jenny Cheshire, J.K. Chambers, Laurie Bauer, Dennis R. Preston, Peter Roach, Nicholas Evans, John H. Esling, and John Algeo. *Language Myths*. London: Penguin Books, 1998. Print.

Vaishampayan, Saumya. "When an Accent Gets in the Way of a Job" *blog.wsj.com*. Dow Jones & Company, Inc. 6 Sept. 2012. Web. 24 Nov. 2015.

Wei, Meifen, Kenneth T. Wang, and Tsun-Yao Ku. "A Development and Validation of the Perceived Language Discrimination Scale." *Cultural Diversity and Ethnic Minority Psychology* 18.4 (2012): 340-351. *PsycARTICLES*. Web. 24 Nov. 2015.

Emily Bienasz

Dr. Mchallian

College Writing

December 8, 2016

The Cell Phone Era

How often is it that you walk down a city street or in any suburban area without seeing a few teenagers staring at their cell phone? This situation seems implausible. Interestingly, the number of children today who have a mobile device compared to twelve years ago has doubled. Nearly seventy percent of kids between the ages of eleven and fourteen have a cell phone, while eighty-five percent of teenagers between the ages of fourteen and seventeen own one as well (Davis par. 3). It is understandable that concerned parents would buy their children a cell phone to obtain a sense of security of knowing that they are just a phone call away. Nevertheless, allowing children full control of a cell phone at too early of an age is detrimental to their development. If children are permitted to have a cell phone, their social development will be stunted, they will be easily distracted from their academics, and they will be discouraged from being involved in physical activities.

Before cell phones became our primary source of communication, the quickest way to reach others was to hold a conversation in person. By communicating with someone in person, the interaction will help develop skills necessary to analyze facial expressions as well as improve the ability to communicate assertively. Today, young adults use texting as their primary method of contacting friends. They hide themselves

Bienasz 2

behind a screen, losing the crucial social skills they would master if they practiced face-to-face communication. A telephone screen cannot teach children how to understand nonverbal emotional cues they can learn from a conversation in person. Dr. Karl Benzio, an executive director of a rehab organization called Lighthouse Nework, states, "Being able to read a person's facial expressions and body language, hear their tone of voice, and look them in the eye allows us to gain so much more from the interaction than even talking to them on the phone. The connection the face-to-face contact brings powerfully deepens the relationship as well, which allows further opportunities to practice and hone more complex aspects of relationship skills" (Kellogg par. 9). How are children supposed to develop powerful relationships if they lack the experience of in-person communication? Although cell phones provide an opportunity for kids to stay connected with friends and family, they discourage children from starting new conversations with new people. Children are deprived of the valuable social skills that will affect them as they mature into adulthood.

It is difficult to not be distracted by a cell phone while it is continuously setting off notifications. WebMD has reported that the average person tends to spend nearly nine hours per day on electronic devices (Davies section 3). It is easy for adults to lose track of time on their phones while surfing the internet, texting or checking emails. If children are given a mobile device, they will be distracted from their academic priorities. Rather than focusing on school, they will have their attention on the top trending game application. At an early age, children do not fully understand the importance of staying concentrated on academics to obtain a prestigious education.

Bienasz 3

Kids seem to find more urgency in responding to a text rather than understanding the significance of reading a novel assigned to them. Technology does serve as a great advantage in the classroom as we move into an era of more technology based teaching; however, it is not always being used with its intended purpose. Joni Siani, a psychologist who studies the digital medial effect on young children says, "You'll get kids saying, 'I'll look something up for English, and while I'm here let me quickly check my Instagram or Twitter feed.' And then it's, 'Oh, I never realized that girl said that to me,' and now they're distracted and not really engaged with their lesson plan" (Matchan par. 4). The distraction of phones and tablets weaken children's ability to learn and focus. Phones benefit teenagers by offering many applications that remind them of major due dates for assignments or help them finish homework. Conversely, a cell phone offers many additional applications that can easily draw their attention away from their work. Children do not have the knowledge of how to moderate their phone use at a young age.

Physical activity is continuously emphasized as having an essential role in maintaining good health. If children are allowed to sit behind a mobile device on a beautiful day, they will begin to establish bad habits that discourage living a healthy lifestyle. Proper growth and development require physical active and exercise. Thus, engaging in physical activity stimulates blood flow which carries essential nutrients and oxygen to cells of developing muscles (Park par. 3). As kids waste daylight sitting in one position playing video games, they do not get the fresh air and exercise their body needs. A recent study conducted by researchers at Kent State University found an association between lower cell phone use and higher levels of physical activity. The students who spent as much as fourteen hours on their phones per day tended to be less fit than those who had only an hour and a half of daily phone use (Chan par. 4). Although mobile devices offer a great variety of applications that promote being active, adults seem to be more intrigued by the fitness motivation programs than children. Encouraging children to participate in a wide range of activities such as basketball, bicycling, and swimming increases the chance that they will find something they enjoy without seeking a phone for entertainment.

Whether we allow ourselves to be consumed by electronic devices or not, we should not promote that type of lifestyle for children. Permitting children to have a phone at a young age impedes their social development. Not only does a phone adversely affect their social skills, but the children will not recognize the importance of academics and will be constantly distracted from it. The more children are on their phone, the less likely they are to be involved in physical activities. In this technological era, introduction of cell phones to young children pose more detriments to development than benefits.

Bienasz 5

Works Cited

Chan, Amanda L. "High Cell Phone Use Linked with Less Physical Activity." *The Huffington Post*. TheHuffingtonPost.com, 11 July 2013. Web. 04 Dec. 2016.

Davies, Madlen. "Average Person Now Spends More Time on Their Phone and Laptop than Sleeping, Study Claims." Daily Mail Online. Associated Newspapers, 11 Mar. 2015. Web. 03 Dec. 2016.

Davis, Susan. "When Is Your Child Ready to Have Their Own Cell Phone." WebMD. WebMD, n.d. Web. 03 Dec. 2016.

Kellogg, Bob. "Study: Smartphones Stunting Students' Social Skills." EAGnews.org. N.p., 27 Aug. 2014. Web. 03 Dec. 2016.

Matchan, Linda. "Cellphones in School: A Teaching Tool or Distraction?—The Boston Globe." BostonGlobe.com. N.p., 16 June 2015. Web. 04 Dec. 2016.

Park, Alice. "How Exercise Works at the Cellular Level." Time. Time, 26 May 2010. Web. 07 Dec. 2016.

Katherine Holliday

Professor MacDonald

College Writing

December 18, 2016

The World of Grimdark Media

What is Grimdark and why has it taken over our media? Grimdark is a subgenera of media that depicts edgy gore, violence, and brutally gruesome content in a beautifully cinematic way, with an anti-hero as the main character and an often dismal outlook for the protagonist. Americans have become enthralled by the stunning violence they witness across their television screens and in big movie theater blockbusters. But why are people so inclined to see these types of films, and so ready to tune into such dark television shows?

People like horror, gore, and grimdark for a few reasons. The first being the brain does interesting things when confronted by an unnerving situation. When in a stressful situation the brain releases a neurotransmitter called norepinephrine, or noradrenaline, which is then converted into epinephrine (adrenaline) in the body. These are the primary triggers of the bodies "fight or flight" mechanism. According to Berit Brogaard, "the adrenal glands produce adrenaline by transforming the amino acid tyrosine into dopamine" (N.p), and dopamine is associated with the reward and pleasure centers of the brain (Evans). This reaction is why people who are so-called "adrenaline junkies" feel a high after doing something that triggers the fight or flight response in their brains, like skydiving or bungee jumping.

Holliday 2

Grimdark does this same thing. The type of images portrayed in a grimdark series or movie triggers a controlled norepinephrine release. According to O'Brien "horror movies are frequently compared to roller coasters; both take you on a journey that feels dangerous but is inherently safe. It's a ride that feels unbridled, but a ride nonetheless" (n.p). While the danger may not be real, the brain is stimulated by images that frighten or cause stress, which then triggers norepinephrine to be released, causing dopamine to convert it to epinephrine, then causing an increased heart rate and perspiration (Klein).

People are attracted to grimdark and horror because they seek an exhilarating sensation. They want to be scared without their life being in danger, as O'Brien puts it "there's a sense of catharsis once the credits roll, a sense of having survived a brief brush with something dark and unexpected" (n.p). In grimdark, the viewer is consistently getting exposed to blood, violence, and mayhem, which triggers the stress signals inducing an almost constant rush of adrenaline. This rush is why after watching an episode of television shows like *Peaky Blinders, Sons of Anarchy,* and *Vikings* or films like *Nightmare on Elm Street,* and *The Blair Witch Project* viewers may feel that their heart is racing and their palms are sweating, and enjoy the feeling. O'Brien explains "viewers who experience fear or anger at the antagonist during a horror movie will feel an amplified positive emotion come the film's resolution, whether it be a happy ending or not" (n.p). Resulting in a shockingly good feeling after being scared, stressed or excited for the duration of the film or show.

When watching movies and shows that are dark and uncomfortable, people often align themselves with a particular character. This alignment is where realism and unrealism come into the picture. When a film or show appeals to the side of realness, it usually focuses on an aspect of society and amplifies it. According to Hess "looking at the history of horror you have mutant monsters rising in the 50s from our fear of the nuclear bogeyman, Zombies in the 60s with Vietnam, Nightmare on Elm Street as a mistrust in authority figures stemming from the Watergate scandals and Zombies again in the 2000s as a reflection of viral pandemic fears" (n.p). The graphics in video games are often said to be super realistic, but in shows and film, it is actual people acting out the scenarios, not animated figures. Individuals who tune into see such shows and go to the theater to see violent, gory, grimdark films might not be going to get an adrenaline rush, but to see a hugely amplified version of their lives. American's witness horror and violence daily, every time we pick up a newspaper or turn on the national news. There are new shocking headlines about bombings and beheadings in the Middle East, or school shootings and church arsons here in the states. So easily there is a draw in seeing a film and television shows that appear farfetched, but when boiled down are only "a reflection of reality" (Metz, n.p.)

Not all the shows and movies in the grimdark or horror category are mimicking society, but in fact, do the opposite. Many people who enjoy the grimdark genera enjoy it for its side of unrealism. In film and television, viewers are asked to cast off their sense of what is real and what is imaginary by using suspension of disbelief. This is a draw to the horror and grimdark category because made up monsters and fantasy

Holliday 4

villains are accepted for the hour of the television show or the two hour run time of the movie. According to Hess along with this sense of "unrealism" comes the fact that "despite the graphic nature of recent horror films, we all know at some level that what we are watching is not real" (n.p) making us understand that the concepts in what we are watching are very unlikely to happen to us, allowing us to view the horrific violence as unfeasible in our world.

According to an article published by The University of Michigan, "More than 60 percent of television programs contain some violence, and about 40 percent of those contain heavy violence" (n.p) which means that when Americans turn on their televisions, more than half the content reaching them is violent and nearly half of all violent television shows have grimdark themes of dark violence. On average Americans are watching five hours of television a day (Hinckley) which causes a serious amount of blood, guts, guns, and crime to be absorbed by audiences.

Grimdark is more common than it used to be, but our world is more inherently violent than it used to be too. Themes of intense torture, savage crime, and brutal death are growing in our world and our media. We seek such media because we are looking for the feeling it gives us. But we also crave the two different sides of horror, the real, and the unreal. When watching such an intense display of unbridled violence people are inclined to either focus on the similarities between the cinematic world and the real one or choose to suspend all disbelief and focus their mind on how they are unlikely to witness such a situation themselves. For those who find themselves fascinated by gory and dark shows and movies, there is nothing better than grimdark. But for those people who do not understand how someone could enjoy watching death, crime, and violence, grimdark seems to be taking over the majority of media and pushing out lighthearted shows and films. With the current trend, it appears that dark media will continue to grow as long as there is an audience that enjoys it.

Holliday 6

Works Cited

Brogaard, Berit. *What happens during an adrenaline rush?* LIVESTRONG.COM,

16 Apr. 2015. Web. 20 Dec. 2016.

Evans, Robert. *Dopamine*. 1991. Web. 20 Dec. 2016.

Hess, J. P. "The psychology of scary movies." *Filmmaker IQ*. 2010. Web. 20 Dec.

2016.

Hinckley, David. *Average American watches 5 hours of TV per day*. NY Daily News,

5 Mar. 2014. Web. 20 Dec. 2016.

Klein, Sarah. "The 3 Major Stress Hormones, Explained." *Huffington Post*. The

Huffington Post, 19 Apr. 2013. Web. 20 Dec. 2016.

O'Brien, Lucy. *The curious appeal of horror movies*. IGN, 9 Sept. 2013. Web. 20 Dec.

2016.

The University of Michigan. "Violent TV, games pack a powerful public health threat."

UMIH.edu. University of Michigan News, 27 Nov. 2007. Web. 20 Dec. 2016.

PART 4

Style Guide

Easy Punctuation

ALL THOSE RULES VERSUS THE FOUR BASIC SENTENCES

If you're like most writers, editing your punctuation can seem pretty intimidating. Where do you start? Every sentence looks different. And what about all those rules? Comma rules are a particular hassle because there are so many. And what's the function of those mysterious punctuation marks—the semicolon, colon, dash, and apostrophe? (For detailed information on all punctuation marks, see **Chapter 16—Punctuation Rules**.)

Editing punctuation can be an easy job if you approach it from the Big Picture. Instead of coming to every sentence as though it's unique, choosing a punctuation mark because "it sounds right," learn the Big Picture patterns that underlie *all* sentences. Once you learn Four Basic Sentence types, you can apply them to any possible sentence. No sentence is unique. You thus need to memorize the Four Basic Sentences.

Let's begin with the simple sentence. Most writers never have a problem punctuating the simple sentence when it requires just a *final* punctuation mark— an *external* punctuation mark.

- ► I drove Sandy to soccer practice.
- ► Will you drive Sandy to soccer practice?
- ► Please drive Sandy to soccer practice!

The problem comes when we need—or think we need—something in the middle of the sentence, or what is called "*internal* punctuation."

WRONG: I drove Sandy, to soccer practice.

WRONG: Will you please drive Sandy; to soccer practice?

WRONG: Please drive Sandy to: soccer practice!

Along with the apostrophe, internal punctuation causes most of our punctuation problems. Internal punctuation includes the comma, semicolon, colon, dash, parentheses, and brackets.

And that long list probably looks like you have to learn a bunch of rules . . .

But you don't.

THE TRICK TO MASTERING PUNCTUATION

There's a trick to mastering punctuation, and especially basic comma rules. If you take all sentences that need internal punctuation and boil them down—reduce them to basic building blocks—you'll end up with just *four* basic sentence types.

So here's the trick: The easy way to master punctuation is to learn what punctuation all four sentence types require. If you do that, then you won't have to check the rules for every sentence you write. You'll know what to do because all sentences, other than the simple ones above, will *always* fall into one of these four types, no matter their infinite number of variations.

All four have a common denominator: *They have two parts* that variously combine the fragment and the sentence. Because all four sentences have two parts, they also share a second common denominator: *internal punctuation*, which is used to separate the two parts. You won't always need internal punctuation with the four sentence types, but when you do, to punctuate properly, you have to be able to tell a fragment from a sentence.

The Fragment

The fragment is a *fragment*—that is, a *part*—of a sentence. By definition, a fragment *doesn't make sense by itself*. To make sense, a <u>fragment</u> needs more information to complete it. That "more information" comes in a short <mark>sentence</mark> that's part of a bigger sentence, the one that ends with the final period.

> *Fragment + Short sentence = Bigger Sentence.*

- <u>Because Andrea was sick,</u> I stayed home.
- <u>If you come to our place tonight,</u> we will cook you dinner.
- <u>After Frank leaves the house,</u> his dog begins to bark.

Note that, for each fragment, you can ask a "more information, please" question that the short sentence answers.

- What happened because Andrea was sick? (I stayed home.)
- What will happen if you come to our place tonight? (We will cook you dinner.)
- What happens after Frank leaves the house? (His dog begins to bark.)

Sometimes fragments are exactly what a writer needs, especially fiction writers who use the fragment for a special effect. But academic writers, who try to present their ideas free of distraction, avoid the fragment when it's not user-friendly. A fragment can distract the reader from the flow; he has to pause to figure things out. Look at the next example. Does the <u>fragment</u> belong to the sentence on the left or to the sentence on the right?

▶ I tried to get off work. <u>Because I wanted to go to the concert.</u> I was   pset that my boss said I couldn't leave.

You can't tell. Writing teachers frown on fragments like this. The reader jerks to a stop. What is the writer trying to say? That ambiguity is one reason why academic writing avoids fragments.

The Dependent Clause

There are two kinds of fragments–the kind that has a <u>subject</u> and a verb and the kind that doesn't. The kind that does is called a *dependent clause*. (It *depends* on more information to make sense; by itself, a dependent clause doesn't make sense because it's a fragment of a complete thought, that is, of a sentence.)

Fragments with a <u>Subject</u> and Verb = Dependent Clauses

▶ because <u>Andrea</u> was sick (what? more information, please)
▶ if <u>you</u> come to our place tonight (what? more information, please)
▶ after <u>Frank</u> leaves the house (what? more information, please)

The Phrase

The kind of fragment that doesn't have a subject and a verb is called a *phrase*. A prepositional phrase is one example of a phrase. (Prepositions are those little words that glue sentence parts together: *in, at, for, by, up, down, with, through, over, out*, etc.). Other kinds of phrases include the infinitive phrase and the participial phrase.

Fragments without a Subject and Verb = Phrases

▶ in the first fifty days
▶ at the last hearing
▶ for each woman

By itself, like the dependent clause, the phrase doesn't make sense. And like the dependent clause, the phrase is a <u>fragment</u>—a fragment of a sentence. To make sense, a phrase needs more information to complete the thought. (Again, that "more information" comes in a short sentence that's part of a bigger sentence, the one that ends with the final period.)

<u>*Fragment*</u> + *Short sentence* = *Bigger Sentence.*

▶ <u>In the first fifty days</u>, the new administration accomplished a great deal.
▶ <u>At the last hearing</u>, our witness testified quite effectively.
▶ <u>For each woman</u>, beating her team's archrival was more than just a victory.

The Sentence (The Independent Clause)

Like a dependent clause, an independent clause has both a <u>subject</u> and a <mark>verb</mark>. But unlike the dependent clause and the phrase, the independent clause *makes sense by itself*. It doesn't need more words to complete the thought. That's why it's called an *independent clause*. (Independently, by itself, the sentence offers a complete thought. It doesn't depend on other words because it stands on its own.)

Sentences = Independent Clauses.

▶ Because Andrea was sick, <u>I</u> <mark>stayed</mark> home.
▶ If you come to our place tonight, <u>we</u> <mark>will cook</mark> you dinner.
▶ After Frank leaves the house, his <u>dog</u> <mark>begins</mark> to bark.

PUNCTUATION TIP

Sentences belong to a context. Every sentence must somehow connect to the sentence it follows and the sentence it precedes; all together, those sentences belong to a bigger context, which may be the argument you're making in a paragraph. Nevertheless, if you pull a sentence out of its context, no matter how obscure or odd it may sound, it's still a sentence because it's a complete thought.

To test whether you have a fragment or a sentence, read the words out loud. The sentence doesn't automatically require more words to complete it. It's independent. But the fragment does—because it's a fragment of a thought. Now read the following sentences and fragments out loud.

▶ Go down to the cellar. (*sentence = complete thought*)
▶ before you go down to the cellar (*dependent clause fragment = incomplete thought*)
▶ Nobody knew anything. (*sentence = complete thought*)
▶ because nobody knew anything (*dependent clause fragment = incomplete thought*)
▶ In the beginning, the seas enveloped the planet. (*sentence = complete thought*)
▶ in the beginning (*phrase fragment = incomplete thought*)

This test isn't foolproof, but if you read a sentence out loud, it tends to sound finished, complete, whereas a fragment sounds unfinished, left hanging: *Before you go down to the cellar—*(?)

THE FOUR BASIC SENTENCES

Each of the four basic sentence types has two parts. Three of the four combine a fragment (F) and a sentence (S). The fourth combines a sentence (S) and a sentence (S).

The fragment can be either a dependent clause ("because Andrea was sick") or a phrase ("in the first fifty days").

1. **Basic Sentence FS** = a fragment *plus* a sentence (= *a bigger sentence*)
2. **Basic Sentence SF** = a sentence *plus* a fragment (= *a bigger sentence*)
3. **Basic Sentence S͡FS** = a fragment *inside* a sentence (= *a bigger sentence*)
4. **Basic Sentence SS** = a sentence *plus* another sentence (= *a bigger sentence*)

(The loop above the third type, S͡FS , indicates that you have one sentence cut in half, not two sentences; only the fourth type, SS, has two sentences.)

These four sentences break into eight patterns. Each pattern is punctuated differently.

1. *Basic Sentence FS*
   Pattern 1 (F,S)
	2. *Basic Sentence SF*
	   Pattern 2 (SF)
	   Pattern 3 (S,F)

3. *Basic Sentence S͡FS*
   Pattern 4 (S͡FS)
   Pattern 5 (S͡,F,S)
	4. *Basic Sentence SS*
	   Pattern 6 (S, CONJ S)
	   Pattern 7 (S./; S)
	   Pattern 8 (S./; TRANS, S)

1. Basic Sentence FS
Pattern 1 (F,S)

After an introductory fragment, use the comma.

►   Because Andrea was sick, I stayed home. (*fragment = dependent clause*)
►   In the first fifty days, the new administration accomplished a great deal. (*fragment = phrase*)

PUNCTUATION TIP

When the introductory fragment is no more than three or four short words, some writers and publications leave out the comma. This is a matter of style and preference. To be safe (and correct), you can always use the comma. Using the comma will give your writing clarity and consistency.

2. Basic Sentence SF
Pattern 2 (SF)

Don't use the comma before an <u>essential fragment</u>. ("Essential" means that you *can't* get rid of the fragment. It's needed to provide essential information about the rest of the sentence. Without that information, the reader is left hanging: *Why?*)

▶ I had to book my hotel online <u>because I was trying to save money</u>. (*Why* did you have to book your hotel online? The essential fragment gives the reason. *fragment = dependent clause*)

▶ I had to book my hotel online <u>to save money</u>. (*Why* did you have to book your hotel online? The essential fragment gives the reason. *fragment = infinitive phrase*)

Pattern 3 (S,F)

Use the comma before a <u>nonessential fragment</u>. ("Nonessential" means that you *can* get rid of the fragment. It provides nonessential information about the rest of the sentence.)

▶ I called my brother, <u>although I had a lot to do at work</u>. (The sentence doesn't need the nonessential information provided by the fragment. The information is perhaps interesting but in no way essential to explain *why* you called your brother. *fragment = dependent clause*)

▶ I called my brother. (The sentence is a complete thought that doesn't require more information to complete it.)

▶ I called my brother, <u>with real regret</u>. (*fragment = prepositional phrase*)

▶ I called my brother, <u>to speak of real regret</u>. (*fragment = infinitive phrase*)

▶ I called my brother, <u>having real regret</u>. (*fragment = participial phrase*)

▶ I called my brother. (The sentence doesn't need nonessential information provided by the fragments.)

It helps to know the words that start essential and nonessential fragments. Some words start only essential fragments, and some start only nonessential, but some can start both (depending on context).

ESSENTIAL	NONESSENTIAL	BOTH	
as . . . as	all of which	after	unless
for	although	as	what
so . . . that	even though	as if	when
than	no matter how/what/why	as though	where
that	none of which/whom	at/by/for/in which	while
until	some of which/whom	because	who
	whereas	before	whom
	which	if	whose
		in order that	

ALWAYS ESSENTIAL: The girl danced as dramatically as she always had.

ALWAYS NONESSENTIAL: The noisy Cub Scouts sang loudly, which annoyed their scoutmaster.

BOTH: I saw the man who was training for the Olympics. (essential) I saw Kenyon, who was training for the Olympics. (nonessential)

3. Basic Sentence S͡F͡S
Pattern 4 (S͡F͡S)

Don't use commas for an <u>essential fragment</u> inside a sentence. (The fragment identifies the subject and thus is essential.)

▶ The man <u>who sells fish</u> also sells aquariums.
(The essential fragment identifies *which* man also sells aquariums–the man <u>who sells fish</u>. Leaving out the fragment will cause confusion: *Which* man do you mean? *fragment = dependent clause*)

▶ The woman <u>wearing the red shirt</u> also sells aquariums.
(The essential fragment identifies *which* woman also sells aquariums–the woman <u>wearing the red shirt</u>. Leaving out the fragment will cause confusion: *Which* woman do you mean? *fragment = participial phrase*)

▶ My brother <u>Bob</u> also sells aquariums.
(The essential fragment identifies *which* brother also sells aquariums. Here we can assume you have more than one brother and need the fragment to distinguish your brother Bob from your brother Tom and your brother Bill. Leaving out the necessary fragment will cause confusion: *Which* brother do you mean? *fragment = appositive, a word or phrase renaming a noun*)

Pattern 5 (S͡,F,S͡)

Use commas for a <u>nonessential fragment</u> inside a sentence. (The fragment isn't needed since the subject is already identified.)

▶ Mr. Mason, <u>who sells fish</u>, also sells aquariums.
(The nonessential fragment isn't needed to identify the subject. He's already identified by name: Mr. Mason. Leaving out the fragment won't cause confusion. *fragment = dependent clause*)

▶ Frieda Wilson, <u>wearing the red shirt</u>, also sells aquariums.
(The nonessential fragment isn't needed to identify the subject. She's already identified by name: Frieda Wilson. Leaving out the fragment won't cause confusion. *fragment = participial phrase*)

▶ My brother, <u>Bob,</u> also sells aquariums.
(The nonessential fragment isn't needed to identify the subject. Here we will assume you have only one brother. The fragment isn't needed to distinguish one brother from another since you have only one. *fragment = appositive*)

- ▶ My brother, <u>however</u>, also sells aquariums.
- ▶ My brother, <u>on the other hand</u>, also sells aquariums.
  (The nonessential fragments interrupt the "flow" of each sentence. Like many interrupting transitions, *however* and *on the other hand* can be left out without causing confusion. *fragment = transition, a word or phrase used to connect one part to another*)

4. Basic Sentence SS
Pattern 6 (S, CONJ S)

Use the comma BEFORE the coordinating conjunctions for, and, nor, but, or, yet, so (*the FANBOYS*) to separate two <u>sentences</u>.

- ▶ I <u>went to the store</u>, for <u>I needed some bread.</u>
- ▶ <u>Bob went to the store</u>, and <u>he bought some bread.</u>
- ▶ <u>The girl went to the store</u>, yet <u>she forgot to buy some bread.</u>

Pattern 7 (S./;S)

Use the period to separate two unrelated <u>sentences</u>; use the period or semicolon to separate two related <u>sentences</u>.

- ▶ <u>Marilyn Monroe was a famous movie blonde "bombshell."</u> <u>George W. Bush moved to Texas.</u> (***unrelated sentences = period***)
- ▶ <u>Marilyn Monroe was a famous movie blonde "bombshell."</u> <u>The movies' first blonde bombshell was Jean Harlow.</u> (***related sentences = period or semicolon***)
- ▶ <u>Marilyn Monroe was a famous movie blonde "bombshell"</u>; the <u>movies' first blonde bombshell was Jean Harlow.</u> (***related sentences = period or semicolon***)

Pattern 8 (S./; TRANS, S)

Use the period or semicolon to separate two related sentences linked with a transition; use the comma after the transition.*

*Excluding one-syllable transitions: *hence, next, now, then, thus,* etc.

- ▶ <u>Marilyn Monroe was a famous movie blonde "bombshell."</u>
  <u>However, the movies' first blonde bombshell was Jean Harlow.</u>
- ▶ <u>Marilyn Monroe was a famous movie blonde "bombshell"</u>;
  <u>however, the movies' first blonde bombshell was Jean Harlow.</u>

The period and the semicolon have the same function—to separate sentences. Writers choose the semicolon over the period when they want to emphasize the relation that one sentence has with another.

HOW CAN JUST *EIGHT* PATTERNS PUNCTUATE *ALL* POSSIBLE SENTENCES?

Easy answer: You can combine each pattern with every other pattern, using as many fragments or sentences as you want. *Any* sentence, as long as it's not just one big fragment, is fine to write as long as you punctuate it properly. If you follow the punctuation required for each pattern, there won't be a problem (though you may end up with some very lengthy, but perfectly punctuated, sentences).

We'll begin with the first pattern: F,S.

To that pattern, we'll add more fragments and sentences, so that we end up with one long (but perfectly punctuated) sentence.

Instead of the two minimum parts (either a *fragment plus a sentence* or *a sentence plus a sentence*), our big sentence will have four parts, each a sentence: $S + S + S + S = S$.

And each S will break into two or three parts:

$$S \quad S \quad S \quad S \quad = \quad S.$$

$$FS + SFF + S + FSF$$

PUNCTUATION TIP

It's fine to add parts to each pattern as long as each part is punctuated properly. In other words, you can have have FFFS as long as commas go in where they're supposed to: F,F,F,S.

To prove that long sentences are not run-ons when they're punctuated properly, we'll choose semicolons over periods to separate each sentence. The five fragments are <u>underlined</u>; the four sentences are highlighted.

Sentence 1   Sentence 2

[F,S] <u>After I left town,</u> I walked into the country; [S,FF] my dog went with me, <u>something she likes to do when I go hiking;</u>

Sentence 3   Sentence 4

[S] we kept a good pace; [F,SF] <u>though we stopped a couple of times to rest,</u> we managed to reach home <u>in time for dinner.</u>

PROPERLY PUNCTUATED WITH SEMICOLONS: After I left town, I walked into the country; my dog went with me, something she likes to do when I go hiking; we kept a good pace; though we stopped a couple of times to rest, we managed to reach home in time for dinner.

PROPERLY PUNCTUATED WITH PERIODS: After I left town, I walked into the country. My dog went with me, something she likes to do when I go hiking. We kept a good pace. Though we stopped a couple of times to rest, we managed to reach home in time for dinner.

IMPROPERLY PUNCTUATED WITH COMMAS: After I left town, I walked into the country, my dog went with me, something she likes to do when I go hiking, we kept a good pace, though we stopped a couple of times to rest, we managed to reach home in time for dinner. (*This improperly punctuated sentence is a run-on! Commas instead of semicolons or periods have created the problem.*)

Easy Grammar

ALL THOSE RULES VERSUS THE BIG PICTURE TROUBLE SPOTS

What's even more intimidating than all those punctuation rules? All those *grammar* rules, let alone the terms: *noun, verb, dangling modifier, object of the preposition* . . . Where do you start?

Editing grammar, like editing punctuation and style, can be an easy job if you approach it from the Big Picture. Learn the Big Picture Trouble Spots, the predictable places where grammar goes wrong. Take care of the Trouble Spots, and most of your grammar problems will disappear.

LEARN THE EIGHT PARTS OF SPEECH

To be on top of grammar, it's important to learn eight grammar terms. It's difficult to edit if you don't know the language. But you probably know these terms better than you think.

The Eight Parts of Speech

1. **Adjective**. Describes a <u>noun</u> or pronoun: the *red* <u>car</u>; <u>it</u> is *red*.
2. **Adverb**. Describes everything other than a noun or pronoun, including a <u>verb</u>, an adjective, another **adverb** or a **group of words**: the car <u>drove</u> *slowly, too slow*, drove *very* **slowly**. *Unfortunately,* **the car drove up slowly**.
3. **Conjunction**. Connects words in a sentence (remember the coordinating conjunctions with the mnemonic <u>**FANBOYS**</u>: **for, and, nor, but, or, yet, so**): The car *and* the bike are here.
4. **Interjection**. Breaks up sentence flow; an exclamation/curse word: *Damn*, I cut my finger!
5. **Noun**. Names a person, place, or thing: *Richard, woman, Chicago, cars.*
6. **Preposition**. Relates a noun or pronoun in a <u>phrase</u> to the rest of the sentence: I saw the car *<u>in the</u> <u>driveway</u>*. It was *<u>out</u> of gas*. Did Richard buy gas *<u>from</u> them*?
7. **Pronoun**. Takes the place of the noun: Richard = *he/him*, woman = *she/her*, Chicago = *it*, cars = *they/them*.
8. **Verb**. Shows <u>action</u> or a lack of action (a state of being): I *<u>drive</u>* the car; I *am* a doctor.

GRAMMAR TIP

The eight parts are easy to identify in a sentence because of their *job functions*.

- Nouns and pronouns (as subjects) control verbs.
- Verbs take orders from nouns and pronouns (as subjects).
- Pronouns replace nouns and (as subjects) control verbs.
- Adjectives go with nouns.
- Adverbs go with everything but nouns and pronouns.
- Prepositions start phrases that relate nouns or pronouns (as objects) to other parts.
- Conjunctions connect one part to another.
- Interjections break up the flow of the parts.

A noun has several functions. One is as a *subject*—the person or thing that controls the verb. Another is as an *object*—a person or thing that reacts to (1) the verb or (2) the preposition.

Noun as subject → **(1) Verb** → **Noun as object**
     Jim   **threw**   **the ball**
(2) Preposition → **Noun as object**
      to   **Bob.**
Jim threw the ball to Bob.

Before we go further, memorize the definitions and the job functions. Quiz yourself to make sure you understand each.

*

A sentence is built up in combinations of the eight parts. At the heart of every sentence is a noun or pronoun used as the *subject*, the motor that runs the sentence and oversees the other seven parts. The parts of the sentence are listed here in order of importance.

Subject (which is a noun or pronoun)
Verb
Adverb-Adjective
Preposition
Conjunction
Interjection

Begin with a <u>noun</u> or <u>pronoun</u> (serving as subject) and add a <mark>verb</mark>:

SUBJECT	Verb
<u>Ice</u>	melts.

Add an <mark>adjective</mark> to describe the subject and an <mark>adverb</mark> to describe the verb.

Adjective	Adverb
Exposed ice	melts quickly.

Then add a <mark>preposition</mark> in a <u>phrase</u> (with a *noun* as object).

Prepositional phrase + noun

Exposed ice   melts quickly <u>on the *street*</u>.

Then add a <mark>conjunction</mark> (with another *noun* as object).

Conjunction + noun

Exposed ice   melts quickly <u>on the street</u> and *sidewalk*.

Finally add an <mark>interjection</mark>.

Interjection

Exposed ice—wow!—melts quickly on the street and sidewalk.

Exposed ice—wow!—melts quickly on the street and sidewalk.

THE BIG PICTURE TROUBLE SPOTS

In order of frequency, from most errors to least, writers have trouble with the following trouble spots:

- **Verbs**
- **Pronouns**
- **Adverbs and Adjectives**
- **Prepositions**
- **Conjunctions**
- **Interjections**

It's not just writers who have trouble. We all do. Listen to a conversation, and you'll hear grammar errors most often with verbs, then pronouns, then adverbs and adjectives; then prepositions, conjunctions, and interjections:

It <u>don't</u> bother me. (doesn't—verb error)

<u>Lay</u> down. (lie—verb error)

She's one of the women who<u>'s</u> going to help us.

(are—verb error)

<u>Me</u> and <u>him</u> want to start our own band.

(He and I—pronoun error)

That money was intended for Molly and <u>I</u>, but we'll give it to somebody else. (me—pronoun error)

I'm worried about doing <u>good</u> on the chem test.

(well—adverb/adjective error)

That dress looks <u>well</u> on her. (good—adverb/adjective error)

He's angry <u>at</u> the governor. (with—preposition error)

You go <u>in</u> the house from the porch. (into—preposition error)

She read many Russian writers, including Tolstoy, Turgenev, <u>and etc</u>. (etc.—conjunction error)

<u>Hey that's</u> a lot to think about! (Hey, that's—interjection/punctuation error)

So it makes sense to look first for problems with these trouble spots. We can take care of them with a Big Picture plan of attack.

That plan will solve two problems every writer faces:
- **Knowing how to spot the error**
- **Knowing how to fix the error**

Before you begin, find a pen and three highlighters in three colors–like yellow (for *verbs*), green (for *pronouns*), and blue (for *adverbs* and *adjectives*).

VERBS—BIG PICTURE PLAN OF ATTACK

Step 1. Underline the subject with a pen.

Step 2. Highlight the verb. Usually it follows the subject.

If you have trouble spotting the right words, remember family relationships.
- **Who or what is the sentence about?** *Ice* is the <u>subject</u> of the sentence below.
- **What verb does the subject control? What happens?** Ice = *melts*.

Exposed <u>ice</u>—wow!—<mark>melts</mark> quickly on the street and sidewalk.

Now we can troubleshoot.

This sentence has no problems with its verb, but what if it did? What kind of verb errors should you look for? What trouble spots?

Troubleshooting Verb Trouble Spots

Verb problems show up in four classic trouble spots.

1. **Irregular Verbs** (*lie* or *lay*?)
2. **Tricky Subject-Verb Agreement** (*is* or *are*?)
3. **Tenses** (*past* or *present*?)
4. **Indicative for Subjunctive** (*was* or *were*?)

1. Irregular Verbs

GRAMMAR TIP

If you have trouble spotting verbs, look for a word that will change if you move from one time to another, like from past to present or from present to future. Because verbs reflect time (present, past, and future), their spelling and their <u>helping verbs</u> change according to the time. *Today I eat lunch. Yesterday I ate lunch. In the past, I <u>have [or had]</u> eaten lunch. Tomorrow I <u>will</u> eat lunch.* No matter the time, the other parts of speech won't change. For example, *lunch* (a noun) stays the same from sentence to sentence, just like *I* (a pronoun).

Definition: A *helping verb* comes before the main verb and gives information about it, like whether it's in the past, present, or future. Common helping verbs: *am, are, was, were, has, have, can, may, could, would, might, will* in sentences like *I <u>have been</u> typing all day.*

Verbs in English break into two groups:
*   **Regular**
*   **Irregular**

Regular verbs account for a good share of our verbs. These verbs are predictable and easy to handle. Speakers and writers don't often make errors with them. To show a regular verb's past tense or past participle, you add *-d* or *-ed* to the present; for the present participle, you add *-ing* to the present. Each verb has four principal parts. The four principal parts of *to call* are *call, called, called, calling*. Begin with the present (*call*). For the past, add *-ed* (*called*) and for the present participle add *-ing* (*calling*).

1. **Present**: Today I call my brother.
2. **Past**: Yesterday I called my brother.

3. **Past Participle**: In the past, I have call*ed* my brother *or* In the past, I had call*ed* my brother.

4. **Present Participle**: Today I am calling my brother. Yesterday, I was calling my brother. In the past, I have/had been calling my brother. In the future, I will be calling my brother.

The errors come with *irregular* verbs because, with a few exceptions, they don't end with *-d* or *-ed*. Instead, to show a new tense, irregular verbs shift vowels (*arise/arose*) or change into new words (*go/went/gone*). Despite their irregularities, most of us know these forms pretty well and get stuck only on ones we don't use daily or have learned incorrectly.

When writers refer to verbs, they sometimes use the term *infinitive*. An infinitive is the present-tense form plus *to: to call, to arise, to become, to begin*, etc. The one exception is the messy verb form that includes *am, is, are, was, were*, and *been*. Its infinitive is *to be*.

This chart of irregular verbs also includes a few asterisked (*) regular verbs that cause confusion. The *italicized* words are the most troublesome irregulars.

PRESENT	PAST	PAST PARTICIPLE (WITH **HAVE, HAS,** OR **HAD**)	PRESENT PARTICIPLE
am, is, are (to be)	*was, were* (Don't confuse them.)	been	being
arise	arose	arisen	arising
become	became	*become* (not became)	becoming
begin	began	*begun* (not began)	beginning
bend	bent	bent	bending
bet	bet or betted	bet or betted	betting
bite	bit	bitten or bit	biting
blow	*blew* (not blowed)	*blown* (not blowed)	blowing
break	broke	*broken* (not broke)	breaking
bring	*brought* (not brung)	*brought* (not brung)	bringing
build	built	built	building

burst	*burst* (not bursted or busted)	*burst* (not bursted or busted)	bursting
buy	*bought* (not boughten)	*bought* (not boughten)	buying
catch	caught	caught	catching
choose	chose	*chosen* (not chose)	choosing
cling	*clung* (not clinged)	*clung* (not clinged)	clinging
come	*came* (not come)	*come* (not came)	coming
cost	*cost* (not costed)	*cost* (not costed)	costing
creep	crept	crept	creeping
cut	cut	cut	cutting
dig	dug	dug	digging
dive	dived or dove	*dived* (not dove)	diving
do	*did* (not done)	*done* (not did)	doing
draw	drew	*drawn* (not drawed)	drawing
dream	dreamed or dreamt	dreamed or dreamt	dreaming
drink	*drank* (not drunk)	*drunk* (not drunken)	drinking
drive	drove	driven	driving
*drown	*drowned* (not drownded)	*drowned* (not drownded)	drowning
eat	*ate* (not eat)	*eaten* (not eat or ate)	eating
fall	fell	fallen	falling
find	found	found	finding
fly	flew	flown	flying
forbid	*forbade, forbad* (not forbid)	*forbidden* (not forbid)	forbidding
forget	forgot	forgotten, forgot	forgetting

forgive	forgave	forgiven	forgiving
freeze	*froze* (not frozed)	*frozen* (not frozed)	freezing
get (not got or gots)	got	gotten, got	getting
give	*gave* (not give)	*given* (not give)	giving
go	*went* (not gone)	*gone* (not went)	going
grow	*grew* (not growed)	*grown* (not growed)	growing
*hang (execute)	*hanged* (not hung)	*hanged* (not hung)	hanging
hang (a picture)	*hung* (not hanged)	*hung* (not hanged)	hanging
have	had	had	having
hide	hid	*hidden* (not hid)	hiding
hold	held	held	holding
hurt	*hurt* (not hurted)	*hurt* (not hurted)	hurting
keep	kept	kept	keeping
know	*knew* (not knowed)	*known* (not knowed)	knowing
lay (set something)	laid	laid	laying
lead	*led* (not lead)	*led* (not lead)	leading
leave	left	left	leaving
let	let	let	letting
lie (recline)	*lay* (not laid or lied)	*lain* (not laid or lied)	lying
lie (speak untruth)	lied	lied	lying
*loosen	*loosened* (not loosed)	*loosened* (not loosed)	loosening
lose (not loose)	lost	lost	losing
make	made	made	making
pay	*paid* (not payed)	*paid* (not payed)	paying
prove	proved	proved, proven	proving

*raise (lift something)	raised	raised	raising
ride	rode	*ridden* (not rode)	riding
ring	*rang* (not rung)	*rung* (not rang)	ringing
rise	*rose* (not arose)	*risen* (not arisen)	rising
run	ran	run	running
say	said	said	saying
see	saw	seen	seeing
sell	sold	sold	selling
set (place something)	set	set	setting
shake	*shook* (not shooken)	*shaken* (not shook or shooken)	shaking
show	showed	showed, shown	showing
shrink	shrank or shrunk	shrunk or shrunken	shrinking
sing	sang or sung	*sung* (not sang)	singing
sink	sank or sunk	*sunk* (not sunken)	sinking
sit	*sat* (not set)	*sat* (not set or satten)	sitting
sleep	slept	slept	sleeping
speak	spoke	spoken	speaking
spin	spun	spun	spinning
spring	sprang or sprung	*sprung* (not sprang)	springing
stand	stood	stood	standing
steal	*stole* (not stold)	*stolen* (not stold)	stealing
sting	stung	stung	stinging
stink	stank or stunk	*stunk* (not stank)	stinking
swear	sworn	sworn	swearing

swim	swam	*swum* (not swam)	swimming
swing	*swung* (not swang)	*swung* (not swanged)	swinging
take	took	*taken* (not took or tooken)	taking
think	thought	thought	thinking
throw	*threw* (not throwed)	*thrown* (not throwed)	throwing
wake	*woke or waked* (not woked)	*waken or woken* (not wakened or awoken)	waking
wear	wore	worn	wearing
write	wrote	*written* (not wrote)	writing

Four Irregular Verb Errors to Watch For: Four irregular verbs cause a number of errors: *to be, to do, to lie*, and *to lay*. (*To lie* seems to cause more errors than any other verb, even among educated speakers and writers. Remember to use *to lie* when you're talking about going to bed or taking a nap. Use *to lay* when you're talking about setting something down.)

Every verb has various endings, depending on who or what controls the verb. Refer to the verb ending by the person or thing in charge. For example, if "I" controls the verb, we call it *first-person singular*. If "it" controls the verb, we call it *third-person singular*. Each of the forms below is a *subject pronoun*—because a pronoun used as the subject controls the verb.

SUBJECT PRONOUNS

First-person singular = **I**
First-person plural = **We**
Second-person singular and plural = **You**
Third-person singular = **He, she, it**
Third-person plural = **They**

You can break down any verb into one of the three main tenses—simple present, simple past, and simple future. Let's break down *to be* and *to do*.

	TO BE	TO DO
Present	I am You are He/she/it is We are They are	I do You do He/she/it does We do They do
Past	I was You were He/she/it was We were They were	I did You did He/she/it did We did They did
Future	I will be You will be He/she/it will be We will be They will be	I will do You will do He/she/it/will do We will do They will do

The most common errors come from choosing the wrong verb for the person—like choosing a third-person verb for a second-person pronoun—or leaving out part of the verb.

WRONG: You was late to class; we was happy to see her. (choosing the wrong verb)

RIGHT: You were late to class; we were happy to see her.

WRONG: We been there; I done it. (leaving out part of the verb)

RIGHT: We've been there; I did it *or* I've done it.

WRONG: It don't matter; she don't care. (choosing the wrong verb)

RIGHT: It doesn't matter; she doesn't care.

WRONG: We do it tomorrow. (leaving out part of the verb)

RIGHT: We will (we'll) do it tomorrow.

We can complicate tenses by adding *progressive tenses*—tenses that show continuous action.

	TO LIE	TO LAY
Simple present (Present progressive)	Today I lie down for a nap. (Today I am lying down for nap.)	Today I lay IT down. (Today I am laying IT down.)
Present perfect (Present perfect progressive)	In the past, I have lain down for a nap. (In the past, I have been lying down for a nap.)	In the past, I have laid IT down. (In the past, I have been laying IT down.)
Simple past (Past progressive)	Yesterday I lay down for a nap. (Yesterday I was lying down for a nap.)	Yesterday I laid IT down. (Yesterday I was laying IT down.)
Past perfect (Past perfect progressive)	In the past, I had lain down for a nap. (In the past, I had been lying down for a nap.)	In the past, I had laid IT down. (In the past, I had been laying IT down.)
Simple future (Future progressive)	Tomorrow I will lie down for a nap. (Tomorrow I will be lying down for a nap.)	Tomorrow I will lay IT down. (Tomorrow I will be laying IT down.)
Future perfect (Future perfect progressive)	Tomorrow I will have lain down for a nap. (Tomorrow I will have been lying down for a nap.)	Tomorrow I will have laid IT down. (Tomorrow I will have been laying IT down.)

To sort out these verbs, replace *lie* with *sit* and *lay* with *set*. Remember that *lay* and *set* always are followed by an object–an "it."

LIE = SIT	LAY = SET
Today I lie/sit down. Yesterday I lay/sat down. In the past, I have (had) lain/sat down. Tomorrow I will lie/sit down. (I am [have been, was, had been, will be, will have been] lying/sitting down.)	Today I lay/set IT down. Yesterday I laid/set IT down. In the past, I have (had) laid/set IT down. Tomorrow I will lay/set IT down. (I am [have been, was, had been, will be, will have been] laying/setting IT down.)

> # GRAMMAR TIP
> Whenever you use an infinitive to talk about the past, use *to* plus the present tense of the verb: Yesterday I wanted to go [not to *went*].

A quick quiz:

1. Right now I want to (lie/lay) down.
2. Yesterday I wanted to (lie/lay) down; yesterday I wanted to (lie/lay) the pen down.
3. Right now I am (lying/laying) the pen on the desk; soon it will be (lying/laying) there.
4. Yesterday before I (lay/laid) down for a nap, I (lay/laid) the pen on the desk.
5. In the past, I have (lay/laid) the pen on the desk before I have (lain/laid) down for a nap.
6. In the past, the pen has been (lying/laying) on the desk while I have been (lying/laying) down for a nap.
7. Tomorrow I will be (lying/laying) down for a nap before you see me (lying/laying) down the pen.

    1. lie
    2. lie, lay
    3. laying, lying
    4. lay, laid
    5. laid, lain
    6. lying, lying
    7. lying, laying

2. Tricky Subject-Verb Agreement

> # WARNING!
> In English, an *-s* ending makes a <u>noun</u> plural but a <mark>verb</mark> singular.
>
> | | |
> |---|---|
> | <u>dog</u> = singular | <u>dogs</u> = plural |
> | runs = singular | run = plural |
>
> The <u>dog</u> runs. (singular noun + singular verb)
> The <u>dogs</u> run. (plural noun + plural verb)

> # GRAMMAR TIP
>
> When a subject and verb are in *agreement*, they agree in number: A singular subject takes a singular verb; a plural subject takes a plural verb.

Look out for problems showing up with:

- Subject-Verb Split: *I, among all my friends, (am/is/are) leaving.*
- Collective Subject + Singular Verb: *Two-thirds of the pie (was/were) eaten.*
- Subject before a *To Be* Verb + Noun: *What mattered (was/were) the rules.*
- A or *The* + Subject + Verb: *A number of voters (was/were) delayed.*
- Compound Subjects with *Either/Or: Either my aunt or my uncles (is/are) retired.*
- Verb before Subject: *(What's/what're) the priorities?*
- *There* + Verb + Plural or Compound Subject: *(There's/there're) some cops here.*
- *Each* or *Every* before a Compound Subject: *Each boy and each girl (is/are) voting.*
- *Each* after a Compound Subject: *The dog and cat each (is/are) eating snacks.*
- Plural Noun + *Who* or *That: Sara is one of the bicyclists who (wants/want) to quit.*
- *None* or *Some* + Verb: *None of the lumber (was/were) sold; none of the trees (was/were) cut down.*

Subject-Verb Split: *I, among all my friends, (am/is/are) leaving.*

> # GRAMMAR TIP
>
> Underline the subject and highlight the verb. *Do words split them up?* That's often the sign of a subject-verb agreement error. When a *fragment* separates the subject from its verb, don't let the fragment's last word determine the verb.

I, *among all my friends,* (am/is/are) leaving. (am)

The lone Republican, *as well as the Democrats,* (wants/want) to reconsider a filibuster. (wants)

Dr. Foxways, *along with the hospital's other staff physicians,* (is/are) planning to leave. (is)

Marcy's sales, *despite competition from that other yard sale,* (promises/promise) many bargains. (promise)

Collective Subject + Singular Verb: *Two-thirds of the pie (was/were) eaten.*

> # GRAMMAR TIP
>
> Underline the subject. Is it a word like *jury, team, congress, senate, series, band, orchestra, a million dollars*? Or a word ending in *-s* like *statistics, athletics, economics, politics, physics, news, mumps,* or *measles*? In other words, is it a <u>collective</u>? *When the subject is a collective, usually use a singular verb.*

> <u>Two-thirds</u> of the pie (was/were) eaten. (was)
>
> The <u>jury</u> (is/are) filing into the courtroom. (is)
>
> The newspaper reported that a <u>million dollars</u> (was/were) missing from the bank. (was)
>
> <u>Statistics</u> (is/are) my favorite class. (is)
>
> <u>Politics</u> (is/are) one of my interests. (is)
>
> <u>Ice cream and cake</u> (is/are) a favorite dessert. (is)

Sometimes you may need a plural when the collective isn't entirely united, like a jury debating a verdict.

> The <u>jury</u> (is/are) arguing among themselves. (are)

Or something is considered separately instead of as a unit.

> A <u>million dollars</u> (was/were) counted out on the table. (were)
>
> The <u>statistics</u> (shows/show) him to be right. (show)
>
> Their <u>politics</u> (is/are) difficult to understand. (are)
>
> The <u>ice cream and</u> the <u>cake</u> (is/are) sold out. (are)

Subject before a *To Be* Verb + Noun: *What mattered (was/were) the rules.*

> # GRAMMAR TIP
>
> Underline the subject. Is it a group of words acting as a unit—as one subject? Does it come before a to be verb (*is, are, was, were,* etc.)? *When <u>what as a subject</u> comes before a to be verb and a noun comes after, the verb agrees with the noun, not the subject.*

<u>What mattered</u> (was/were) the **rules**. (were)

(The rules were what mattered.)

<u>What she really wanted to buy</u> (was/were) both **DVDs**. (were)

(Both DVDs were what she really wanted to buy.)

The logic becomes clear when you consider:

<u>What the telescope reveals</u> is the **man**.

(The man is what the telescope reveals.)

<u>What the telescope reveals</u> are the **men**.

(The men are what the telescope reveals.)

A or *The* + Subject + Verb: *A number of voters (was/were) delayed.*

GRAMMAR TIP

Underline the subject. Is it a collective noun? Does *the* or *a* come before the subject? *When* the *comes before, the verb is usually singular; when* a *comes before, the verb is usually plural.*

The <u>number</u> of voters (was/were) unexpected. (was)

A <u>number</u> of voters (was/were) delayed. (were)

Compound Subjects with *Either/Or: Either my aunt or my uncles (is/are) retired.*

A compound subject has more than one subject, like *my aunt and my uncles, neither my aunt nor my uncles,* or *neither my uncles nor my aunt.*

GRAMMAR TIP

Underline the subject. Is it a compound? *With* either/or *and* neither/nor, *the* <u>subject</u> *next to the verb controls the verb.*

---

1. My <u>aunt and my uncles</u> (is/are) retired. (are)
2. My <u>uncles and my aunt</u> (is/are) retired. (are)
3. **Either** my aunt **or** my <u>uncles</u> (is/are) retired. (are)

4. **Neither** my uncles **nor** my <u>aunt</u> (is/are) retired. (is)

5. **Neither** Bob **nor** <u>I</u> (am/is/are) going to take care of that issue. (am)

   1. aunt and uncles = plural = **are**

   2. uncles and aunt = plural = **are**

   3. uncles = plural = **are**

   4. aunt = singular = **is**

   5. I = singular = **am**

Verb before Subject: (*What's/what're) the priorities?*

GRAMMAR TIP

Underline the subject and highlight the verb. Usually the subject comes before the verb. *But when the verb comes before the <u>subject</u>, make sure they still agree—singular subject with singular verb; plural subject with plural verb.*

(**What's**/what're) the <u>priorities</u>? (what're = what are)

   (The priorities we're supposed to follow are what?)

In this databank (is/**are**) many reliable <u>sources</u>. (are)

   (Many reliable sources are in this databank.)

Beyond the orchard (was/**were**) the storm <u>cave</u> and the <u>shed</u>. (were)

   (The storm cave and the shed were beyond the orchard.)

There + Verb + Plural or Compound Subject: (*There's/there're) some cops here.*

GRAMMAR TIP

Using the *Find* command, search for *there*. *When a plural or compound <u>subject</u> follows* there *and the verb, use a plural verb.*

---

1. (**There's**/there're) some <u>cops</u> here. (there're = there are)

2. (**There was**/there were) a tool <u>chest</u> and some old garden <u>tools</u> in the garage. (were)

   1. cops = plural = **are**

   2. chest and tools = compound = **were**

Each or *Every* before a Compound Subject: *Each boy and each girl (is/are) voting.*

> # GRAMMAR TIP
>
> Using the *Find* command, search for *each* and *every*. Does a <u>subject</u> follow? Is the subject compound? *When* each *or* every *comes before a compound subject, use a singular verb.*

<u>Each</u> <u>boy</u> and each <u>girl</u> (is/are) voting. (is)
Every <u>mentor</u> and every <u>mentee</u> (was/were) instructed to meet in Bascom Hall. (was)

Each after a Compound Subject: *The dog and cat each (is/are) eating snacks.*

> # GRAMMAR TIP
>
> Using the *Find* command, search for *each*. Does a <u>subject</u> come before it? Is the subject compound? *When* each *comes* after *a plural subject, use a plural verb.*

The <u>dog</u> and <u>cat</u> each (is/are) eating snacks. (are)
The <u>animals</u> each (is/are) eating their food. (are)

Plural Noun + *Who* or *That*: *Sara is one of the bicyclists who (wants/want) to quit.*

> # GRAMMAR TIP
>
> Using the *Find* command, search for *who* and *that*. Does a plural <u>noun</u> come before it? *When you have a* <u>plural noun</u> + *who or that, proceed with caution: You may need a singular or plural verb.*

1. Sara is one of the <u>bicyclists</u> who (wants/want) to quit. (want)
2. Sammy is one of the <u>volunteers</u> who (comes/come) to visit. (come)
3. Ignacio is the only one of the <u>volunteers</u> who (comes/come) to visit. (comes)
4. Chicken pox is among those <u>diseases</u> that (is/are) curable. (are)

5. Jack is the only one of the <u>bicyclists</u> who (wants/want) to quit. (wants)
6. *Monopoly* is just one of the <u>games</u> that (was/were) invented in during the 1930s. (were)

Here's the logic of this common and difficult error:

1. MANY bicyclists want to quit. Sara is ONE of them.
2. MANY of the volunteers come to visit. Sammy is just ONE of them.
3. No volunteer comes to visit except Ignacio: He's the ONLY one.
4. MANY diseases are curable. Chicken pox is ONE of them.
5. No bicyclist wants to quit except Jack. He's the ONLY one.
6. MANY games were invited in the 1930s. *Monopoly* is just ONE of them.

None or *Some* + Verb: *None of the lumber (was/were) sold; none of the trees (was/were) cut down.*

GRAMMAR TIP

Unlike the personal pronoun, the *indefinite pronoun* doesn't refer to specific people or things (see **9. Singular or Plural Indefinite Pronoun**, page 130). Using the *Find* command, find these indefinite pronouns: *none, some, all, any, more,* and *most.*

Some indefinite pronouns can be <u>singular</u> or plural, depending on the words they refer to.

None of the <u>lumber</u> (was/were) sold; none of the trees (was/were) cut down.
   (lumber = singular = <u>was</u>; trees = plural = were)
Some of the vegetables (has/have) spoiled; some of the <u>food</u> (has/have) spoiled.
   (vegetables = plural = have; <u>food</u> = singular = <u>has</u>)
Most of the university's original buildings (was/were) built before 1900. (were)

3. Tenses

Writers face three common tense problems:

- Picking the Wrong Past Tense for Irregular Verbs
- Using the Wrong Tense for an Event That Happens before Another Event
- Jumping from One Tense to Another

Picking the Wrong Past Tense for Irregular Verbs: See **above, 1. Irregular Verbs,** for a list of irregular verbs, including *to be, to do, to lie,* and *to lay.*

GRAMMAR TIP

Next to the computer, keep a list of your verb mistakes. (The list probably won't be long.) If you make these mistakes once, you'll make them again unless you train yourself to recognize and fix them. Practice reciting principal parts you're not sure of, like *lie, lay, lain, lying.* Then write out quizzes for yourself as though you were studying French or German verbs.

Using the Wrong Tense for an Event That Happens before Another Event: In the WRONG sentences, A and B seem to take place at the same time. In each case, this is logically impossible. The event that comes first *must* have an earlier tense.

> **WRONG: She plans [A] to call him by the end of the week, but he is [B] out of the office.**
> **RIGHT: She has planned to call him by end of the week, but he is out of the office.**

In this situation, on Monday she has decided to call him; on Tuesday he leaves the office. One event precedes another, so the tenses can't both be in the present. One must be earlier.

> **WRONG: I was employed [A] for five months before I was fired [B].**
> **RIGHT: I had been employed for five months before I was fired.**

Here the speaker had been employed in January but was fired in June.

> **WRONG: The movie started [A] just a few minutes before we arrived [B].**
> **RIGHT: The movie had started just a few minutes before we arrived.**

In this situation, the movie had started at 1:50 p.m., but we arrived at 1:54 p.m.

> **WRONG: Gerry thinks [A] she might go, but she'll [B] have to borrow money for the trip.**
> **RIGHT: Gerry has thought she might go, but she'll have to borrow money for the trip.**

In the past, Gerry has thought she might go, but before she can leave in the future, she'll have to borrow money.

GRAMMAR TIP

Keep the four principal parts of the verb handy (see page 100, **Verb Trouble Spots, 1. Irregular Verbs**). Remember that English has three basic past tenses: *I chose, I have chosen, I had chosen*. And remember that each refers to a *different* time. Hence, for each different time in the past, you must use a different tense (*chose, have chosen, had chosen*).

Jumping from One Tense to Another:

> **WRONG: Hilda runs out to the curb, hops into her car, and drove off.**
> **RIGHT: Hilda runs out to the curb, hops into her car, and drives off.**
>   (*Or* **Hilda ran out to the curb, hopped into her car, and drove off.**)

Once you begin in a tense, generally you should stay there. If you're in the past, stay in the past; if you're in the present, stay in the present. This advice becomes especially important when you write about the arts: Writing about fiction, poetry, music, the graphic arts—whatever the art—you want to stay in *present* tense when discussing the artwork itself. (Here Shakespeare says . . . Beethoven begins the symphony by . . . Austen creates her characters to show that . . .)

However, it's fine to use two different tenses in a situation like this—here, a past tense followed by three present tenses:

> *In 1935, Tom Kromer published his only novel.* Waiting for Nothing *tells the harrowing story of a young teacher who is forced on the road after losing his job. Kromer spares the reader no misery or glimpse into the underbelly of the Great Depression.*

When one time exists outside another time (the novel's 1935 publication took place in the historical past, outside the story's eternal present), then it makes sense to begin in the past (published) but then shift to the present (tells, is, spares) to talk about the novel's plot. Because the novel, like any artwork, exists in an eternal present, the three present-tense verbs make perfect sense.

GRAMMAR TIP

Jumping tenses can happen when a writer gets distracted: When the phone rings or somebody knocks on the door, it's not hard to forget the tense we're working in. Sometimes, too, we unconsciously pick up the tense of a source we're reading. If you break off work or consult a source, make sure that you continue and stay in the right tense.

---

4. Indicative for Subjunctive

In grammar, every sentence falls into one of three *moods*. Mood refers to the "attitude" of the sentence—that is, what it wants to express. Sentences can express:

- A fact or what could be a fact (**indicative mood**)
- Something clearly not a fact (**subjunctive mood**)
- A command to do something (**imperative mood**)

A verb in the *indicative* mood expresses what it says as *fact: He is old; he looks like he is old.* A verb in the *subjunctive mood* often expresses what is *clearly not a fact*, like a wish or an impossibility: *I wish I were young.* (But the speaker can never be young; it's impossible.) A verb in the *imperative mood* expresses a command for somebody to do something: *Please find out how much that costs.*

We use the indicative and imperative for most sentences, so it's not hard to forget the exceptions that need the subjunctive: sentences that state something *clearly not a fact*. Verbs in the subjunctive use a slightly different form. Often they exchange one form (*was*) for another (*were*) or drop an ending (like -*s* from a third-person singular: appears becomes appear).

GRAMMAR TIP

Highlight the verb. *Does it express a fact or a command? Or does it express something clearly not a fact—like a wish, a doubt, an impossibility, a demand, a request, or a recommendation?* If it doesn't express a fact or a command, use the subjunctive.

He wishes he (was/were) young. (wish = were)

If she (was/were) a better singer, she would receive a scholarship. (doubt = were)

Glen delivered the speech as though he (was/were) Barack Obama. (impossibility = were)

The judge demands that Winston (appears/appear) in court tomorrow. (demand = appear)

Myron insists that Brenda (submits/submit) the proposal. (request = submit)

The landlady asked that each tenant (pays/pay) on the first of the month. (request = pay)

Mrs. Springdale recommended that the recipe (is/be) followed precisely. (recommendation = be)

Subjunctive forms:

am, is, are = **be**

was = **were**

singular verbs ending in -*s* = **drop the -*s*** (appears = **appear**)

PRONOUNS—BIG PICTURE PLAN OF ATTACK

Step 1. Highlight the verb.
Step 2. Highlight the pronoun. (See **Personal Pronouns Box below**.)

A pronoun takes the place of the noun. Instead of *computer* or *computers*, we say *it* or *they/them*. We'll look at four kinds of personal pronouns: subjective (used for a sentence subject), objective (used for an object), possessive (used for possession), and reflexive (used for emphasis).

PERSONAL PRONOUNS			
SUBJECTIVE	**OBJECTIVE**	**POSSESSIVE**	**REFLEXIVE**
I	me	my, mine	myself
you	you	your, yours	yourself(ves)
he	him	his	himself
she	her	her, hers	herself
it	it	its	itself
we	us	our, ours	ourselves
they	them	their, theirs	themselves
who*, whoever	whom, whomever	whose	(no word)

*Though *who* and its forms are relative pronouns, they're treated here like personal pronouns.

In sentences, <u>subjective</u> pronouns usually come *before* the verb; objective pronouns come *after*.

<u>SUBJECTIVE</u> PRONOUN	VERB	**OBJECTIVE PRONOUN**
I	TOLD	him.
You	VISITED	whom?
He	INVITED	us.
She	MAILED	it.
It	DELIGHTED	me.
We	TEASED	them.
They	SAW	you.
Who	CALLED	her?

Errors take place when a writer puts an objective pronoun *before* the verb instead of *after*. Or puts a subjective pronoun *after* the verb instead of *before*.

GRAMMAR TIP

Use the *Find* command to find the pronouns in your project (all are listed **above** in the **Personal Pronouns** box).

Does the pronoun come *before* or *after* the verb?
    Tommy and him WENT to the movies.
    (WRONG: him = objective pronoun)
    (Tommy and he WENT to the movies.)

WARNING!

Nervous about their grammar, many speakers and writers automatically reject *me* and choose *I*, ending up with errors like *between you* and *I*. *I* has its place in a sentence, but so does *me*, as in the grammatically correct *between you and me*.

Troubleshooting Pronoun Trouble Spots

Pronoun problems show up in eleven classic trouble spots.

1. **Subjective or Objective Pronoun as Subject?** *Bob and (I/me) saw the Grand Canyon.*
2. **Subjective or Objective Pronoun in a Comparison?** *He's taller than (I/me).*
3. **Subjective or Objective Pronoun after a Verb?** *Dan told (we/us) workers the truth.*
4. **Subjective or Objective Pronoun after a *To Be* Verb?** *Yes, this is (he/him).*
5. **Subjective or Objective Pronoun after a Preposition?** *She gave money to Jim and (I/me).*
6. **Subjective *Who* or Objective *Whom*?** *The boy (who/whom) is tall is here.*
7. **Noun + *That, Which,* or *Who/Whom*?** *The corporation (that/which/who/whom) we contacted needs workers.*
8. **Singular or Plural Possessive Pronoun Agreement?** *A writer needs to write (his/her/their) own essays.*
9. **Singular or Plural Indefinite Pronoun?** *Everyone completed (his or her/their) assignment.*
10. **Reflexive, Subjective, or Objective Pronoun?** *Tom and (I/myself) will pay the bill.*
11. **Possessive or Objective Pronoun before a Gerund?** *(His/him) singing is terrible.*

1. *Subjective or Objective Pronoun as Subject?* Bob and (I/me) saw the Grand Canyon.

Definitions: A *subjective* pronoun is used as the <u>subject</u> of a verb: *I saw him.* An *objective* pronoun is used as the <u>object</u> of the verb: He saw <u>me</u>.

> # GRAMMAR TIP
>
> (1) Highlight the VERB. Does the pronoun come *before* or *after* the verb? Usually, before = subjective; after = objective. (2) With a compound subject like Bob and (*I/me*), delete everything but the pronoun. Say the sentence: (*I/me*) *saw the Grand Canyon.* Which pronoun sounds more natural?

Bob and (I/me) **SAW** the Grand Canyon. (I)

   (<u>I</u> saw the Grand Canyon.)

Clarise and (she/her) **ARE MAILING** the report. (she)

   (<u>She</u> is mailing the report.)

I believe that Samantha and (he/him) **WILL PLAY** cards tomorrow. (he)

   (I believe that <u>he</u> will play cards tomorrow.)

Hannah suggested that Dell and (he/him) **SHOULD COME** for supper. (he)

   (Hannah suggested that <u>he</u> should come for supper.)

(I/me) and (she/her) **HOPE** to take the train to New Orleans.

   (always put the *I* last: <u>She</u> and <u>I</u> hope to take the train to New Orleans.)

Nevertheless, despite being broke, Alicia and (they/them) **TOOK** the trip. (they)

   (Nevertheless, despite being broke, <u>they</u> took the trip.)

MAY LaKiesha and (I/me) **LEAVE** early? (I)

   (May <u>I</u> leave early?)

2. *Subjective or Objective Pronoun in a Comparison?* He's taller than (I/me).

> # GRAMMAR TIP
>
> In a comparison, try putting a verb like *am* or *do* after the comparison. If the sentence sounds natural, use the <u>subjective</u> pronoun. If the sentence reads ambiguously, you may need an <u>objective</u> pronoun.

He's taller than (I/me). (I)

    (He is taller than <u>I</u> [am].)

Cynthia plays violin better than (he/him). (he)

    (Cynthia plays violin better than <u>he</u> [does].)

The historian admires Richard Nixon more than (we/us). (we)

    (The historian admires Richard Nixon more than <u>we</u> [do].)

But: **The historian admires Richard Nixon more than [the historian admires] <u>us</u>.**

    (The sentence reads ambiguously: *more than <u>we</u> admire Richard Nixon* or *more than the historian admires <u>us</u>?*)

3. *Subjective or Objective Pronoun after a Verb?* Dan told (we/us) workers the truth.

> # GRAMMAR TIP
>
> Other than in a question, normal sentence order is <u>Subject</u>-Verb-<u>Object</u> (*I like baseball*). Question order is Verb-<u>Subject</u>-<u>Object</u> (*Do <u>you</u> like <u>baseball</u>?*) In normal sentence order, use an objective pronoun after a verb unless it's a *to be* verb (see 4, next).

Highlight the verb. (1) Does the pronoun come before or after? (2) Leave out words before or after the pronoun to hear what sounds natural.

    Dan **TOLD** (we/us) workers the truth. (us)

        (Dan told <u>us</u> the truth.)

    They **MAILED** Amber and (I/me) a present. (me)

        (They mailed <u>me</u> a present.)

    Bette **WILL LEAD** Brian and (I/me) to the office. (me)

        (Bette will lead <u>me</u> to the office.)

4. *Subjective or Objective Pronoun after a* To Be *Verb?* Yes, this is (he/him).

> # GRAMMAR TIP
>
> Though an objective pronoun usually comes *after* the verb, *to be* verbs cause the exception. After a *to be* verb, use the <u>subjective</u> pronoun. If it sounds too odd or formal, in everyday conversation use the <u>objective</u>, like *me*, instead of *I*. But remember: Academic writing prefers a <u>subjective</u> pronoun. (And you always have the option of revising the sentence to get rid of the formal pronoun.)

Hello? Yes, this *is* (he/him). (he)

   (<u>He</u> *is* here not <u>Him</u> *is* here.

Are we all of the volunteers? Yes, all the volunteers *are* (we/us). (we)

   (<u>We</u> are all of the volunteers.)

The mysterious caller *had been* (she/her). (she)

   (<u>She</u> *had been* the mysterious caller.)

5. *Subjective or Objective Pronoun after a Preposition?* **She gave money to Jim and (I/me).**

> # GRAMMAR TIP
>
> (1) Using the *Find* command, find the preposition. (See page 154, under **Prepositions**, the **Prepositions** box.) (2) Use the <u>objective</u> pronoun after a <u>preposition</u>. (3) Leave out words between the preposition and the pronoun to hear what sounds natural.

She gave money <u>to</u> Jim and (I/me). (me)

   (She gave money to <u>me</u>.)

Deciding what protocol to follow was <u>for</u> (we/us) women to decide. (us)

   (Deciding what protocol to follow was for <u>us</u> women to decide.)

Just <u>between</u> you and (I/me), her theory is pure nonsense. (me)

   ([To] <u>me</u>, her theory is pure nonsense.)

<u>Except for</u> Sandra, Keith, and (he/him), we have no reliable workers. (him)

   (Except for <u>him</u>, we have no reliable workers.)

6. *Subjective* **Who** *or Objective* **Whom?** **The boy (who/whom) is tall is here.**

> # GRAMMAR TIP
>
> Use a simple trick to choose *who* and *whom* correctly: Since *who* needs a verb and *whom* doesn't, match up every VERB with a <u>subject</u>. If there's a word left over, the word left has to be *whom* (since it doesn't need a verb). That word is an <u>object</u>.

An infinitive (*to + verb*) can't have a subject; thus don't try to match it with a subject.

1. **The boy (who/whom) IS tall IS here. (who)**
2. **The boy (who/whom) he SAW IS here. (whom)**
3. **Willie TOLD Brenda (who/whom) to hire. (whom)**
4. **DO you REMEMBER (who/whom) WON the U.S. Open in 1997? (who)**
5. **You HAVE a pizza delivery for (who/whom)? (whom)**
6. **You HAVE a pizza delivery for (whoever/whomever) LIVES upstairs? (whoever)**
7. **You HAVE a pizza delivery for (whoever/whomever) they WANT to give it to? (whomever)**
8. **(Who/whom) DOES she RECOMMEND? (whom)**
9. **(Who/whom) DO you THINK WILL BE GOING tomorrow? (who)**

   1. <u>Boy</u> matches with first IS. Second IS needs a subject = <u>who</u>.
   2. <u>He</u> matches with SAW. <u>Boy</u> matches with IS. Word left over = <u>whom</u>.
   3. <u>Willie</u> matches with TOLD. *To hire* is an infinitive and can't have subject. Leftover word = <u>whom</u>.
   4. <u>You</u> matches with DO REMEMBER. WON needs a subject = <u>who</u>.
   5. <u>You</u> matches with HAVE. Word left over (with preposition) = <u>whom</u>.
   6. <u>You</u> matches with HAVE. LIVES needs a subject = <u>whoever</u>. (Though the preposition **for** needs *whomever*, the verb LIVES has more power and matches with whoever.)
   7. <u>You</u> matches with HAVE. <u>They</u> matches with WANT. *To give* = infinitive = no subject. Leftover word = <u>whomever</u>.
   8. <u>She</u> matches with DOES RECOMMEND. Leftover word = <u>whom</u>.
   9. <u>You</u> matches with DO THINK. WILL BE GOING needs a subject = <u>who</u>.

7. *Noun* + That, Which, *or* Who/Whom? The corporation (that/which/who/whom) we contacted needs workers.

GRAMMAR TIP

(1) *That* refers to animals, things, and types or classes of people.

(2) *Which* refers to animals, things, and groups of people.

(3) *Who/whom* refer to individual people, groups of people, and animals with names.

That, which, and *who* all refer to groups. But remember this distinction:

- When a group is an *it*, referring to the collective unit, use *that* for essential fragments and *which* for nonessential (the <u>company</u> *that* we've audited; <u>Sims & Pierce</u>, *which* we've audited)
- When a group is a *they*, referring to the people who make it up, use *who/whom* (the <u>managers</u> of Sims & Pierce, whom we've interviewed)

The <u>corporation</u> (that/which/who/whom) we contracted needs workers.

> (corporation = it = *that*)

The <u>executives</u> at Smythe, Chadwick, and Co., (that/which/who/whom) received large bonuses, have been criticized for their salaries.

> (executives = they = *who*)

Lilia is the <u>kind of painter</u> (that/which/who/whom) will win fame and money.

> (kind of painter = a type of something = *that*)

Have you seen the <u>cat</u> (that/which/who/whom) got stuck in the tree?

> (cat = unnamed animal = *that*)

Have you seen <u>Tiger</u>, (that/which/who/whom) got stuck in the tree?

> (Tiger = named animal = *who*)

GRAMMAR TIP

When *that* follows another *that* somewhere in the sentence, change the second *that* to *which*: *That* is a movie (that/which) I wish I'd seen. (which)

---

8. *Singular or Plural Possessive Pronoun Agreement?* A writer needs to write (his/her/their) own essays.

Definition: A *possessive* pronoun shows possession: *my* car, *his* apartment, *their* house. A <u>singular</u> noun matches with a <u>singular</u> possessive pronoun (*writer = his* or *her*); a <u>plural</u> noun matches with a <u>plural</u> possessive pronoun (*writers = their*).

> A <u>writer</u> needs to write (his/her/their) own essays. (his or her)
>
> Is that the <u>firefighter</u> who had (his/her/their) picture in the paper? (his or her)
>
> We found the <u>dog</u> that ran away from (its/his/her/their) home. (its, his, or her)
>
> How well did that <u>nun</u> do on (her/their) driving test? (her)
>
> We knew a <u>priest</u> from Rome who had (his/their) novel published. (his)

Because a collective noun like *jury, team,* and *committee* is usually singular, use a singular pronoun.

> The <u>jury</u> has come to (its/their) decision. (its)
>
> The <u>team</u> is playing (its/their) best. (its)
>
> The <u>committee</u> will submit (its/their) final report. (its)

But if members of the collective are acting independently and not as a unit, use a plural pronoun.

> The <u>jury</u> have argued (its/their) individual positions for the last three hours. (their)

GRAMMAR TIP

To avoid sexism and the awkwardness of *his/her*, try several strategies:

1. Change the gender-biased noun or pronoun to *you*:
   Each *man* will be responsible for *his* leave reports.
   = You are responsible for your leave reports.

2. Change gender-biased words to neutral words:
   Each *man* will be responsible for *his* leave reports.
   = Each will be responsible for leave reports.

3. Use plural nouns and pronouns:
   Each *man* will be responsible for *his* leave reports.
   = All workers are responsible for their leave reports.

4. Use job titles:
   Each *man* will be responsible for *his* leave reports.
   = All firefighters are responsible for their leave reports.

5. Use *the*, *a*, and *an* instead of pronouns:
   Each *man* will be responsible for *his* leave reports.
   = Each worker will be responsible for the leave reports.

6. Alternate pronouns: One time use *he* or *him*; the next, *she* or *her*.

7. Choose a singular pronoun and use it consistently through a text. Some writers add a prefatory note that says the consistent use of *he* or *she* does not intend sexism.

WARNING!

In conversation, many people make this grammar error: *A writer needs to write their own essays.* **Academic writing, however, still expects a singular noun to match with a singular pronoun, a plural noun to match with a plural pronoun:** *A writer needs to write his (or her) own essays.*

9. *Singular or Plural Indefinite Pronoun?* Everyone completed (his or her/their) assignment.

Definition: Unlike the personal pronoun, the *indefinite* pronoun doesn't refer to specific people or things. Instead of listing the states by specific name (Alabama, Alaska, etc.), we say *each* state, *some* states, or *all* states.

> # GRAMMAR TIP
> Use the box **below** to identify indefinite pronouns.

INDEFINITE PRONOUNS		
ALWAYS SINGULAR	**SOMETIMES SINGULAR, SOMETIMES PLURAL**	**ALWAYS PLURAL**
another	all	both
anybody	any	few
anyone	more	many
anything	most	several
each	none	
either (see **Note***)	some	
everybody		
everyone		
everything		
much		
neither*		
no one		
nobody		
nothing		
one		
somebody		
someone		
something		

*Although *either* and *neither* usually require singular possessive pronouns, they may require a plural pronoun with a compound subject (like *the singers or the actor*). If *either/neither* is the subject, it controls the verb. Otherwise, the <u>subject</u> next to the verb controls the possessive pronoun.

Either the singers or the <u>actor</u> left (her/their) shoes. (her)

Either the actor or the <u>singers</u> left (her/their) shoes. (their)

But here *neither* becomes the <u>subject</u>:

<u>Neither</u> of the cashiers was in (her/their) checkout lane. (her)

(*of the cashiers* = a prepositional phrase, not the subject)

Always <u>singular</u>:

<u>Everyone</u> completed (his or her/their) assignment. (his or her)

<u>Every one</u> of the clan practiced (his/her/their) hunting skills. (his or her)

<u>One horse</u> left (its/their) oats untouched. (its)

<u>No one</u> else on the men's team has mounted (his/their) bike. (his)

<u>Each member</u> of the women's team ran (her/their) personal best. (her)

<u>Each violinist</u> tuned (his/her/their) instrument. (his or her)

<u>Anybody</u> can plan (his/her/their) own vacation. (his or her)

Sometimes <u>singular</u>, sometimes plural:

<u>All</u> of the employees acted as if (his or her/their) jobs were in danger. (their)

<u>All</u> of the <u>juice</u> has lost (its/their) flavor. (its)

Do you know if <u>any rose</u> has sent out (its/their) first bud? (its)

Do you know if any roses have sent out (its/their) first buds? (their)

Always plural:

Few of the geese have (his or her/their) nests built. (their)

Several of the girls, including Maggie, have finished (her/their) chores. (their)

10. *Reflexive, Subjective, or Objective Pronoun?* Tom and (I/myself) will pay the bill.

Definition: Within a sentence, a *reflexive* pronoun reflects an earlier noun or pronoun like a mirror reflects an image:

The *woman* saw *herself* on TV. (woman = herself)

He cut *himself* shaving. (he = himself)

The reflexive *emphasizes* the noun or pronoun. Like subjective, objective, and possessive pronouns, the reflexive is a personal pronoun. It also shares *-self* endings with the *intensive* pronoun, which, like the reflexive, is used to emphasize (see **below, Intensive Pronoun**).

> # GRAMMAR TIP
>
> Find pronouns ending in -*self* or -*selves*: *myself, yourself, yourselves, himself, herself, itself, ourselves.* Look for misspellings: *hisself, theirself,* and *theirselves.*

Two rules govern the use of the reflexive pronoun:
- SUBJECT: Don't use it unless the sentence has a subjective noun or pronoun that the reflexive reflects. (The woman saw *herself* on TV; he cut *himself shaving.*)
- OBJECT: Don't substitute it for the <u>objective pronoun</u>. (*Give it to Bob or <u>me</u>*, not *Give it to Bob or myself.*)

We can use *herself* because we've already used *woman*; we can use *himself* because we've already used *he.* Both *woman* and *he* are *antecedents*–the nouns or pronouns used *before* the reflexive can be used (*ante* = before).

Failing to remember this basic rule leads to grammar errors:

SUBJECT ERROR: Tom and myself will pay the bill. (I)

(The antecedent *I* hasn't been set up, so *myself* can't be used.)

SUBJECT-VERB ERROR: Hey, how're you? Fine, how's *yourself*? (are you)

(No antecedent, so the subjective pronoun must follow a plural *to be* verb.)

OBJECT ERROR: The plan was discussed by Ralph and *himself.* (him)

OBJECT ERROR: The estate was split between the Pattersons and *ourselves.* (us)

OBJECT ERROR: Give it to Bob or *myself.* (me)

> # WARNING!
>
> In an imperative sentence—a sentence that commands somebody to do something—the subject <u>you</u> serves as the antecedent. Since <u>you</u> in an imperative is *understood* (that is, not present in the sentence), the reflexive pronoun is correct (see below).

- Please present *yourselves* to the Queen.

  (The plural subject/antecedent *you* is understood: *[You] please present yourselves to the Queen.*)
- Go over the budget yourself.

  (The singular subject/antecedent *you* is understood: *[You] go over the budget yourself.*)

Intensive pronoun:

Definition: The *intensive* pronoun, a personal pronoun, uses *-self* to *intensify* a noun or pronoun—that is, to *emphasize* it.

- I *myself* will take care of planning the party.
- Mrs. Steinberg wanted to speak with the supervisors *themselves*.
- The President *himself* will speak to the press.

GRAMMAR TIP

Never use commas with an *intensive* pronoun. Because it's an *essential* appositive emphasizing a noun or pronoun, commas aren't necessary.

WRONG: I, *myself*, will take care of planning the party.

(I myself will)

WRONG: Mrs. Steinberg wanted to speak with the supervisors, *themselves*. (supervisors themselves)

WRONG: The President, *himself*, will speak to the press.

(The President himself)

11. *Possessive or Objective Pronoun before a Gerund?* (His/him) singing is terrible.

Definitions: A _possessive pronoun_ shows who owns something: *my house* or *the house is mine, your/yours, his, her/hers, its, our/ours, their/theirs*. A gerund is a word that comes from a verb, ends in *-ing*, and functions as a noun—either as a subject (*Dancing is fun*) or as an object (*I like dancing*). A **_present participle_** also comes from a verb and ends in *-ing*, but unlike the gerund, it functions as a verb (*I am singing*).

GRAMMAR TIP

Use a possessive pronoun before a gerund but not before a present participle. Likewise, show possession by using a noun + apostrophe in front of a gerund.

(His/him) singing is terrible. (His)

(gerund = subject)

I hate (his/him) singing. (his)

(gerund = object)

BUT ALSO RIGHT: I hate him <u>singing</u>.

(singing = a present participle: I hate him [when he is] singing.)

(You/your) working so many hours will see a bigger paycheck. (<u>your</u>)

(gerund = subject)

BUT ALSO RIGHT: You, <u>working</u> so many hours, will see a bigger paycheck.

(working = a present participle: You [who are] working so many hours . . .)

(Jill/Jill's) studying will make a difference on the test. (Jill's)

(gerund = subject)

ADVERBS AND ADJECTIVES—BIG PICTURE PLAN OF ATTACK

Step 1. Highlight the adverb.

Step 2. Underline the adjective.

> # GRAMMAR TIP
>
> Adverbs answer questions about the words they describe: *how?* (carefully) *how often?* (never) *where?* (here) *when?* (early).
>
> Adverbs also act as transitions—words like *also, consequently, finally, furthermore, hence, however, moreover, nevertheless, otherwise, similarly, therefore, thus, whereas.* (See the chart of **Common Transition Words and Phrases**, pages 59–60.) And some adverbs serve as negatives, like *no, not, scarcely, seldom.*

Adverbs can appear just about anywhere in a sentence (Slowly I walked; I slowly walked; I walked slowly.) By contrast, <u>adjectives</u> come in front of nouns (<u>the purple</u> car) or on the other side of certain verbs, especially *to be* verbs (The car is <u>purple</u>). (See **6. Adjectives, Linking Verbs, and Adverbs**, page 145.)

Just as the key to the adjective is the noun, the key to the adverb is usually the verb. And, luckily, many adverbs end in *-ly*: slowly, quickly, really, surely, jumpily, happily, cautiously, early, accidentally, badly, recently, etc.

However, look for a handful of common short adverbs that don't end in *-ly*.

COMMON SHORT ADVERBS NOT ENDING IN *-LY*				
above	*close	high	not	sort of
again	*deep	inside	now	then
ahead	*direct	just	nowhere	there
almost	down	kind of	often	thus
also	enough	*last	outside	today
always	ever	less	over	tomorrow
apart	*fair	little	perhaps	tonight
as	far (distance)	*loud	*quick	too
as (soon) as	far (future)	low	seldom	up
away	fast	maybe	*slow	very
back	first, second,	more	so	well
before	*etc.*	much	somehow	*wide
below	forever	near	sometime(s)	worse
best	forward	never	somewhat	worst
better	*hard	next	somewhere	yesterday
but	hence	no	soon	
	here			

Though the adverbs in the box don't end in *-ly*, you can use a few (marked with *) either way. You can say *Play fair* or *Play fairly*, *Drive slow* or *Drive slowly*. And you can use many of the adverbs as adjectives, words like *best, better, close, deep, direct, fair*, and *but* and *so* as conjunctions. You can even have the same word used as both <u>adjective</u> and adverb in the same sentence: *A <u>better</u> truck will drive <u>better</u>*.

Comparisons use a word called the *positive* to set up the comparison. You then compare two things in the *comparative*, three or more in the *superlative*.

He is <u>smart</u>. (positive)
Of the two boys, Grover is the <u>smarter</u>. (comparative)
Of the three [or three thousand] boys, Grover is the <u>smartest</u>. (superlative)

Most adjectives and adverbs use a regular form to make an adjective or adverb comparison. You add *-er* or *more* to the positive, *-est* or *most* to the superlative. Some adjectives and adverbs, however, use an irregular form to make the comparison (see the box **below, Adverb and Adjective Comparisons**).

ADVERB AND ADJECTIVE COMPARISONS			
	POSITIVE (one)	**COMPARATIVE** (two)	**SUPERLATIVE** (three or more)
REGULAR FORM			
ONE SYLLABLE			
Adverb	fast	faster	fastest
Adjective	tall	taller	tallest
TWO SYLLABLES			
Adverb	often	more often	most often
Adjective	pretty	prettier OR more pretty	prettiest OR most pretty
THREE SYLLABLES +			
Adverb	effectively	more effectively	most effectively
Adjective	effective	more effective	most effective
IRREGULAR FORM			
Adverb	badly far (distance) far (future) late much well	worse farther further later more better	worst farthest furthest last most best
Adjective	bad OR ill far (distance) far (future) good OR well late less little (in size) little (amount of) many	worse farther further better later lesser littler lesser more	worst farthest furthest best latest OR last least littlest least most

> # GRAMMAR TIP
>
> When you compare one thing to another, make sure to compare an <u>apple</u> to an <u>apple</u> and not an <u>apple</u> to an orange. For example, in *This year's budget is lower than last year*, the writer compares an apple (<u>this year's budget</u>) to an orange (last year). To compare them as apples, the writer needs to revise: *This year's budget is lower than last year's budget.* (<u>this year's budget</u> = apple; <u>last's year's budget</u> = apple)
>
> This tip holds true for both adverbs and adjectives. If you compare a member of a group to other members of the group, use *other* or *else* to compare an apple to an apple and not an apple to an orange (see **below**).

Adjective:

> **WRONG:** <u>John</u> is *older* than <u>any man in Ringgold County</u>.
>
> **RIGHT:** <u>John</u> is *older* than <u>any other man in Ringgold County</u>.
>
>> (Leaving out *other* sounds like John doesn't live in Ringgold County, and it compares an <u>apple</u> to an orange.)

Adverb:

> **WRONG:** <u>Mrs. Foster's cake</u> baked *quicker* than <u>anyone's</u>.
>
> **RIGHT:** <u>Mrs. Foster's cake</u> baked *quicker* than <u>anyone else's [cake]</u>.
>
>> (Leaving out *else* compares an <u>apple</u> to an orange.)

> # WARNING!
>
> **Some adverbs and adjectives shouldn't be used in comparisons.**

Writing books advise against "more unique" because *unique* means it's *absolutely unique*—there's no way to get *more* unique. Still, we do say sentences like:

I generally never cook broccoli.

That's a rather unique idea.

The software has been almost universally adopted.

When we say such sentences, people appreciate the distinction between *never* and *generally never* (though *never* means *never*), and no less than the Preamble to the U.S. Constitution speaks of a "more perfect Union." Overall, though, academic writing doesn't look favorably at illogical constructions like *most correct* or *completely round*.

See the box **below** for a list of absolute adverbs and adjectives.

ABSOLUTE ADVERBS AND ADJECTIVES	
ADVERBS	**ADJECTIVES**
always	(no equivalent)
completely	complete
correctly	correct
dead	dead
exactly	exact
forever	(no equivalent)
fully	full
once, twice, *etc.*	once, twice, *etc.*
perfectly	perfect
round	round
singly	single
square	square

Troubleshooting Adverb-Adjective Trouble Spots

Adverb and adjective problems show up in eleven classic trouble spots.

1. **Adverbs and *-ly*:** *He drives (pretty careful/pretty carefully).*
2. **Adverbs and Double Negatives:** *I (could/couldn't) hardly hear you.*
3. **Redundant Adverb-Verb Phrases:** *Begin/First begin? Refer? Refer back?*
4. **Adverb Placement:** *Only Jan can win the prize/Jan can only win the prize/Jan can win only the prize.*
5. **Adverb Word-Pair Confusions:** *A part/Apart? All ready/already? Every day/Everyday?*
6. **Adjectives, Linking Verbs, and Adverbs:** *Good/Well? Bad/Badly? Real/Really? Sure/Surely?*
7. **Adverbs, Adjectives, and the Hyphen:** *Rapidly dwindling food/Rapidly-dwindling food? Eighteenth century novel/Eighteenth-century novel?*

8. Proper Adjectives and Capital Letters: *French fries/french fries?*
9. Demonstrative Pronouns and Singulars/Plurals: *These/Those kind? These/Those kinds?*
10. Dangling Modifiers: *Driving recklessly, my car went over the cliff.*
11. Misplaced Modifiers: *I bought a used Harley from a Hell's Angel with a leak somewhere.*

1. Adverbs and -ly: He drives (pretty careful/pretty carefully).

Because adverbs often end in *-ly*, don't forget to use an *-ly* on the many that require it.

He drives (pretty careful/pretty carefully). (pretty carefully)

> ## GRAMMAR TIP
>
> To determine if an adverb needs an *-ly*, find the verb and then highlight the word describing it. Remember that adverbs describe verbs but also adjectives and other adverbs; they explain *how*, *when*, and *where*. Then: Does the word end in *-ly*? Check the box on page 136 called **Common Short Adverbs Not Ending in -ly** (*Careful* isn't on the list, so it needs an *-ly* ending.)

2. Adverbs and Double Negatives: I (could/couldn't) hardly hear you.

Definition: Negative adverbs express negative ideas—something denied or refused or refuted, like *I do not want to stay home tonight.* Negative adverbs include *barely, but, hardly, little, never, no, not, nowhere, rarely, scarcely,* and *seldom*.

A basic grammar rule is *Don't use two negatives to talk about one negative idea.* "Two negatives" are called a *double negative,* which we see in a sentence like *I do not want no spinach.* Just as in math, in grammar two negatives = a positive, so when you say *I do not want no spinach,* you're really saying *I do want some spinach.*

> ## GRAMMAR TIP
>
> Use one negative for one idea. If you give each negative its own fragment or sentence, you won't have a problem.

WRONG: I couldn't hardly hear you.

(**n't** and **hardly** = two negatives for one idea)

RIGHT: I could hardly hear you.

(**hardly** = one negative for one idea)

WRONG: Vivian never told nobody the truth.

(**never** and **nobody** = two negatives)

RIGHT: Vivian never told anybody the truth.

(**never** = one negative for one idea)

You can use two negatives as long as you give each idea in a sentence its own clause—like a (1) dependent clause and (2) an independent clause.

(1) If Boyd does not turn down his music, (2) I will never renew his lease.

Sometimes two negatives will emphasize an idea more emphatically than a positive. Here we combine a negative adverb (*not*) and a negative adjective (*unprepared*) to make a stronger case than the positive:

Wanda is not unprepared for the test.

versus

Wanda is prepared for the test.

Though they mean the same thing, the first sentence suggests that Wanda seems *more* than prepared for the test. Sometimes, then, a double negative can emphasize a quality that the reader doesn't notice with a positive.

3. *Redundant Adverb-Verb Phrases:* Begin/First begin? Refer/Refer back?

A number of verbs pick up unnecessary adverbs that mean the same as the verb. If an adverb is *redundant*, cut it from the sentence.

We will (begin/first begin) with the rules of French pronunciation. (begin)

Please (refer/refer back) to page twelve. (refer)

The logic is clear. If you begin, you *first* begin; if you refer, you necessarily refer *back*—you can't refer *forward*.

GRAMMAR TIP

Consult the box **below** for a list of redundant adverb-verb phrases. In each case, cut the adverb.

REDUNDANT ADVERB-VERB PHRASES		
assemble **together**	finish **off**	plan **ahead**
cancel **out**	finish **up**	refer **back**
continue **on**	**first** begin	repeat **again**
convert **over**	**first** meet (**first** met)	repeat **back**
cooperate **together**	**first** start	revert **back**
copy **off**	follow **after**	
edit **out**	meet **together**	

4. *Adverb Placement:* Only Jan can win the prize/Jan can only win the prize/Jan can win only the prize.

Because many adverbs can move around in the sentence (Slowly I walked; I slowly walked; I walked slowly), a problem develops: Moving some adverbs can radically change the meaning.

Only Jan can win the prize. (Nobody but Jan can win the prize.)

Jan can only win the prize. (Jan can't lose the prize—maybe the contest is fixed in her favor.)

Jan can win only the prize. (Jan can't win anything else, like a scholarship.)

These three sentences show a basic rule about adverb placement: The adverb should be as close as possible to the word you want to describe. Do you want to describe *Jan, win*, or *prize*? To describe *Jan*, don't put the adverb somewhere else, as in *Jan can win only the prize*, which creates a different meaning.

Just Timothy knows the answer.

Timothy just knows the answer.

Timothy knows just the answer.

GRAMMAR TIP

Try to place the following adverbs *right before the word they describe.* The closer, the better.

almost	ever	nearly	too
also	just	only	
even	merely	scarcely	

5. *Adverb Word-Pair Confusions:* A part/Apart? All ready/already? Every day/ Everyday?

Try this quiz:

> **Cynthia has always stood (a part/apart) from the group even though she wants to be (a part/ apart) of it.**
>
> **(All together/altogether), we are (all together/altogether) ready to leave.**
>
> **(Every day/Everyday) I wear my (every day/everyday) clothes.**

Answers:

> **apart, a part; all together, altogether; every day, everyday.**

See **Chapter 18—Word Confusions**. On page 445, you'll find a long list of Word Confusions, including adverbs confused with nouns (*a part* or *apart*?), other adverbs (*altogether* or *all together*?) adjectives (*every day* or *everyday*?), and verbs (*may be* or *maybe*?). In particular, pay attention to:

all most/almost	every day/everyday	quiet/quite
all ready/already	farther/further	real/really
all together/altogether	good/well	some day/someday
all ways/always	hopefully/I hope*	some time/sometime/
any time/anytime	last/latest	sometimes
any way/anyway	like/as	sure/surely
a part/apart	may be/maybe	to/too/two
a while/awhile	meantime/meanwhile	when/where
bad/badly	over time/overtime	

---

*GRAMMAR TIP

Hopefully has long meant *in a hopeful manner*, used in sentences like *He approached each day hopefully*. In recent years, careful writers have pointed out that sentences like *Hopefully, he will come home* aren't saying what the speaker intends. The speaker intends to say *I hope that he will come home*, but the sentence is really saying *He will come hopefully*, which means *He will come with hope*, which means *with a hopeful manner*, which is not what the speaker intends. A similar sentence would be *Presently, he will come home*, which means the same thing as *He will come home presently* and means what the speaker intends.

Recent dictionaries point out the disdain that most careful writers have for the illogic of *Hopefully, he will come home*. However, these dictionaries also point out the new, implied second meaning for the word: *It is to be hoped*. Thus *It is to be hoped = I hope that he will come home*.

If you choose to say a sentence like *Hopefully, he will come home*, you probably won't encounter a problem. But in academic prose if you write a *Hopefully* sentence, then prepare for the worst. Hopefully, you won't write one . . .

6. Adjectives, Linking Verbs, and Adverbs: Good/Well? Bad/Badly? Real/Really? Sure/Surely?

Definition: A linking verb links the SUBJECT to a **noun**, **pronoun**, or <u>adjective</u> that follows the verb: *The DOG is a **collie*** or *TERRY looks <u>sick</u>*.

GRAMMAR TIP

One trick for remembering linking verbs is that five of them deal with the five senses: *feel, look, smell, sound, taste.*

LINKING VERBS			
***TO BE* VERBS**			
am/is/are am being/is being/are being has been/have been/had been may be/might have been		was/were was being/were being will be/will have been	
OTHER LINKING VERBS			
appear become feel get go	grow keep lie look prove	remain resemble run seem smell	sound stay taste turn

Most of us handle routine *-ly* adverbs without a problem. The adverb errors we do make come from confusing the <u>adjective</u> with the adverb, or vice versa, in the following pairs.

- <u>good</u>/<u>well</u>
- <u>bad</u>/<u>badly</u>
- <u>real</u>/<u>really</u>
- <u>sure</u>/<u>surely</u>

> ## GRAMMAR TIP
> Writers rarely make errors with well or badly describing an <u>adjective</u> or adverb. We naturally say a *well-<u>deserved</u> award, a badly <u>written</u> novel*, or *The ball landed well over the line*. But be careful with the word that describes the verb: Choose well instead of <u>good</u>, badly instead of <u>bad</u>, really instead of <u>real</u>, surely instead of <u>sure</u>.

The adjective <u>good</u> describes the noun: a <u>good</u> exam. Here the adverb well describes the verb DID.

Shawn thought it was a good exam, and he DID (good/well) on it. (well)

The confusion lies in deciding whether to use <u>good</u> or well to talk about health. <u>Good</u> refers to psychological health; well refers to physical health: *I'm in good spirits* [psychologically] *because I feel well* [physically].

I got over my cold; I'm feeling (good/well). (wll)
I'm no longer depressed; I'm feeling (good/well). (good)

The adjective <u>bad</u> describes the noun: a <u>bad</u> exam. Here the adverb badly describes the verb DID:

Shawn thought it was a bad exam, and he DID (bad/badly) on it. (badly)

> ## GRAMMAR TIP
> Writers rarely make errors *with really* describing verbs (few would say *He real involved himself with the club*). The errors come with describing <u>adjectives</u> (*real <u>concerned</u>*) and other adverbs (*real soon*).

The adjective <u>real</u> describes the noun: a <u>real</u> test. Here the adverb really describes the adverb well:

Shawn thought the exam was a real test of his knowledge, and he did (real/really) well on it. (really)

GRAMMAR TIP

Writers often make errors with *surely* describing verbs (*He sure involved himself with the club*), <u>adjectives</u> (*sure concerned*), and other adverbs (*sure soon*).

The adjective <u>sure</u> describes the noun: a <u>sure</u> thing. Here the adverb surely describes the adjective <u>surprised</u>.

Shawn thought the exam grade was a sure thing, so he was (sure/surely) <u>surprised</u> when he did so badly. (surely)

WARNING!

In conversation, many of us choose *real* and *sure* over <u>really</u> and <u>surely</u> (*I'm real tired, I'm sure happy*). In fact, in some situations <u>surely</u> may sound awkward or pretentious when used correctly. Nevertheless, academic writing expects the adverb, not the adjective, to describe verbs, adjectives, and other adverbs.

---

7. *Adverbs, Adjectives, and the Hyphen:* Rapidly dwindling food/Rapidly-dwindling food? Eighteenth century novel/Eighteenth-century novel?

See **Chapter 16—Punctuation Rules: The Hyphen**, page 399, for information on the following:

- When to hyphenate before a noun (*second-place winner, well-written novel, fast-moving train, true-false quiz*)
- When to hyphenate after a verb (*the winner won second place, the novel is well written, the train is fast-moving, the quiz is true-false*)

Among the many and complex hyphen rules, you should remember four—the first two dealing with adverbs; the second two dealing with adjectives.

1. **Rule 1A. Don't use the hyphen with an *-ly* adverb in phrases like these—both before and after the <u>noun</u>:**

   The rapidly dwindling <u>food</u>. (The <u>food</u> is rapidly dwindling.)
   Clearly defined <u>goals</u>. (Our <u>goals</u> are clearly defined.)

   > # WARNING!
   >
   > Don't confuse an *-ly* adjective (*friendly, kindly*) with an *-ly* adverb. Common adjective word pairs use the hyphen before and after the noun:
   >
   > *friendly-looking <u>dog</u> (the <u>dog</u> is friendly-looking)*

2. **Rule 1B. Use the hyphen before a noun with an adverb phrase that doesn't end in *-ly*** (see **Common Short Adverbs Not Ending in *-ly*,** page 136).

   often-cited <u>quotation</u>, seldom-seen <u>politician</u>
   clear-cut <u>answer</u>

   But don't use the hyphen with an adverb phrase that belongs to the <u>verb</u>:

   That quotation <u>is</u> very often cited.
   We <u>have</u> seldom seen that writer.

   Use the hyphen with an adverb phrase that doesn't belong to the <u>verb</u>:

   That quotation <u>appears</u> to be often-cited.
   After all these years, the novelist <u>is</u> still seldom-seen.
   The answer <u>seems</u> pretty clear-cut.

3. **Rule 2A. In general, hyphenate adjective phrases before but not after a <u>noun</u>.**

   eighteenth-century <u>novel</u> (The <u>novel</u> comes from the eighteenth century.)
   up-to-date <u>styles</u> (Those <u>styles</u> are up to date.)
   get-well <u>card</u> (The <u>card</u> said to get well.)
   thank-you <u>letter</u> (The <u>letter</u> said thank you.)

WARNING!

Don't use the hyphen to connect well-known compounds or compounds with proper names.

    middle school volunteer

    real estate salesman

    social security guidelines

    Mickey Mouse politics

4. **Rule 2B. Use the hyphen for adjective phrases before and after a noun when the phrases are common word pairs.**

    brain-dead response (the response was brain-dead)

    customer-friendly staff (they employ a staff that's customer-friendly)

    user-friendly transition (the transition seems user-friendly)

    smoke-clogged bar (the bar is smoke-clogged)

    habit-forming drug (the drug proved habit-forming)

    panic-stricken passengers (the passengers were panic-stricken)

    fair-minded judge (the judge may be fair-minded)

    round-faced boy (the boy was round-faced)

    deep-rooted desire (the desire is deep-rooted)

    dirty-looking street (the street is dirty-looking)

    long-held beliefs (the beliefs are long-held)

    rough-talking cowboy (the cowboy is rough-talking)

    kindly-looking doctor (the doctor appeared kindly-looking)

8. *Proper Adjectives and Capital Letters:* French fries/french fries?

For a detailed list of rules, see **Chapter 17—Spelling and Mechanics Rules: Capitalization**, page 428.

Capitalize adjectives when they come from proper nouns, like German from *Germany*, Victorian from *Queen Victoria*, or African-American from *Africa* and *America*.

However, don't capitalize such proper-noun adjectives when they're no longer associated with the country or person they came from.

    Bobby loves (French fries/french fries). (french fries = no longer associated with France)

    Bobby also loves Chinese food/chinese food) (Chinese food = still associated with China)

    The (Pasteurized/pasteurized) milk has been heated to a specific temperature. (pasteurized = no longer associated with Louis Pasteur)

    LaRue has undergone (Freudian analysis/freudian analyis). (Freudian analysis = still associated with Sigmund Freud)

9. *Demonstrative Adjectives and Singulars/Plurals:* These/Those kind? These/Those kinds?

Definition: A *demonstrative adjective* is a word like *this, that, these,* or *those* used to point out a noun that's near or distant. *This* hat, *that* hat, *these* hats, *those* hats. *This* and *that* are singular; *these* and *those* are plural. Thus the noun that follows *this* and *that* must be singular, and the noun that follows *these* and *those* must be plural.

> ## GRAMMAR TIP
>
> Highlight the verb. If the verb is singular, use *this* or *that.* If the verb is plural, use *these* or *those.*
>
> > (*This/these*) (*kind/kinds*) of cookie is my favorite. (is = singular = *This kind*)
> >
> > (*That/those*) (*type/types*) of songs are hardcore heavy metal. (are = plural = *Those types*)

10. *Dangling Modifiers:* Driving recklessly, my car went over the cliff.

Definition: A *modifier* is any word or phrase describing another word or phrase somewhere in a sentence. When a modifier *dangles*, it forgets to hook up logically to the word or phrase it's supposed to—that is, that it's supposed to modify (or describe).

> ## GRAMMAR TIP
>
> If a sentence begins with a fragment (usually followed by a comma), look for a dangling modifier.

You can spot a dangling modifier by any of the following signs:

- The fragment starts with a word that ends in -*ing* (*driving, making, using,* etc.)
- The fragment starts with a word that ends in a past tense (*driven, made, used,* etc.)
- The fragment starts with an infinitive: *to + verb* (*to drive, to make, to use,* etc.)
- The fragment starts with a clause word (*if, when, since, because, while,* etc.)

To fix a dangling modifier, give the sentence a subject that logically hooks up to the fragment. Put the subject in the <u>fragment</u> or right after the comma.

> **WRONG:** <u>Driving recklessly</u>, my car went over the cliff. (How can a car drive recklessly? The <u>fragment</u> needs a logical subject—somebody to drive the car.)
> **RIGHT:** <u>Because I was driving recklessly</u>, my car went over the cliff. (subject in fragment)
> **ALSO RIGHT:** <u>Driving recklessly, I</u> caused my car to go over the cliff. (subject after comma)
> **WRONG:** <u>Driven to alcohol by his problems</u>, vodka brought about his death.
> **RIGHT:** <u>Driven to alcohol by his problems, Jack</u> brought about his death through vodka.
> **WRONG:** <u>To be considered for this special offer</u>, the reply card should be sent.
> **RIGHT:** <u>To be considered for this special offer, you</u> should send the reply card.
> **WRONG:** <u>When at the age of six</u>, my parents moved to Texas.
> **RIGHT:** <u>When I was six</u>, my parents and I moved to Texas.

11. *Misplaced Modifiers:* I bought a used Harley from a Hell's Angel with a leak somewhere.

Definition: Like a dangling modifier, a *misplaced modifier* describes another word or phrase somewhere in a sentence. But unlike the dangling modifier, the misplaced modifier has a noun it refers to. The problem is that this modifier has been placed too far from the noun—sometimes with comic results. That's why it's *misplaced*.

> ## GRAMMAR TIP
> Place the misplaced modifier as close to its <u>noun</u> as possible.

> **WRONG:** I bought a used <u>Harley</u> from a Hell's Angel with a leak somewhere.
> **RIGHT:** I bought a used <u>Harley</u> with a leak somewhere from a Hell's Angel.
> **WRONG:** Sandy put the <u>sandwich</u> into the garbage that she had not yet eaten.
> **RIGHT:** Sandy put the <u>sandwich</u> that she had not yet eaten into the garbage.

PREPOSITIONS—BIG PICTURE PLAN OF ATTACK

Step 1. Familiarize yourself with the prepositions in the box below.

Step 2. Look for the preposition trouble spots. Highlight the preposition.

PREPOSITIONS			
about	between	in regard to	round
above	beyond	in spite of	since
according to	but	in terms of	through
across	by	including	throughout
after	by means of	inside	till
against	by reason of	instead of	to
along	by way of	into	toward(s)
along with	concerning	like	under
apart from	despite	near	underneath
around	down	next to	unlike
as	due to	of	until
as for	during	off	up
as regards	except	on	up to
as to	except for	on account of	upon
aside from	excepting	onto	with
at	for	on top of	with reference to
because of	from	out	with regard to
before	in	out of	with respect to
behind	in addition to	outside	with the exception
below	in case of	over	of
beneath	in front of	past	within
beside(s)	in lieu/place of	regarding	without

Troubleshooting Preposition Trouble Spots

Preposition problems show up in five classic trouble spots.

1. **Word Pairs and Prepositions:** *Angry at/Angry with? Different from/Different than? Between/Among?*
2. **Necessary Prepositions:** *Couple coffees/Couple of coffees? This type shoe/This type of shoe?*
3. **Necessary Prepositions in a Series:** *by car, bus, and on the train.*
4. **Unnecessary Prepositions:** *Where's he (going/going to)?*
5. **Unnecessary Colons with Prepositions:** *a novel (by/by:) J.D. Salinger*

1. *Word Pairs and Prepositions:* **Angry at/Angry with? Different from/Different than? Between/Among?**

GRAMMAR TIP

Certain words require certain prepositions. The box below lists Difficult Word Pairs with Prepositions.

DIFFICULT WORD PAIRS WITH PREPOSITIONS

accompanied by/accompanied with	confer on/confer with
account for/account to	consist in/consist of
admit into/of/to	contend against/for/with
agree on/agree upon	convenient for/convenient to
agree to/agree with	correspond to/correspond with
all/all of	couple/couple of
among/between	deal in/deal with
angry about/angry at/angry with	defect in/defect of
annoyed at/by/with	differ about/from/in/on/over/with
apply for/apply to	different from/different than
argue about/argue with	due to/because of /on account of
at/at about	end in/end with
based in/off of/on/upon	except/except for
beside/besides	from/off
bored by/bored with	grateful for/grateful to
compare to/compare with	impatient at/for/with
comply to/comply with	in/into/in to
independent from/independent of	speak to/speak with

intervene between/intervene in	style/style of
invest in/invest with	suspect of/suspect with
like/as/as if	to/too/two
mastery of/mastery over	toward/towards
off/off of	true to/true with
on/on to/onto	type/type of
opposite/opposite from/of/to	up/up on/upon/on
part from/part with	what/of what
reconcile to/reconcile with	

I hope you're not (angry at/angry with) me. (with)

This car is (different from/different than) that car. (different from)

(Between/Among) the three of us, Colonel Wilson is the best leader. (Among)

2. *Necessary Prepositions:* Couple coffees/Couple of coffees? This type shoe/This type of shoe?

> # GRAMMAR TIP
>
> Keep track of your preposition mistakes. Make a list of the errors and have it handy as you write. If you make the error once, you'll probably continue to make it until somebody calls attention to it. See the box **above, Difficult Word Pairs with Prepositions**, for common errors.

The salesman ordered a (couple/couple of) coffees. (couple of)

I really like this (type/type of) shoe. (type of)

(What/Of what) use is this old computer? (Of what)

WARNING!

Some writing resources still warn against ending a sentence with a preposition. Writers have always ended sentences with prepositions, and they always will. To avoid awkwardness, some sentences need to have the preposition at the end.

> **AWKWARD:** That's the show at which I don't like to look.
>
> **BETTER:** That's the show I don't like to look at.

In conversation and writing, even in academic writing, choose the natural over the unnatural. If the "proper version" sounds odd or awkward, you may want to end with the preposition: *Do you know the man of whom she spoke?* versus *Do you know the man she spoke of?*

3. Necessary Prepositions in a Series: by car, bus, and on the train

If you set up a series that uses the same preposition for each item in the series, you can delete all but the first.

> **We exercise by running, by swimming, and by lifting weights.**
> **(We exercise by running, swimming, and lifting weights.)**

But if you set up a series that uses a different proposition for each item in the series, make sure not to delete a necessary preposition.

> **WRONG: I hope to travel by car, bus, and on the train.**
> **RIGHT: I hope to travel by car, by bus, and on the train.**
> **WRONG: She has a great fascination, not to mention a serious respect for, old stamps.**
> **RIGHT: She has a great fascination in, not to mention a serious respect for, old stamps.)**

4. Unnecessary Prepositions: Where's he (going/going to)?

GRAMMAR TIP

Some words pick up unnecessary prepositions that redundantly say the same thing as the word. (See the box **below**. In each case, you can delete the highlighted preposition.)

calm (yourself) down	it up (Cut it up into equal pieces.)
clean up (the room)	keep on (working)
climb up (the ladder)	later on (we'll talk)
close up (the store)	lift up (your eyes)
come on (to the party)	meet up with (friends)
continue on (down the street)	off of (the roof)
dress up (as a clown)	open up (the window)
end up (the movie)	out of (the window)
escape from (prison)	raise up (children)
except for (him)	sit down (on the couch)
finish up (the project)	start off (for home)
go to (Where did she go to?)	start out (for home)
help out (my brother)	stir up (the chili)
hurry up (the food)	topple down (the government)
inside of (an hour)	up until (my last birthday)

Where's he (going/going to)? (going)
We have to (start/start off) for home. (start)
(Keep/keep on) working! (keep)

WARNING!

Sometimes a writer will add the preposition to emphasize or add zest to tone: *Eat up your food!* has more kick than *Eat your food!*

5. *Unnecessary Colons with Prepositions:* a novel (by/by:) J.D. Salinger

> # GRAMMAR TIP
>
> Prepositions can function as colons—that is, they can direct the reader from one idea to another. Just as we can say *Today's mailings: Cleveland and Fort Worth*, we can also say *Mail this today to Cleveland and Fort Worth*. Because a preposition can function as a colon, it is usually redundant to use a colon after a preposition.

WRONG: This novel is by: J.D. Salinger.

RIGHT: This novel is by J.D. Salinger.

WRONG: This is for: the people who have helped me to succeed.

RIGHT: This is for the people who have helped me to succeed.

WRONG: Please contact every office, including: Rome, Seville, and New York.

RIGHT: Please contact every office, including Rome, Seville, and New York.

> # WARNING!
>
> You can, however, introduce a *vertical list* with a preposition and colon.
>
> Please contact every office, including:
>
> 1. Rome
> 2. Seville
> 3. New York

CONJUNCTIONS—BIG PICTURE PLAN OF ATTACK

Step 1. Learn the FANBOYS: the coordinating conjunctions *for, and, nor, but, or, yet, so.*

Step 2. Highlight the conjunctions. Follow the advice below.

Troubleshooting Conjunction Trouble Spots

Conjunction problems show up in four classic trouble spots:

1. Job Function of the Coordinating Conjunction: *and/but?*
2. Sentence Parts That Aren't Parallel: . . . *and which?/which . . . but which?*
3. Conjunctions, Commas, and Semicolons: *Bob, and Mary/Bob and Mary?*
4. And: *etc., and so on, &*

1. Job Function of the Coordinating Conjunction: and/but?

Definition: *Coordinating conjunctions* connect words or parts of sentences equal in some way to each other. <u>*Bob*</u> *or* <u>*Mary*</u>. The general knew <u>that his troops were exhausted</u> and <u>that they needed food</u>.

Since the job of a coordinating conjunction is to *coordinate*, it must do so logically. Each conjunction has a specific job that you must follow.

Job Functions

For signals cause and effect (**for** = **because:** *Bob wins a thousand dollars, for [because] he has a winning lottery ticket.*)

And signals addition (**and** = **plus:** *Bob buys a lottery ticket each week, and [plus] he has a winning lottery ticket.*)

Nor signals a negative alternative (**nor** = **and not:** *Bob doesn't have a winning lottery ticket, nor does he [and he does not] ever have a winning lottery ticket.*)

But signals a contrast (**but** = **however:** *Bob has a winning lottery ticket, but [however] he has misplaced it.*)

Or signals an alternative (**or** = **as another possibility:** *Bob has a winning lottery ticket, or [as another possibility] he has a losing lottery ticket.*)

Yet signals a contrast (**yet** = **still:** *Bob buys many lottery tickets, yet [still] he never wins.*)

So signals cause and effect (**so** = **therefore:** *Bob has a winning lottery ticket, so [therefore] he wins a thousand dollars.*)

My mentor has an extensive business background, (and/but) he doesn't know how to communicate his knowledge. (*but* signals a contrast = however)

My mentor has an extensive business background, (and/so) he often gives me good business advice. (*so* signals cause and effect = therefore)

2. Sentence Parts That Aren't Parallel: . . . and which?/ which . . . but which?

When coordinating conjunctions connect sentence parts, each item connected must look like every other item. If you connect apple + apple + orange, something has gone wrong.

GRAMMAR TIP

Find the key parallel word and use it to set up the rest of the parallel.

Key parallel word = running.

apple   apple   orange

WRONG: He likes running, rowing, and to swim for exercise.

running and rowing = **gerunds** (-*ing* verbs used as nouns) = *apples*

to swim = **infinitive** (to + verb) = *orange*

swimming = **gerund** = *apple*

To keep the parallel:

apple   apple   apple

RIGHT: He likes running, rowing, and swimming for exercise.

orange orange   orange

ALSO RIGHT: He likes to run, to row, and to swim for exercise.

(ALSO RIGHT: He likes to run, row, and swim for exercise.)

Key parallel words = to shape up

apple   orange

WRONG: I was told either to shape up or I would be shipping out.

apple   apple

RIGHT: I was told either to shape up or to ship out.

to shape up = **infinitive** = *apple*

I would be shipping out = sentence with **present participle** (shipping out) = *orange*

to ship out = **infinitive** = *apple*

Key parallel word = important

                    apple   *orange*

WRONG: Elections are important and a <u>tradition</u>.

                    apple   *apple*

RIGHT: Elections are important and traditional.

    important = **adjective** = *apple*

    a <u>tradition</u> = **noun** = *orange*

    traditional = **adjective** = *apple*

GRAMMAR TIP

Using the *Find* command, search for *that, where, which, who, whom,* and *whose*. Now look for *and* or *but*. Does *and* or *but* precede one of these six words? If so, you may have a problem with parallel sentence parts.

Look for two clauses in a single sentence. Each has to start with *that, where, which, who, whom,* or *whose*. Between them will come *and* or *but*. If you can't find the first clause, fix it with one of the six clause words. The <u>first clause</u> must be parallel with the <u>second clause</u>.

    which . . . but which

NOT:

    . . . but which

WRONG: In 1867, Dr. David Livingstone found the Lualaba River, mistakenly assumed to be the Nile but which actually flows into the Upper Congo Lake.

RIGHT: In 1867, Dr. David Livingstone found the Lualaba River, <u>which he mistakenly assumed to be the Nile</u> but which actually flows into the Upper Congo Lake.

GRAMMAR TIP

After *no, not,* and *never*, use *nor* to continue a later negative clause that's parallel with an earlier negative clause.

WRONG: I have never appreciated sushi, and I won't ever.

RIGHT: I have never appreciated sushi, nor will I ever appreciate it.

3. *Conjunctions, Commas, and Semicolons:* **Bob, and Mary/Bob and Mary?**

For an overview of commas and semicolons, see **Easy Punctuation** and **Punctuation Rules**.

Writers make four common errors with conjunctions, commas, and semicolons.

Comma:

1. **Don't put a comma before a conjunction if a complete sentence doesn't follow.**
   WRONG: Patti drove all the way to Chicago, <u>and spent the night there</u>. (<u>incomplete sentence</u>)
   RIGHT: Patti drove all the way to Chicago and spent the night there.
   ALSO RIGHT: Patti drove all the way to Chicago, and she spent the night there. (complete sentence)

WARNING!

The exception to the first comma rule is the series. With a series of three or more items, you can put a comma in front of a conjunction, but the comma is optional.

    RIGHT: George Clooney is tall, dark, and handsome.
    ALSO RIGHT: George Clooney is tall, dark and handsome.

---

2. **Don't put a comma after a conjunction unless there's a sentence interrupter.**
   WRONG: Yet, the weather continued to grow colder.
   RIGHT: Yet, though it was now late June, the weather continued to grow colder.
   ALSO RIGHT: Yet the weather continued to grow colder.

Semicolon:

3. **Don't put a semicolon before a conjunction separating two sentences; use a comma.**
   WRONG: She read through the Harry Potter novels; and then she watched all the movies.
   RIGHT: She read through the Harry Potter novels, and then she watched all the movies.
4. **Don't put a comma between a series of items that have internal punctuation; use a semicolon.**
   WRONG: I visited New York, New York, Chicago, Illinois, and Duluth, Minnesota.
   RIGHT: I visited New York, New York; Chicago, Illinois; and Duluth, Minnesota.

4. *And:* etc., and so on, &

Etc. is an abbreviation for the Latin *et cetera*, meaning *and other things, and the like, and so forth.*

1. Use the abbreviation; don't write out the full *et cetera.*
2. Generally, don't italicize the abbreviation unless you're using it in a special way (see 3, next).
3. Some authorities caution against using the abbreviation within the body of a text and suggest saving it for parenthetical references: *(see Smith, Jones, etc.)* If you do use it in the body, use commas before (and after when it comes in the middle of a sentence: *See Smith, Jones, etc., before you call).*
4. If the abbreviation comes at the end of a sentence, don't use two periods.

   WRONG: She studied harmony, counterpoint, etc..

   RIGHT: She studied harmony, counterpoint, etc.
5. Don't use the redundancy "and etc." The *et* part of the abbreviation means *and*.
6. Remember: It's spelled and pronounced *et cetera,* not *ek cetera.*
7. Likewise, it's never abbreviated *ect.*

And so on is the choice of some editors for *etc.* to conclude a list. Along with these editors, you too may feel that it's more graceful and hence is a matter of style rather than of grammar.

   WEAK: She studied harmony, counterpoint, etc.

   BETTER: She studied harmony, counterpoint, and so on.

&:

Reserve the **ampersand (&)** for two occasions:

1. To quote material that includes the ampersand, like "Brown & Co." Here the ampersand belongs to the company name and thus must be quoted exactly. Otherwise, avoid it in academic writing except for 2, below.
2. To use an APA parenthetical citation or Reference entry: Jones and Smith = Jones & Smith.

WARNING!

In APA style, don't use the ampersand within the text, as in *According to Smith and Jones (2010).* Reserve for parenthetical citations (Smith & Jones, 2010) and for References: *Smith, J., & T.R. Jones (2010).*

WRONG: She studied harmony & counterpoint.
RIGHT: She studied harmony and counterpoint.

INTERJECTIONS—BIG PICTURE PLAN OF ATTACK

Step 1. See the box below—Common Interjections.

Step 2. Then highlight the interjections in your writing.

COMMON INTERJECTIONS			
absolutely	anyway(s)	cheers	gadzooks
achoo	argh	ciao	gee; gee whiz
adios	as if	congratulations	god
agreed	attaboy	crikey	golly
ah	attagirl	cripes	good grief
aha	aww	crud	gosh
ahem	bah, humbug	damn (curses, etc.)	great; great Scott
ahoy	bam	dang	ha-ha
alack	behold	darn	hallelujah
alas	bingo	dear me	heigh-ho
all right	blah	drat	hello
all righty	bless you	duh	hem
all righty-roo	boo	eek	hey
aloha	bravo	eh	hi
amen	brrr	encore	hi-ho
anyhoo	bye	eureka	hmm
anyhow	cheerio	fiddlesticks	holy buckets
holy cow	nah	pshaw	ugh
holy smoke	nope	rats	voilà
hot dog	oh	right; righto	waa
huh	oh dear	scat	well
humpff	oh my	shhh	well, well
hurray	oh my god	shoo	what
hush	oh well	shoot	whoa
indeed	okay	shucks	whoops
jeepers	okey-dokey	shush	whosh
jeepers creepers	oops	so long	wow
jeez	ouch	thanks	yay
lo and behold	ow	there, there	yeah
mmm	phew	touché	yikes
my god	phooey	tush	yippie
my goodness	please	tut-tut	yo
my lord	poo	uh-huh	yuck
my word	pow	uh-oh	yup

Troubleshooting Interjection Trouble Spots

Interjection problems show up in two classic trouble spots.

1. Interjection + Sentence: *Punctuation/No punctuation?*
2. Interjections and Tone: *The Requirements of Academic Prose*

1. Interjection + Sentence: Punctuation/No punctuation?

Use a punctuation mark with an interjection—comma, period, dash, question mark, or exclamation point.

Gee, it's cold.

Gee. It's cold.

Gee—it's cold.

Gee? It's cold.

Gee! It's cold.

The kind of interjection, ranging from a soft one like *gee* or *darn* to a harsher one like *damn*, will suggest the right mark to choose. But whatever the mark, choose *something*. If it comes at the start of a sentence, put a mark after it. If it comes in the middle, put two marks around it. If it comes at the end, put a mark before it.

WRONG: Damn it's cold.

RIGHT: Damn, it's cold.

WRONG: All I know okay is that it's cold.

RIGHT: All I know, okay, is that it's cold.

WRONG: It's cold huh?

RIGHT: It's cold, huh?

2. Interjections and Tone: The Requirements of Academic Prose

Academic writing tends to frown on interjections. The writer who begins a sentence with *Well, I think that* or *Yes, global warming is a problem* moves the tone toward the informal—and academic writing prefers the formal. *Well* at the beginning of a sentence gives it a conversational tone, just as *yes* sounds as though the writer were offering an answer to a question that an off-page speaker has just asked. Both words, however much charm conversational prose may offer, are *too* conversational. Your writing teachers will no doubt suggest you delete them and ask that you keep your writing professional, academic, and formal.

Nevertheless, a skilled shift in tone—perhaps the occasional interjection—can bring welcome variety to a page of straitlaced formality.

Easy Style

ALL THOSE RULES VERSUS SEVEN HOW-TO APPROACHES FOR WRITING WITH STYLE

A good style is more than "packaging" or putting your ideas into a fancy suit of clothes. Style manages content, and *how* you say something can alter that content. Three writers with three different styles approaching the same content will produce three different realities.

How well each person thinks and pays attention to the world shapes his or her style. A good style, one rooted in clear thought and accurate observation, smoothly leads the reader from one idea to the next, avoids abstract or pretentious words, offers wit and metaphor, and takes pleasure in saying efficiently what it says. Because style as a subject seems resistant to rule-making—how can you set down rules for *style?*—it probably intimidates writers more than grammar and punctuation.

But you *can* learn time-honored methods for improving style. These methods break into seven how-to approaches—which then break into forty-seven editorial strategies.

1. **How to Emphasize Ideas**
2. **How to Get Rid of Vagueness**
3. **How to Get More out of Verbs**
4. **How to Get Rid of Wordiness**
5. **How to Choose the Right Word**
6. **How to Balance Sentence Parts**
7. **How to Repeat Words**

1. HOW TO EMPHASIZE IDEAS

STRATEGY 1. Don't split the subject from the verb.

Bill Clinton, after serving as governor of Arkansas and then as president of the United States for eight years, has continued to participate in national and international politics.

Emphasis problem: The verb belongs next to the subject, but the fragment pushes it to the middle of the sentence.

EDITING TIP

The sentence subject belongs next to the <u>verb</u>—or as close as you can manage.

Revision: <u>After serving as governor of Arkansas and then as president of the United States for eight years,</u> Bill Clinton **has continued** to participate in national and international politics.

WARNING!

An exception comes with the <u>appositive</u> (a word or phrase that renames the subject). But try to keep the appositive short so that the split is short: Bill Clinton, <u>ex-president,</u> <u>has continued</u> to participate in national and international politics.

STRATEGY 2. Don't delay the subject.

This past fall, a trail-blazing film on mountain climbing <u>was completed</u> after years of setbacks, including a series of dead-ended production deals, the firing of the main actor, and a near-fatal car wreck that hospitalized his writing partner, by the young French-Canadian director Laurent Chatagny.

Emphasis problem: We don't learn the subject controlling the verb until the end of the sentence.

EDITING TIP

The sentence subject belongs next to the <u>verb</u>—or as close as you can manage.

Revision: This past fall, the young French-Canadian director Laurent Chatagny <u>completed</u> a trail-blazing film on mountain climbing after years of setbacks, including a series of dead-ended production deals, the firing of the main actor, and a near-fatal car wreck that hospitalized his writing partner.

STRATEGY 3. Don't forget to start a sentence with the main idea.

Patrons must check out materials by nine forty-five, complete their online searches, and finish photocopying because Memorial Library closes at ten.

Emphasis problem: We don't learn the main business of the sentence until the end of the sentence.

EDITING TIP

Don't bury the main idea at the sentence end for two reasons:

1. **Starting with the main idea tells the reader *what's important*.**
2. **Starting with the main idea can hook the sentence to the preceding sentence; the main idea functions as a *key-word transition*.**

Main idea = *What's important*

Revision: Memorial Library closes at ten, so patrons must check out materials by nine forty-five, complete their online searches, and finish photocopying.
  Main idea = *Key-word transition* hooking two sentences

With just a campus ID, patrons can use the many services offered

by the entire campus library system. Memorial Library closes at ten, so patrons . . .

STRATEGY 4. Don't forget to end a new-idea sentence with the new idea.

Using three kinds of cheese is the secret to making great macaroni and cheese.

Emphasis problem: We learn the new before the old can orient us.
  New idea at end = *Suspense* and *transition from familiar to unfamiliar*.

Revision: The secret to making great macaroni and cheese is using three kinds of cheese.

EDITING TIP

Not all sentences need to start with the main idea. If the main idea is a *new* idea, it can work effectively at the end.

1. **Ending with the new idea provides suspense:** *And the winner is . . . [something new].*
2. **Starting with an old idea before the new transitions the reader from the familiar into the unfamiliar.** Here the familiar = *making macaroni and cheese*; the unfamiliar = *using three kinds of cheese.*
3. **Ending with the new sets up a steady supply of key-word transitions**.

New idea at end = Key-word transition

The secret to making great macaroni and cheese is using three kinds of

cheese. Try a variety of cheese types, including Parmesan, feta, and blue cheese.

STRATEGY 5. Don't use more than one main idea per sentence.

In 2007, scientists finished mapping the genome of the rhesus macaque, which lives on a wider range of the planet than any other primate except man and which is the second primate after man to be mapped, discovering that the monkey and man share approximately 93% of their DNA and had a common ancestor twenty-five million years in the past.

Emphasis problem: We can't pick out the sentence's main idea because there are too many ideas.

EDITING TIP

To fix long sentences crammed with more than one main idea:

1. **Mark each idea to sort both main and minor ideas.**
2. **Move each main idea into a single sentence.**
3. **Attach minor ideas to major ideas.**
4. **Order the new sentences from most to least important, cutting and replacing words.**

MAIN IDEA:	In 2007, SCIENTISTS FINISHED MAPPING THE GENOME OF THE RHESUS MACAQUE,
minor idea:	which lives on a wider range of the planet than any other primate except man
minor idea:	and which is the second primate after man to be mapped,
MAIN IDEA:	DISCOVERING THAT THE MONKEY AND MAN SHARE APPROXIMATELY 93% OF THEIR DNA
MAIN IDEA:	AND HAD A COMMON ANCESTOR
COMPLETED:	TWENTY-FIVE MILLION YEARS AGO.

Revision: The rhesus macaque monkey and man share approximately 93% of their DNA. They had a common ancestor twenty-five million years ago. In 2007, scientists finished mapping the genome of the rhesus macaque, which is the second primate after man to be mapped. The monkey lives on a wider range of the planet than any other primate except man.

STRATEGY 6. Don't shift the topic midstream.

A Des Moines-based wind energy company has decided to suspend plans to develop wind turbines in Johnson County. Brightwell Energy, Inc., had announced last year it would build a 98-megawatt farm in Johnson County and was considering farms in neighboring counties. Wind turbine use has multiplied across the state in recent years because of increasing oil prices. Tensions in the Mideast have contributed to high prices and uncertainty over supply. Congress has been considering legislation to allow oil drilling in national parks.

Emphasis problem: A paragraph should stick to the same topic so we don't get confused.

> # EDITING TIP
>
> A paragraph should stick to its topic (here, suspending wind turbine development) from the first word to the end of the paragraph. A paragraph may bring in subtopics, but the subtopics (increasing oil prices, tensions in the Mideast, drilling in national parks) can't take over and shift the topic midstream in the paragraph. Note how increasing oil prices triggers the shift from wind turbines to oil. In the revision, the writer continues with wind-turbine material.

Revision: A Des Moines-based wind energy company has decided to suspend plans to develop wind turbines in Johnson County. Brightwell Energy, Inc., had announced last year it would build a 98-megawatt farm in Johnson County and was considering farms in neighboring counties. Wind turbine use has multiplied across the state in recent years because of increasing oil prices. Brightwell Energy, Inc., gave no reason for the suspension, but their Web site voices concerns over "increased governmental wind-turbine legislation."

STRATEGY 7. Don't write structurally correct sentences that still use faulty logic.

(1) The United States Congress should legalize marijuana because it <u>will definitely reduce organized crime, provide tax relief, and save millions of lives through medical benefits</u>. (2) If Congress doesn't legalize marijuana, <u>only two options</u> present themselves: We organize a mass protest to march on Washington, or we flood the office of every member of Congress with e-mails.

Emphasis problem: A writer should come as close to the truth as possible. Though the two sentences have no errors in grammar or punctuation, they still have errors in logic: Sentence (1) commits a <u>hasty generalization</u> fallacy; sentence (2), a false dilemma fallacy.

EDITING TIP

Avoid the Thirteen Logical Fallacies

1. **Argumentum ad hominem**—Attacking the person instead of the argument. *You're so stupid, who can believe anything you say?*

2. **Red herring**—Avoiding the real issue by bringing up another. *Why should we send money overseas when we have problems at home?*

3. **Bandwagon**—Arguing that because everybody else is doing it, you should too. *The whole floor is coming to the party—what's the matter with you?*

4. **Begging the question**—Restating a point without answering *why*: in other words, begging for the basic *why* question to be answered. *He procrastinates because he doesn't like to work.* (But *why* doesn't he like to work?) This fallacy is sometimes called a **circular argument**.

5. **False analogy**—Falsely assuming that because one thing resembles another in one way, they will resemble each other in other ways. *I don't need to go to Disneyland because I've been to Disney World.*

6. **False authority**—Assuming that an expert in one field can be an expert in another. *We need a smaller government, to quote my dentist.*

7. **False cause**—Assuming that because one event follows another, the first causes the second. *She ate a lot of potato chips, so I'm not surprised she has high blood pressure.*

8. **False dilemma**—Assuming that only two choices exist. *We have only two choices: Vote for the Democrat or vote for the Republican.*

9. **Guilt by association**—Attempting to blame one person for the beliefs or actions of another. *They're brothers, so he must be a thief too.*

EDITING TIP, *continued*

10. **Hasty generalization**—Generalizing based on little or no evidence. *The Irish drink too much* or *The homeless could get jobs if they wanted them.*

11. **Non sequitur**—Stating a conclusion that doesn't logically follow a premise. *I have a college degree, so I know I'll find a good job.*

12. **Oversimplification**—Making a claim that ignores details. *It really doesn't take that much work to learn Spanish.*

13. **Slippery Slope**—Assuming that if you take a first step, it will lead to disaster. *If we let gay people marry, it will lead to the collapse of marriage as an institution.*

Revisions: (1) The United States Congress should legalize marijuana because it may reduce organized crime, provide tax relief, and save lives through medical benefits. (2) If Congress doesn't legalize marijuana, two possible options present themselves: We organize a mass protest to march on Washington, or we flood the office of every member of Congress with e-mails. (Adding may and possible shows that the writer understands his claims are open to question—neither a generalizing statement nor a two-option choice.)

STRATEGY 8. Don't forget to start a sentence with date/time/place.

In 1887, Eadweard Muybridge set up twenty-four cameras to photograph the sequential motion of racing horses. In 1889, George Eastman invented celluloid film. Thomas Edison, using Eastman's film, secured a patent for a motion picture camera he called the Kinetograph in 1897.

Emphasis problem: We need signs at the start of sentences to orient us to changes in date, time, and place.

EDITING TIP

To orient the reader within sentences that use date, time, or place references, move each date, time, or place reference to the *start* of a sentence. The references function like road signs that signal changes: *In 1887 . . . In 1889 . . . In 1897 . . .* **Or** *At 5:45 a.m. . . . At 9:43 a.m. . . . At 12:02 p.m. . . .* **Or** *In Los Angeles . . . In Chicago . . . In New York . . .*

Revision: In 1887, Eadweard Muybridge set up twenty-four cameras to photograph the sequential motion of racing horses. In 1889, George Eastman invented celluloid film. In 1897, Thomas Edison, using Eastman's film, secured a patent for a motion picture camera he called the Kinetograph.

2. HOW TO GET RID OF VAGUENESS

STRATEGY 9. Don't leave the subject out of the sentence.

The effort on behalf of a desire to address the failure within the city to address a plan for recycling precipitated a change in direction in recycling efforts whereby a mayoral initiative was submitted and was duly instituted.

Vagueness problem: We need a subject that controls the sentence.

EDITING TIP

To fix a sentence that lacks a subject:

1. **Mark each idea.**
2. **Figure out *who* or *what* controls each idea:** Add grammatical subjects as needed.
3. **Keep the subject *as short as possible*.**
4. **Rewrite the sentence in plain language.**

The effort on behalf of a desire | to address the failure within the city | to address a plan for city-wide recycling | precipitated a change in direction in recycling efforts | whereby a mayoral initiative was submitted | and was duly instituted. (= six ideas)

1. **What happened?** *The city failed to "address" [write, submit] a recycling plan.*
2. **What else happened?** *Somebody wanted to fix the problem and submit a plan.*
3. **So who controls the sentence?** *The mayor, under whose "mayoral initiative" a plan was written and submitted.*
4. **Who else controls the sentence?** *The city's Board of Directors = Those responsible for instituting the plan.*

Revision: Because the city had no recycling plan, the mayor submitted one, which the Board of Directors then put into practice.

STRATEGY 10. *Don't leave* it *hanging.*

(1) Reinhold discussed <u>child abuse</u>, looking at <u>bullying</u>, <u>oral humiliation</u>, and <u>physical assault</u>, giving each <u>rationale</u> for <u>corporal punishment</u>, like the <u>religious</u> and the <u>cultural</u>, and observing that *it* needs further study. (2) Tina's dad is a <u>trombone player</u>, so Tina wants to study *it*.

Vagueness problem: We don't know which underlined topics *it* refers to.

> ## EDITING TIP
> 1. When *it* follows a series of nouns, the reader often has no idea which noun *it* refers to. Replace *it* with a noun.
> 2. When *it* has no noun to refer to, replace *it* with a noun or insert a noun earlier in the sentence that *it* can refer to.

Revisions: (1) Reinhold discussed child abuse, looking at bullying, oral humiliation, and physical assault, giving each rationale for corporal punishment, like the religious and cultural, and observing that child abuse needs further study. (2) Tina's dad is a trombone player, so Tina wants to study trombone *or* Tina's dad plays trombone, so Tina wants to study it.

STRATEGY 11. *Don't leave* this, that, *and* which *hanging.*

(1) I hope <u>to learn more about China, Japan, and Southeast Asia</u> and <u>practice my language skills</u> on my <u>trip</u>; this is something I'm really excited about. (2) Tommy <u>traveled to Asia</u> and <u>wrote about it</u>, which is one reason I want to go.

Vagueness problem: What underlined topics do *this* and *which* refer to?

> ## EDITING TIP
> When *this (these)*, *that (those)* and *which* follow a series of nouns, the reader often has no idea which noun these words refer to.
>
> 1. Insert a noun after *this* or *that*.
> 2. Replace *which* with a noun.

Revisions: (1) I hope to learn more about China, Japan, and Southeast Asia on my trip next year; this trip is something that I'm really excited about. (2) Tommy traveled to Asia and wrote about it; his blog on the trip is one reason I want to go.

3. HOW TO GET MORE OUT OF VERBS

STRATEGY 12. Don't use more nonaction verbs than action verbs.

The lamp is bright.

Nonaction verb problem: The *to be* verb *is* shows no action; it doesn't create a picture.

EDITING TIP

To be verbs don't cause sentences to come alive the way action verbs do. To create pictures that pull in the reader and give your prose momentum, replace *to be* verbs with action verbs.

To Be Verbs
am/is/are	was/were
am being/is being/are being	was being/were being
has been/have been/had been	will be/will have been
may be/might have been	

---

                    glows brightly.
Revision: The lamp ~~is bright~~.
                  ^

STRATEGY 13. Don't use the passive without good reason.

(1) The check was sent by Christy. (2) The check was sent.

Passive verb problem: (1) The passive delays the subject until the end of the sentence. (2) The passive deletes the subject: We don't know who sent the check.

EDITING TIP

Most sentences have *active* order: *Subject* - *Verb* - *Object*
                                 Christy   sent   the check.

Passive order inverts the order: *Object* - *Verb* - *Subject*
                                 The check   was sent by   Christy.

Writers avoid the passive for four reasons:

1. The passive *uses more words* than the active.
2. The passive *uses nonaction* (to be) *verbs*.
3. The passive *delays the subject* till the end of the sentence.
4. Worse, the passive can *delete the subject*.

To turn passive into active:

1. Move the delayed subject to the sentence start.
2. Or insert *by* + the deleted subject and move the subject to the sentence start.

Revisions:

(1) Christy [delayed subject moved to start] sent the
    ^
    ~~The~~ check ~~was sent by Christy~~.

(2) Christy [deleted subject inserted and moved to start] sent the
    ^
    ~~The~~ check ~~was sent~~ [~~by Christy~~].

EDITING TIP

Use the passive in five situations.

1. When the active emphasizes the <u>wrong subject</u> over the right subject.

    ACTIVE: <u>We</u> advise that you make routine virus checks.

    PASSIVE: Routine virus checks are advisable. [**the subject <u>we</u> deleted**]

2. When the active introduces trivial, obvious information.

    ACTIVE: The mail carrier delivered the mail.

    PASSIVE: The mail was delivered.

3. When the active produces a pointlessly long sentence with trivial, obvious information.

    ACTIVE: A team of heart surgeons performed his heart replacement at St. John's.

    PASSIVE: His heart replacement was performed at St. John's.

4. When the active offers more information than you want to give.

    ACTIVE: I made the decision to spend company money.

    PASSIVE: A decision was made to spend company money.

5. When the passive produces a padded-verb transition (<u>resign</u> = resignation) that hooks two sentences.

    I decided to <u>resign</u>. My resignation was criticized by the supervisor.

STRATEGY 14. Don't split infinitives without good reason.

Lucia didn't want to <u>just</u> sail solo across the Pacific. What she wanted was to <u>really</u> write about a book about her trip.

Split infinitive problem: Splitting to sail with <u>just</u> could make us think that Lucia wanted to do something more than simply *sail* solo across the Pacific—maybe she also wanted to fly or swim across the Pacific. Splitting to write with <u>really</u> makes us think that she wanted to write with great energy or intensity: to *really* write.

> # EDITING TIP
>
> *To* + a verb forms an infinitive: *to play, to appear*, etc. An old rule of style says *Never split an infinitive*. Academic writing generally follows this rule unless moving the word from the infinitive makes the sentence awkward or changes the meaning.
>
> **SPLIT INFINITIVE:** Try not to "accidentally" lose your allowance.
>
> **REVISED BUT AWKWARD:** Try not to lose your allowance "accidentally."

Revision: Lucia didn't want just to sail solo across the Pacific. What she really wanted was to write a book about her trip.

4. HOW TO GET RID OF WORDINESS

STRATEGY 15. *Get rid of word twins and triplets.*

Each and every person should learn the basics and fundamentals of good driving and then take a driving examination that submits one's knowledge and skills to thorough testing, assessment, and evaluation. (31 words)

Wordiness problem: These word twins and triplets repeat themselves. Does the writer think that we have to be told twice—or thrice? *Once is enough.*

> # EDITING TIP
>
> Writers love the sound of word twins and triplets. Sometimes twins and triplets aren't redundant (*willing and able; red, white, and blue*), but often they are. When you write a word twin or triplet, ask if you're using it because it sounds good or because it's needed. As a general practice, be wary of patterns that break into twins. Be downright suspicious of patterns that break into triplets. Check the *end* of your sentences, where triplets love to congregate: First and last, we must try and understand the economic, social, and political factors influencing poverty, joblessness, and high unemployment rates.

Revision: Each person should learn the basics of good driving and then take a driving examination that submits one's knowledge to thorough testing. (22 words)

STRATEGY 16. *Get rid of redundant word pairs.*

It's absolutely essential to have mutual cooperation as we plan ahead for testing our new innovation before the company releases the end product. (23 words)

Wordiness problem: As with word twins, redundant word pairs say things twice. *Once is enough.*

EDITING TIP

Delete the ~~redundancy~~. Watch for redundant word pairs formed with:

    Noun + Noun

    Verb + Preposition or Adverb

    Adjective + Noun

    Adverb + Adjective

EDITING TIP, *continued*

Noun + Noun	*Verb + Prep. or Adv.*	*Adjective + Noun*	*Adverb + Adj.*
ATM ~~machine~~	allow ~~for~~	~~advance~~ planning	~~absolutely~~ essential
~~cash~~ money	copy ~~off~~	~~end~~ product	~~currently~~ anticipated
~~end~~ product	edit ~~out~~	~~honest~~ truth	~~exactly~~ alike
HIV ~~virus~~	~~first~~ met	~~mutual~~ cooperation	~~fundamentally~~ basic
Rio Grande ~~River~~	plan ~~ahead~~	~~new~~ innovation	~~obviously~~ apparent
subject ~~matter~~	refer ~~back~~	~~qualified~~ experts	~~personally~~ responsible

---

Revision: It's essential to have cooperation as we plan for testing our innovation before the company releases the product. (18 words)

STRATEGY 17. Get rid of formula phrases and clichés.

It goes without saying, once the professor collects all of the bluebooks, it is obvious that students will rush outside and at that point of time pull out their phones in order to begin to check for messages. (38 words)

Wordiness problem: We're given a sentence that's bloated with gas. Why not trim it to essentials?

EDITING TIP

Look for four kinds of formula phrases:

1. **Phrases you can *completely* cut.**
   it goes without saying   in order
   needless to say   in the final analysis
2. **Phrases you can *partly* cut.**
   all of   whether or not   begin to check
3. **Phrases you can extract a *key word* from.**
   it is obvious that = **obviously**
   there is no question that = **unquestionably**
4. **Phrases you can *replace*.**
   at that point in time = **then**
   regardless of the fact that = **although**
   at this point in time = **now**
   in short supply = **scarce**
   went on to say = **added**
   take appropriate action = **act**

EDITING TIP

A cliché is a word, phrase, or idea that's lost its freshness. Clichés like *Have a good one* help us through the day but, typed on the page, signal a lazy writer. A writer *may* be able to express clichéd thinking without using clichéd language, but probably can't. Where you find one cliché, you find another.

Clichés take the place of real thought. Faced with a tough problem, we reach for a "groupthink" cliché. Using groupthink is easier than thinking for ourselves. Readers skim over a page of clichés because there's nothing to digest. To make the reader slow down and pay attention:

EDITING TIP, *continued*

1. Refuse to use other people's *thinking*. If you've heard it before, don't use it.
2. Refuse to use other people's *language*. If you've heard it before, don't use it.

WARNING!

Using a recent cliché can make us feel like we belong to the club. And that's all the more reason not to use it.

However: Don't cut *all* clichés from your writing. Elderly clichés like happy as a clam and needle in a haystack can be dusted off and used for comic effect, as Woody Allen knows: "Life doesn't imitate art; it imitates bad television" and "My one regret in life is that I am not someone else."

Revision: Once the professor collects all the bluebooks, obviously students will rush outside and then pull out their phones to check for messages. (22 words)

STRATEGY 18. Get rid of padded verbs and nouns.

(1) Arthur <u>came to a decision</u> to change careers. (8 words) (2) The lawyer argued for an exhumation of the body. (9 words)

Wordiness problem: By extracting verbs from nouns, we can shorten the padded verb <u>came to a decision</u> and the padded noun an exhumation of.

EDITING TIP

Many nouns begin as <u>verbs</u> but acquire "padding" that turns them into nouns. (Note typical padded-verb endings: *-tion, -sion, -ment, -ance*.)

decision = <u>decide</u>	solution = <u>solve</u>
investigation = <u>investigate</u>	replacement = <u>replace</u>
performance = <u>perform</u>	discussion = <u>discuss</u>

Adding a verb phrase to a padded verb produces a wordy, sometimes awkward phrase that further "pads" the verb. Cut the padding and rescue the verb.

Verb Phrase	*Padded Verb*	*Revision*
had been	+ supportive of	= supported
triggers	+ a provocation of	= provokes
takes into	+ consideration	= considers

Some noun phrases used as objects begin as verbs. They can also be cut and revised by extracting the verb and using it as an <u>infinitive</u> or <u>shorter noun</u>.

<u>to complete</u>
She planned ~~the completion of~~ the garden by May.
∧

<u>completing</u>
She planned ~~the completion of~~ the garden by May.
∧

Revisions: (1) Arthur <u>decided</u> to change careers. (5 words) (2) The lawyer argued for <u>exhuming</u> the body. (7 words)

WARNING!

Generally try to reduce padded verbs and nouns. However, the occasional padded verb can serve as a transition that hooks sentences by repeating words. *The modern grocery store is <u>equipped</u> with computers, scanners, and ATMs. Such <u>equipment</u> guarantees the customer will quickly pass through the checkout lane.*

STRATEGY 19. Get rid of redundant general descriptions.

The cake was small in size, blue in color, and sour in taste. (13 words)

Wordiness problem: The redundant general descriptions add nothing to the sentence.

EDITING TIP

Look for descriptions that have two parts: a specific description followed by a general description:

1. The specific description (*small, blue, sweet*)
2. The general description (*size, color, taste*)

Sharpen your prose by keeping the specific and cutting the general.

Specific	General		Specific	General
appreciate/depreciate	in value		grow/shrink	in size
big/small	in size, etc.		longer/shorter	in length
blue, etc.,	in color		massive/tiny	in size, etc.
brief/long	in duration		oval/rectangular/round/square	in shape
cacophony	of noise			
cosmetic	in appearance		puzzling	in nature
disappear	from sight		shiny	in appearance
earlier/later	in time		short/tall	in height/stature
evolve	over time		soft/harsh	in texture/touch
fast/slow	in speed		sour/sweet	in taste
few/many	in number			

Revision: The cake was small, blue, and sour. (7 words)

STRATEGY 20. Get rid of unnecessary qualifiers.

Essentially, he's incredibly different from Brian and kind of like Mark in virtually every way, from being very focused to utterly and definitely committed to political activism. (27 words)

Wordiness problem: These qualifiers add nothing to the sentence. We can ~~totally~~ cut them.

EDITING TIP

Qualifiers *qualify* words. Sometimes they're needed—more often, they're not. We use them because they "sound good" or, more likely, because they've become verbal tics, like *like* and *you know*.

almost	given	pretty	sort of
basically	hardly	quite	surely
certain	incredibly	rather	totally
certainly	individual	really	tremendously
clearly	just	said	unbelievably
consistently	kind of	scarcely	unusually
definitely	moderately	simply	utterly
essentially	nearly	slightly	very
fairly	personal	so	virtually
generally	practically	somewhat	

Revison: He's different from Brian and like Mark in every way, from focus to commitment to political activism. (17 words)

STRATEGY 21. *Get rid of* that, which, *and* who *clauses.*

(1) The novel that was a mystery became a bestseller. (9 words) (2) *The Murder at the Vicarage*, which is a mystery novel, became a bestseller. (13 words) (3) The woman who is buying this book likes mysteries. (9 words) (4). Agatha Christie, who regularly published, wrote mysteries. (7 words)

Wordiness problem: The *that, which*, and *who* clauses add unnecessary words.

EDITING TIP

Try cutting *that, which*, and *who* clauses in one of two ways:

1. **With *to be* verbs, cut all but the key words (the last word or two).**
   ~~that was~~ **a mystery**
   ~~which is~~ **a mystery novel**
2. **With other verbs, cut all but the main verb and the key words.**
   ~~who is~~ **buying this book**
   ~~who~~ **regularly published**

Then, depending on what's possible, do one of two things:

1. **Turn the remaining words into an essential or a nonessential fragment.**
   The woman **buying this book** likes . . .
   The novel, a mystery, became . . .
   The Murder at the Vicarage, a mystery novel, became . . .

2. *Or* **move and revise the clause words to modify the subject.**
   The **mystery** novel became . . .
   Mystery novel *The Murder at the Vicarage* became . . .
   Publishing regular Agatha Christie wrote . . .

Revisions: (1) The novel, a mystery, became a bestseller. (7 words) (2) Mystery novel *The Murder at the Vicarage* became a bestseller. (10 words) (3) The woman buying this book likes mysteries. (7 words) (4) Publishing regular Agatha Christie wrote mysteries. (6 words)

STRATEGY 22. Get rid of that *and* that of.

(1) Mrs. Conway believed that her daughter was a gifted musician; Mr. Conway knew that she wasn't, and little that he could say would change his wife's mind. (27 words) (2) The preacher went on for so long that the congregation grew uneasy. (12 words) (3) The most common reaction is that of dismay, and I'm sad that they should feel this way. (17 words)

Wordiness problem: That and that of chew up space and provide an unwelcome repetition of unimportant words. (See **Strategy 45, Don't repeat unimportant words.**)

EDITING TIP

Cut that in four situations:

1. **With verbs like *say, think,* and *order*.** *Roberta demanded ~~that~~ Carlos pay the bill.*
2. **With that clauses.** *Little ~~that~~ she can say . . . Here's the DVD ~~that~~ Amazon.com sent.*
3. **With adjectives.** *I'm happy ~~that~~ you called. She's glad ~~that~~ her roses bloomed.*
4. **With *so/that* and *such/that*.** *Jane had such a wonderful experience ~~that~~ she's returning.*

WARNING!

In *so/that* and *such/that* sentences, insert a comma to replace that. *Jane had such a wonderful experience, she's returning.*

EDITING TIP

Cut that of after a <u>subject</u> + a <u>to be</u> verb. *The most common <u>reaction</u> <u>is</u> that of dismay . . .*

The most common reaction is dismay.

WARNING!

Don't cut that in two situations and that of in one situation:

1. **With a formal balance:** *Having an aquarium means that you must feed the fish regularly and that you must clean the tank regularly.*
2. **With an interrupter:** *Jonathan says, <u>as he has always said</u>, that poker is more psychology than luck.*
3. **With a comparison:** *The picture of Sam is torn like that of Rob.* (**Without that of, the sentence would say** *The picture of Rob is torn like Sam.*)

Revisions: (1) Mrs. Conway believed her daughter was a gifted musician; Mr. Conway knew she wasn't, and little he could say would change his wife's mind. (24 words) (2) The preacher went on for so long, the congregation grew uneasy. (11 words) (3) The most common reaction is dismay, and I'm sad they should feel this way. (14 words)

STRATEGY 23. Get rid of unnecessary parallel words: that/that, which/which, not only/but also.

(1) Wilson claimed that his vinyl record collection was the best in the city and that it was worth fifty thousand dollars. (21 words) (2) Wilson claimed his vinyl record collection, which he thought was the best in the city and which he had insured for a large sum, was worth fifty thousand dollars. (29 words) (3) Sylvester the cat not only sneaked around but also got into mischief. (12 words) (4) Sylvester the cat not only sneaked around but also ate every canary that came into the house. (17 words)

Wordiness problem: We need to keep phrases parallel, but we don't always need to keep every word in the parallel.

EDITING TIP

1. **When parallel that or which clauses share common words (including pronoun replacements like *it*), cut repeated words in the second clause:** *that his vinyl collection was the best in the city and ~~that it was~~ worth fifty thousand dollars; which he thought was the best in the city and ~~which he~~ had insured for a large sum.*
2. **If not only means *some of this* and *some of that*, keep but also:** *Pedro O'Toole was not only Spanish but also Irish.*
3. **But if not only means *some of this* but *more of that*, cut also:** *Pedro O'Toole was not only a resident of Spain but ~~also~~ the heir to the Spanish throne.*

Revisions: (1) Wilson claimed that his vinyl record collection was the best in the city and worth fifty thousand dollars. (18 words) (2) Wilson claimed his vinyl record collection, which he thought was the best in the city and had insured for a large sum, was worth fifty thousand dollars. (27 words) (3) Sylvester the cat not only sneaked around but also got into mischief. (12 words) (4) Sylvester the cat not only sneaked around but ate every canary that came into the house. (16 words)

STRATEGY 24. Get rid of a, an, the.

(1) Try to buy a travel mug and a guidebook. (9 words) (2) Ship the couch, the bed, and the refrigerator by a moving van. (12 words) (3) The sunset always comes early in the winter. (8 words)

Wordiness problem: We can often cut indefinite (a, an) and definite (the) articles.

EDITING TIP

Cut **a, an, and the:**

1. **With a pair or series after establishing the first a, an, or the:** the couch, bed, and refrigerator.
2. **With words that show the *only* example of something:** the seasons (*winter*) and time of day (*sunset*).
3. **With words that don't need articles:** *by moving van, aboard ship.*

WARNING!

Warning: Don't cut **a, an, and the:**

1. **With one list item starting with a consonant and another starting with a vowel:** *I ate a banana and an orange.*
2. **With ambiguity:** *The secretary and treasurer contacted the group.* **Do we have one person** (*secretary-treasurer*) **or two** (*the secretary and the treasurer*)?
3. **With *either/or* and *neither/nor* to keep the parallel:** *Neither a borrower nor a lender be.*

Revisions: (1) Try to buy a travel mug and guidebook. (8 words) (2) Ship the couch, bed, and refrigerator by moving van. (9 words) (3) Sunset always comes early in winter. (6 words)

STRATEGY 25. *Get rid of* **to, to be,** *and* **being.**

(1) For language practice, he began to read German magazines, to eat lunch at the German House, and to watch German movies. (21 words) (2) The convenience store likes to stay open late to catch late-shift workers. (12 words) (3) Mrs. R. C. Haase thought the fuss to be unnecessary. (10 words) (4) Bea realized her employee wasn't being truthful about hours worked. (10 words)

Wordiness problem: To be, being, and the repetitions of to add nothing to these sentences.

EDITING TIP

1. **After establishing the first to in a series of infinitives, keep the first and cut the rest:** *to read, to eat, to watch.*
2. **When one infinitive follows another (*to stay open late to catch*), change the first to an *-ing* word:** *to stay = staying.*
3. **If the sentence works fine without them, cut to be and being:** *the fuss to be unnecessary; wasn't being accurate.*

WARNING!

Keep to if you want to create a memorable series, as is common in a speech: *Americans must learn to sacrifice, to help one another, and to contribute to the community.*

Revisions: (1) For language practice, he began to read German magazines, eat lunch at the German House, and watch German movies. (19 words) (2) The convenience store likes staying open late to catch late-shift workers. (11 words) (3) Mrs. R. C. Haase thought the fuss unnecessary. (8 words) (4) Bea realized her employee wasn't truthful about hours worked. (9 words)

STRATEGY 26. Get rid of unnecessary prepositions.

(1) Roland fell off of the roof and was carried inside of the house. (13 words) (2) I hope you can edit out the mistakes, copy off the draft, and distribute from between fifteen and twenty copies. (20 words) (3) Take the boy in to work. (6 words) (4) It's clear that all of her complaints happened because she was near to exhaustion. (14 words) (5) Second of all, you need to prepare early on. (9 words) (6) Here are the directions for roasting vegetables, for making a cheese sauce, and for baking a lemon cake. (18 words)

Wordiness problem: These prepositions add nothing to these sentences.

EDITING TIP

Cut unnecessary prepositions sticking to:

1. **Other prepositions:** *off of, inside of, outside of, from between*
2. **Verbs:** *edit out, copy off, take in*
3. **Adjectives:** *large in (size), pink in color*
4. **Adverbs:** *second of (all), early on*
5. **A series of items:** for roasting, for making, and for baking **(keep the first preposition—***for, in, by, at,* etc. **—and cut others when possible)**

Revisions: (1) Roland fell off the roof and was carried inside the house. (11 words) (2) I hope you can edit the mistakes, copy the draft, and distribute between fifteen and twenty copies. (17 words) (3) Take the boy to work. (5 words) (4) It's clear that all her complaints happened because she was near exhaustion. (12 words) (5) Second, you need to prepare early. (6 words) (6) Here are the directions for roasting vegetables, making a cheese sauce, and baking a lemon cake. (16 words)

STRATEGY 27. Get rid of unnecessary prepositional phrases.

Dr. Hutchins' relatives from Brooklyn went with him to the sale of men's clothing at a mall on the West Side. (21 words)

Wordiness problem: A sentence with more than two or three prepositional phrases probably needs cutting.

EDITING TIP

Too many prepositional phrases can kill a sentence quicker than the passive, *to be* verbs, or vagueness. Prepositional phrases stacked up like boxcars cause prose to sound jerky and repetitive—and the drone can put a reader to sleep.

Follow these steps to reduce prepositional phrases:

1. **Cut all but the key words (usually the last word or two).**
2. **Move the key word(s) to modify an earlier noun.**

>   Brooklyn
> Dr. Hutchins' relatives ~~from~~ Brooklyn went with him to the
>   ^

>   men's clothing   West Side
>   sale ~~of~~ men's clothing at a mall ~~on the~~ West Side.
> ^   ^

Revision: Dr. Hutchins' Brooklyn relatives went with him to the men's clothing sale at a West Side mall. (17 words)

STRATEGY 28. Get rid of unnecessary expletives.

(1) There are over one million bats that have died from a fungus infection called the white-nose syndrome. (16 words) (2) It is the disease that has ranged across fifteen states and two Canadian provinces, threatening the ecological balance. (18 words)

Wordiness problem: Expletives are such phrases as *there are* and *it is*. Cut them to reduce wordiness.

EDITING TIP

Look for sentences starting with *there* or *it + to be* verb (is, are, was, were, has been, have been, might be). Cut the expletive and *that*.

~~There are~~ over one million bats ~~that~~ have died . . .

  (Over one million bats have died . . .)

~~It is~~ the disease ~~that~~ has ranged . . .

  (The disease has ranged . . .)

Expletives:
1. **Slow down the sentence.**
2. **Delay the subject.**
3. **Add words.**

WARNING!

Routine editing cuts most expletives. On occasion, use the expletive for its "bad" qualities—to slow down the sentence and to delay the subject. Use the expletive to set up important ideas: *There are three reasons why you should volunteer. It is a lie that Christopher Columbus discovered America.* **(Here emphasis is more important than wordiness.)**

Revisions: (1) Over one million bats have died from a fungus infection called the white-nose syndrome. (13 words) (2) The disease has ranged across fifteen states and two Canadian provinces, threatening the ecological balance. (15 words)

STRATEGY 29. Get rid of unnecessary -ing verbs.

The subcommittee will be reviewing the company's brand while the main committee is examining the mission. (16 words)

Wordiness problem: A heavy use of *-ing* verbs can signal a style that's pompous and official-sounding. Don't write like a government bureaucrat.

EDITING TIP

You can express a verb in two ways—*one-time* action or *continuous* action.

One-time action   **Continuous action**

(1) He *runs* [**present**] vs. (2) He *is running* [**present progressive**]

(1) He *ran* [**past**] vs. (2) He *was running* [**past progressive**]

(1) He had *run* [**past perfect**] vs. (2) He *had been running* [**past perfect progressive**]

Use *-ing*, or progressive, verbs only when they're necessary. If one action takes place *before* the other, use it. The *-ing* tells the reader which action takes place before the other. But if two actions take place *at the same time*, don't use it.

1. **TAKES PLACE BEFORE:** When the shot *fired*, he was *running*. (He was already running **before the shot fired**.)
2. **TAKES PLACE AT THE SAME TIME:** When the shot *fired*, he *ran*. (He started running **at the same moment the shot fired**.)

Thus: Cut -*ing* with 2: when both actions happen at the same time.

The subcommittee will ~~be~~ review~~ing~~ the company's brand

                                              es
while the main committee ~~is~~ examin~~ing~~ the mission.
                                             ^

Revision: The subcommittee will review the company's brand while the main committee examines the mission. (14 words)

STRATEGY 30. Get rid of sentences by combining sentences.

(1) Brittney e-mailed the CEO of Myer Industries about an internship. Brittney also asked for an appointment. (*same subject*; 16 words) (2) Brittney knows the CEO of Myer Industries. Carl also knows the CEO of Myer Industries. (same verb; 15 words) (3) Brittney wants to work for a nonprofit company. She believes that working for a nonprofit company will deeply satisfy her. (same topic; 20 words)

Wordiness problem: Too many sentences of similar length (each has six to twelve words) may cause wordiness. Combining sentences will let you cut common words and avoid repetitive sentence lengths.

EDITING TIP

1. **If two sentences share the same subject, combine them:** *Brittney e-mailed the CEO of Myer Industries and asked . . .*

2. **If two sentences share the same verb, combine them:** *Brittney and Carl know the . . .*

3. **If two sentences share the same topic, combine them, putting one sentence into a fragment with a synonym:** *Brittney wants to work for a nonprofit company, believing the experience. . .* **(Put the minor idea into the fragment.)**

Revisions: (1) Brittney e-mailed the CEO of Myer Industries about an internship and asked for an appointment. (15 words) (2) Brittney and Carl know the CEO of Myer Industries. (9 words) (3) Brittney wants to work for a nonprofit company, believing the experience will deeply satisfy her. (15 words)

STRATEGY 31. Get rid of I in the picture.

I first plan to show how stem cell research faces wide public hostility because, in essence, opponents claim that it violates common morality by "murdering" babies. I want to show that to understand the current state of research, I must look at its history, focusing on moral and legal challenges to advancing the research. I have discovered in my research that proponents claim that stem cell research must proceed without restriction. My intention in this essay is to argue that stem cell research, like other controversial medical research in the recent past, must proceed without restriction because of two pressing imperatives: I will prove that there is a medical need to cure disease that can be cured. I will then prove that there is a moral need to cure disease that can be cured. (134 words)

Wordiness problem: Don't write an overview of the essay that says what you're going to do. Cut I from the picture and let the essay speak for itself.

EDITING TIP

Use I only in academic essays that call for a personal response, like a response paper or a theater review. Many published academic essays do use I–but often at the peril of the topic because I can trigger awkward transitions (*I first plan . . .*) or irrelevant digression (*which reminds me that . . .*). At its worst, the "personal experience" of I substitutes for hard thought and data, and the real topic gets lost in a show of ego.

If you handle transitions carefully, the parts of a project will naturally unfold without stage directions. To avoid directions like *I first plan*, organize the essay with user-friendly conventions:

1. **Place the thesis in a logical position: at the start or end of the Introduction.**
2. **If the writing model permits, use headings to set up sections.**
3. **Make each section organically lead to the next section.**
4. **Use transitions that lead the reader through the project:** *however, next, finally.*
5. **Use a reverse outline to check the project's logic, paragraph by paragraph.**

Revision: Stem cell research faces wide public hostility. In essence, opponents claim that it violates common morality by "murdering" babies. To understand the current state of research, one must look at its history, focusing on moral and legal challenges to advancing the research. Proponents claim that stem cell research must proceed without restriction. Stem cell research, like other controversial medical research in the recent past, must proceed without restriction because of two pressing imperatives: the medical and moral needs to cure diseases that can be cured. (85 words)

STRATEGY 32. Get rid of writing about the writing.

It is the goal of this section to look at Charles Calverley's poetry, which is noted for its skillful handling of meter and rhyme. The first part of the section will look at his original poetry. After that will follow a detailed examination of the miscellaneous poems. The second part will survey Calverley's translations of Greek and Roman classics. The goal of this section is to show Calverley's ease with classical forms. The next section will discuss Calverley's translations from English into Latin and Greek. The final section will look at three of his articles, all on the subject of Greek and Roman poetry. (104 words)

Wordiness problem: The writer provides too many road signs—writing about the writing that adds wordiness.

EDITING TIP

Writing about the writing can help the reader navigate a text. But limit the number of times you provide writing about the writing. The example above uses seven road signs; the writer can reduce wordiness by cutting five.

As general practice:

1. Limit the **writing about the writing.**
2. Use <u>transitions</u> that point the reader forward without obviously saying *The next section will . . .*

Revision: Charles Calverley's poetry is noted for its skillful handling of meter and rhyme. The essay will look first at the classical influences on his original poetry, <u>with</u> a detailed examination of the miscellaneous poems. Calverley's masterly translations of Greek and Roman classics <u>also</u> show his ease with classical forms. <u>After</u> discussing Calverley's translations from English into Latin and Greek, the essay will conclude with three of his articles on Greek and Roman poetry. (73 words)

STRATEGY 33. Get rid of empty thought.

In our world of today, we need better communication between our children, who are the leaders of tomorrow, and their elders, who are the leaders of today. Although many children and adults share a bounty of blessings, from church to family vacations, some children feel they cannot talk to their parents because of a "communication gap." One means to address this gap is greater awareness. Without awareness, we cannot move forward as a society and nation. (76 words)

Wordiness problem: The paragraph substitutes clichés for serious thought. What is "better communication"? What is the "communication gap"? What is "greater awareness"? Once the writer moves away from fact (*many children feel they cannot talk to their parents*) toward "answers," the passage falls back on clichés picked up from society, television, and the Internet. Empty thought causes wordiness.

EDITING TIP

Faced with hard thought, many writers fall back on empty thought: language and ideas that come from the media and group-think. Cut three kinds of empty thought:

1. **Obvious statements:** *children . . . the leaders of tomorrow, elders . . . the leaders of today*
2. **Clichés of thought and language:** *in our world of today, we need better communication, greater awareness, we cannot move forward as a society and nation*
3. **Assumptions of shared belief:** *A bounty of blessings* (**not all readers share a belief in a god or the Christian God**)

Revision: Some children feel they cannot talk to their parents. (9 words.) (At this point, the passage stripped of empty thought, the writer must dig deeply to explain why *some children feel they cannot talk to their parents.* Hard, original thought, coupled with research that goes beyond skimming the Internet, will provide answers and free the passage of wordiness.)

5. HOW TO CHOOSE THE RIGHT WORD

STRATEGY 34. Don't worry about starting a sentence with and *(but, etc.).*

Paul went to the library. <u>And checked out books.</u> But he didn't read them right away.

Word choice problem: The problem is not the sentences starting with *and/but*. The problem is the <u>fragment</u>: Give it a verb or hook it to the sentence before.

EDITING TIP

It's myth that you can't start a sentence with *and*. Start a sentence with any conjunction—or any word—that you wish. A long time ago, English teachers "invented" this rule no doubt to steer their students from <u>fragments</u>:

> *Paul went to the library.* <u>*And checked out books.*</u>

The fragment worry has thus led to years of writers convinced that *You can't start a sentence with "and."* Of course you can. Here's one of America's greatest writers, Henry David Thoreau. The passage comes from *Walden; or, Life in the Woods* (1854):

> *In eternity there is indeed something true and sublime. But all these times and places and occasions are now and here. God himself culminates in the present moment, and will never be more divine in the lapse of all the ages. And we are enabled to apprehend at all what is sublime and noble only by the perpetual instilling and drenching of the reality that surrounds us.*

Revision: Paul went to the library. And he checked out books. [*Or* Paul went to the library and checked out books.] But he didn't read them right away.

STRATEGY 35. Don't use the wrong word.

(1) The "Synchronous Learning" chapter provides an extended discussion of how such ubiquitous learning takes place in grade schools. (2) She studied the ascetics of music. (3) He provided a verbal analysis of how the affects of radiation effect us. (4) I could care less about politics.

Word choice problem: The highlighted words show how dramatically the wrong word can change meaning. In sentence (4), the writer means the *opposite* of what he says!

EDITING TIP

As Strategy 43 warns, *Use the thesaurus only when you're looking for a precise word—not when you're concerned about repetition.* In sentence (1), the writer worries about repeating *synchronous*, turns to the thesaurus, finds words like *simultaneous* and *omnipresent*, and makes his way to the inappropriate *ubiquitous*. With *synchronous* learning, the same groups of students learn the same things at the same time in the same place. *Ubiquitous*, which means *everywhere at the same time*, dramatically changes the meaning.

In sentence (2), the writer means *aesthetics* (*ascetics* are religious people like monks who give up material comforts). In (3), the writer confuses *verbal* (an adjective referring to both spoken and written words) with *oral* and *effect* (a noun meaning *result*) with *affect* (a verb meaning *change*). In (4), the writer should say *I could <u>not</u> care less about politics.*

(See **Chapter 18 —Word Confusions**.)

Revisions: (1) The "Synchronous Learning" chapter provides an extended discussion of how synchronous learning takes place in grade schools. (2) She studied the aesthetics of music. (3) He provided an oral analysis of how the effects of radiation affect us. (4) I could not care less about politics.

STRATEGY 36. Don't use big words for plain.

Borges' story is enigmatical to the extreme, pretending to the verisimilar and thus linear but inclining to aleatoric peregrinations into the phantasmagorical.

Word choice problem: Six big words in a twenty-two word sentence places a burden on the reader. Do we really need all six?

EDITING TIP

Big words can be *long* words or *fancy* words—those one-hundred dollar words we pull out to flash a rich vocabulary. Many of these words come from French and Latin. By contrast, many plain words come from Old English. We have a world of plain words—*do, give, live, say, see*—and an alternative world of French-Latin words that mean about the same thing—*perform, present, inhabit, declare, observe.* Some big words have one or two syllables, but many have three or more. By contrast, plain words usually have just one or two syllables.

A good style needs both plain and big words. Good nonfiction stylists generally stay in the plain world with occasional raids into the big. But a steady diet of either can wear out the reader. Unless you're writing technical prose, try a ratio of about 75% plain, 25% big. Here's Mark Twain in Chapter XI of *Life on the Mississippi* (1883):

> Sometimes, in the big river, when we would be feeling our way cautiously along through a fog, the deep hush would suddenly be broken by yells and a clamor of tin pans, and all in an instant a log raft would appear vaguely through the webby veil, close upon us; and then we did not wait to swap knives, but snatched our engine bells out by the roots and piled on all the steam we had, to scramble out of the way! One doesn't hit a rock or solid log craft with a steamboat when he can get excused.

Of the 99 words, Twain uses just two words that have more than two syllables (and this paragraph is not unusual in the book). Seventeen of the words have two syllables; the remaining eighty have one.

Revision: Borges' story is puzzling to the extreme, pretending to be true and thus linear but inclining to chance journeys into the dream-like.

WARNING!

If you can't find a synonym for the big word, keep it. Here *linear* works better than a wordy "synonym" like *straightforward in its narrative line.*

STRATEGY 37. Don't use too many abstract and general words.

(1) Some things that concern students are life and love. (2) That car is awesome. (3) Dude, your dog is worthless.

Word choice problem: We can't connect to these sentences because the abstract and general words don't trigger emotions. Without specifics—the who, what, where, when, and why that personalize ideas—it's hard for the reader to care.

EDITING TIP

Abstract words present big concepts: *life, love, good, evil.* They're hard to picture. How do you picture *life, love, good, evil? General words* present vague pictures–*students, car, dog.* To picture them fully, we need specifics. *Which* students? *What* car? *Which* dog? Our writing needs abstract and general words, but it also needs concrete words—words that you picture, touch, smell, taste, hear; words that emotionally connect you to the writer.

1. **Limit abstract/general words to the start or end of a section. Use them to set up specifics:** *Life* sets up career → law → Native American law. **Or to wrap up specifics:** Native American law **returns to the general topic of** *life.*
2. **Work through a chain that ends with specifics:**
   things → aspects of future → choices to make → whether to marry
   car → 1930s vintage car → Cord → 1936 Cord 810 convertible coupe
   dog → Labrador retriever mix → young teething Labrador retriever mix
3. **Change nonaction verbs to action:** *is* worthless → *chewed up* my Doc Martens
4. **Use modifiers to specify abstract/general words:** *vintage car, teething Labrador mix*

Revisions: (1) Many law school students wonder whether they should practice corporate or community law and whether they should marry or remain single until they pay off their school loans. (2) That 1936 Cord 810 convertible coupe has been completely restored: the engine repaired, the interior reupholstered, and new faces silk-screened on the gauges. (3) Dude, your Lab mix puppy has started teething and just chewed up my Doc Martens.

STRATEGY 38. Don't use wrong word endings.

(1) Both musicologist study old-fashion music with cliché lyrics. (2) Roger Staubach's muchly celebrated 1975 Hail Mary pass is historical and will go down in the historic record. (3) She is quite prejudice about the matter and claims it's what we use to do, so I don't know what I'm suppose to do. (4) Anyways, this criteria is not at all clear.

Word choice problem: Most academic readers have a good grasp of word endings. To choose the wrong one opens up your writing to immediate criticism.

EDITING TIP

Wrong word endings fall into three groups:

1. *Dropped* **endings (given here with the corrected endings)**
   musicologists, old-fashioned music, clichéd lyrics, prejudiced, used to, supposed to
2. *Added* **endings**
   muchly, anyways
3. *Confused* **endings**
   historical/historic, criterion/criteria

Because grammar checks fail to catch many wrong endings, keep a list of the ones you regularly miss. (See **Chapter 18—Word Confusions**.)

Revisions: (1) Both musicologists study old-fashioned music with clichéd lyrics. (2) Roger Staubach's much-celebrated 1975 Hail Mary pass is historic and will go down in the historical record. (3) She is quite prejudiced about the matter and claims it's what we used to do, so I don't know what I'm supposed to do. (4) Anyway, this criterion is not at all clear [*Or* these criteria are not at all clear].

6. HOW TO BALANCE SENTENCE PARTS

STRATEGY 39. *Keep phrases parallel.*

(1) She had experience working as a server and she spent a year in the Peace Corps.) (2) For fun, he likes to surf the Internet, to play video games, and riding his bicycle around the lake. (3) It is neither a good movie nor do they handle the history accurately. (4) Kelly managed to learn French and he can get along in Spanish. (5) She was told either to shape up or she would be shipping out. (6) Frank was not only tall, but he also weighed very little.

Parallel phrase problem: Sentences like parallel sequences: *two-part* like apple and apple; *three-part* like apple, apple, and apple. Mixing fruit upsets the balance—apple and orange *Or* apple, apple, and orange.

EDITING TIP

Two ways to spot *two-part* or *three-part* sequences:

1. They often come at the sentence end: **X and Y** *Or* **X, Y, and Z.**
2. Two-part sequences often use formulas that set up the parallel:

   X as well as Y (tall as well as thin)

   X rather than Y (tall rather than thin)

   either . . . or . . . (either tall or thin)

   neither . . . nor . . . (neither tall nor thin)

   when [because, since, etc.] . . . not when [because, since, etc.] (when tall, not when thin)

   whether . . . or . . . (whether tall or thin)

   both . . . and . . . (both tall and thin)

   that [who, which, etc.] . . . and/but that [who, which, etc.] . . . (who is tall but who is thin)

   not only [just, simply, merely] . . . but also . . . (not only tall but also thin)

   not only [just, simply, merely] . . . but . . . (not only tall but seven feet high)

(See **Strategy 23** on when to cut *also* in not *only/but* also.)

EDITING TIP, *continued*

Three ways to make phrases parallel:

1. **Find a sequence of two, three, or more items.**
2. **Pick a key parallel word or phrase to set up the parallel.**
3. **Don't mix apples and oranges. Make all the items apples (or oranges).**

spending a year in the Peace Corps.
She had experience working as a server and ~~also she spent a year in the Peace Corps~~.   ^

to ride
For fun, he likes to surf the Internet, to play video games, and ~~riding~~ his bicycle around the lake.   ^

(For parallels with conjunctions, see **Easy Grammar, Conjunctions: 2. Sentence Parts That Aren't Parallel**)

Revisions: (1) She had experience working as a server and spending a year in the Peace Corps. (2) For fun, he likes to surf the Internet, to play video games, and to ride his bicycle around the lake. (3) It is neither a good movie nor an accurate history. (4) Kelly managed to learn both French and intermediate Spanish. (5) She was told either to shape up or to ship out. (6) Frank was not only tall but thin.

WARNING!

Remember to use parallel forms with both vertical *and* horizontal lists.

STRATEGY 40. Complete two-part parallels.

(1) He's so rich. (2) Jake's temperature is lower than Tiffany. (3) Many people of New Mexico are Latino like Texas.

Complete parallel phrase problem: These sentences share the same illogic. The first half of the sentence doesn't parallel the second half.

EDITING TIP

1. **So often sets up a *so/that* parallel the writer fails to complete.** *He's so rich . . . So rich that what?* **If so sets up a parallel, complete it:**

   He's so rich that he can spend a million dollars without thinking about it.

   She was so talented that she won first place.

   Remember: In a *so/that* parallel, you can leave out *that*, but a comma must replace it:

   He's so rich, he can spend a million dollars without thinking about it.

   She was so talented, she won first place.

2. **A two-part parallel can't compare an apple to an orange. To complete a two-part parallel, compare *like* to *like*—apple to apple, orange to orange:**

   Jake's temperature = apple; Tiffany = orange

   Many people of New Mexico = apple; Texas = orange

   Jake's temperature = Tiffany's temperature

   Many people of New Mexico = many people of Texas

Revisions: (1) He's so rich that he can spend a million dollars without thinking about it. (2) Jake's temperature is lower than Tiffany's. (3) Many people of New Mexico are Latino like many people of Texas.

STRATEGY 41. *Don't mismatch verb tense, voice, and mood.*

(1) Michael wrote a novel, published it at twenty, and soon after starts script writing in Hollywood. (2) Josh hit the ball, and it was fielded by Dwayne. (3) Lola called a cab before she left for the airport.

Mismatched verb problem: In sentences (1) and (2), apples need to go with apples. In sentence (3), an apple needs to go with an orange—not an apple.

EDITING TIP

1. **Present tense goes with present, past with past, and future with future. (orange with orange)**

            started **(all three verbs now in past tense)**
   wrote, published, ~~starts~~
         ∧

2. **Active voice goes with active, passive with passive. (orange with orange)**

            Dwayne fielded it. **(both verbs now active)**
   Josh hit the ball, and ~~it was fielded by Dwayne~~.
         ∧

   The ball was hit by Josh, and it was fielded by Dwayne. **(both verbs now passive)**

3. **An exception to 1: In the past, if one verb action takes place *before* another verb action, add *had* (*has* or *have*). (apple with orange)**

      had   (had called = *past perfect*; left = *simple past*)
   Lola called a cab before she left for the airport.
    ∧

(On mismatched verb problems, see **Easy Grammar: Verbs, 3. Tenses.**)

Revisions: (1) Michael wrote a novel, published it at twenty, and soon after started script writing in Hollywood. (2) Josh hit the ball, and Dwayne fielded it. (3) Lola had called a cab before she left for the airport.

STRATEGY 42. Use a short-to-long cadence.

(1) I'm not sure if I want to buy a Magnavox or a SONY. (2) Bronwyn saw the rough-and-tumble, cheerful child. (3) Christina decorated her apartment with colorful Oriental and Native American rugs, wicker furniture, and a number of flowering plants. (4) Joey hopes to buy a dachshund, a Burmese cat, and a German shepherd.

Short-to-long cadencing problem: Each sentence violates a natural short-to-long cadence, going from long to short (1, 2) or mixing phrases (3, 4).

EDITING TIP

Cadence refers to the rhythm and order of words in a sentence. Just like a musical cadence, verbal cadence tends to lengthen as it approaches the end—of a sentence, paragraph, or a project's final sentence. A cadence can be dramatic, effective, and conclusive. It provides a natural balance to the rest of the sentence, a way to end that's as memorable as a bold opening.

Order words and phrases from short-to-long—that is, by the number of syllables in each item:

      Magnavox (3 syllables), SONY (2) = SONY (2), Magnavox (3)

      rough-and-tumble (4), cheerful (2) = cheerful (2), rough-and-tumble (4)

      colorful Oriental and Native American rugs (15), wicker furniture (5), a number of flowering plants (8) = wicker furniture (5), a number of flowering plants (8), and colorful Oriental and Native American rugs (15)

      a dachshund (3), a Burmese cat (4), a German shepherd (5) = a Burmese cat (4), a dachshund (3), a German shepherd (5)

WARNING!

When a series mixes categories (*cats and dogs*), **group similar elements even if grouping violates short-to-long cadence: cat (4) + dog (3) + dog (5). Likewise, if short-to-long cadence violates convention** (*Bach, Beethoven, and Brahms; red, white, and blue*), **stick with convention** (not *Bach, Brahms, and Beethoven* or *red, blue, and white*).

Revisions: (1) I'm not sure if I want to buy a SONY or a Magnavox. (2) Bronwyn saw the cheerful, rough-and-tumble child. (3) Christina decorated her apartment with wicker furniture, a number of flowering plants, and colorful Oriental and Native American rugs. (4) Joey hopes to buy a Burmese cat, a dachshund, and a German shepherd.

7. HOW TO REPEAT WORDS

STRATEGY 43. Repeat key words.

A pump is a tool for lifting or transferring liquids or gases by pressure or suction. This extractor-transporter operates by physical or mechanical means. There are three groups of such mechanisms: direct lift, displacement, and gravity devices.

Repetition problem: We're confused by the synonyms; new material should repeat key words to reduce the reader's workload.

EDITING TIP

Repeat *key* words—the words that identify or explain your main idea. But don't repeat *unimportant* words—the words that play no major role in main ideas. Repeat key words:

1. **To help the reader process new or technical information. The repetition functions as an *old* idea (see Strategy 4) by orienting the reader with the familiar.**
2. **To hook sentences and paragraphs to other sentences and paragraphs. The repetition functions as a *key-word transition*. (See Strategy 44, below.)**

Revision: A pump is a tool for lifting or transferring liquids or gases by pressure or suction. A pump operates by physical or mechanical means. There are three groups of pumps: direct lift, displacement, and gravity pumps.

WARNING!

Many writers fear repeating words because of an old "rule": *Don't repeat words; use the thesaurus.* **Wrong. Key-word repetition is a powerful strategy to create flow and unity. A thesaurus can lead to comic results, like inaccurately replacing** *red* **with** *carmine, russet, crimson,* **and** *vermilion.* **Use the thesaurus only when you're looking for a precise word—not when you're concerned about repetition.**

STRATEGY 44. Repeat transition words.

(1) *Star Trek* fans go to conventions costumed as favorite characters. Their <u>dress</u> aims at over-the-top effects. (2) Mr. Ramirez decided to examine his plants for aphids. <u>This</u> didn't please Mrs. Ramirez, who wanted to catch the matinee of *Les Misérables*. (3) The cook stumbled on the old rubber mat and, trying to stop his fall, seared his palm on the flat grill, an accident waiting to happen.

<u>Because of potential dangers</u>, this restaurant needs to replace worn-out equipment.

Repetition problem: These pairs of sentences miss good transition opportunities. The second sentence in each pair should repeat a key (theme) word from the first sentence.

EDITING TIP

Three transitions hook sentences and paragraphs; they can also unify sentences and paragraphs:

1. *Key-word transition.* **Repeat key words from sentence to sentence, paragraph to paragraph:** *costumed → costumes*

2. *Padded-verb transition.* **Use a key verb in one sentence; repeat the padded version of it in another sentence:** *decided → decision*

3. *Parallel word-and-phrase transition.* **Repeat key phrases to hook one paragraph to another:** *accident waiting to happen → other accidents waiting to happen*

Revisions: (1) *Star Trek* fans go to conventions costumed as favorite

characters. Their costumes aim at over-the-top effects. (2) Mr. Ramirez

decided to examine his plants for aphids. This decision didn't please Mrs. Ramirez, who wanted to catch the matinee of *Les Misérables*. (3) The cook stumbled on the old rubber mat and, trying to stop his fall, seared his palm on the flat grill, an accident waiting to happen.

Because of other accidents waiting to happen, this restaurant needs to replace worn-out equipment.

STRATEGY 45. Don't repeat unimportant words.

To adjust the temperature to individual requirements, turn the temperature **control dial** clockwise to increase the desired individual temperature and counter-clockwise to decrease the desired individual temperature. To activate the temperature **control dial**, use the temperature **control dial** only when the O/I switches are in the ON temperature position.

Repetition problem: Aiming for precision, the writer unleashes a string of repetitions that fog rather than clear the directions.

EDITING TIP

Repeat a word to:

1. **Make new material easier to understand, using key (theme) words.**
2. **Hook sentences and paragraphs.**
3. **Unify sentences and paragraphs.**

But don't repeat a word to:

1. **Repeat it for no reason (that is, when the word isn't a key word).**
2. **End two phrases or sentences with the same last word (and create an unintentional echo. (See Strategy 47, Don't repeat monotonous word echoes.)**

To cut unimportant words, follow three steps:

1. **Cut as many unimportant repetitions as possible.**
2. **Replace repetitions with synonyms** (temperature = heat).
3. **Replace repetitions with pronouns** (temperature = it).

To adjust the temperature ~~to individual requirements~~, turn the

heat
~~temperature~~ control dial clockwise to increase the ~~desired individual~~
                                                      ∧

it
~~temperature~~ and counter-clockwise to decrease ~~the desired~~
                                                  ∧

~~individual temperature. To activate the temperature control dial.~~ Use the ~~temperature control~~ dial only when the O/I switches are ~~in the~~ ON ~~temperature position.~~

Note: Repeat *dial* **as a key word**.

Revision: To adjust the temperature, turn the control dial clockwise to increase the heat and counter-clockwise to decrease it. Use the dial only when the O/I switches are ON.

STRATEGY 46. Don't repeat monotonous sentence words, patterns, and lengths.

(1) The cat had myriad toys to play with. These toys came from a myriad of pet stores. (2) After eating his food, <u>the cat—a Siamese—ran around the house</u>. Before taking a nap, <u>he—the Siamese cat—washed himself</u>. Following the cat's nap, <u>Kenneth—the cat's companion—took a catnap himself</u>. (3) <u>Kenneth drove to the store</u>. <u>He bought some cat food</u>. <u>Then he drove back home</u>. <u>Then he fed the cat</u>. <u>The cat ate all his food</u>.

Repetition problem: These sentences put us to sleep because of their monotony—monotonous *words* (myriad, myriad), *patterns* (each beginning with a fragment followed by a small sentence with dashes), and *lengths* (each five words long).

EDITING TIP

Monotony takes place when sentences:

1. **Repeat an unimportant word (rather than a key word or transition).**
2. **Repeat the same pattern (same beginning, middle, or end).**
3. **Repeat the same length.**

To avoid monotonous words:

1. **Don't repeat unimportant words.**
2. **Don't use all plain words or all big words. Unless you're writing technical prose, use about 75% plain and 25% big. (See Strategy 36.)**

To avoid monotonous patterns, try a variety of sentence beginnings. (For definitions of each grammar term below, see the **Glossary of Terms**.)

- *Subject-verb:* <u>Kenneth drove</u> to the store.
- *Common transition:* <u>Therefore</u>, Kenneth drove to the store.
- *Adverb:* <u>Obviously</u>, Kenneth drove to the store.
- *Adverb phrase:* <u>Because of his cat</u>, Kenneth drove to the store.
- *Adjective:* <u>Happy</u>, the cat purred loudly.
- *Adjective phrase:* <u>Happy with his treats</u>, the cat purred loudly.
- *Present participle:* <u>Purring loudly</u>, the cat climbed onto Kenneth's lap.
- *Past participle:* <u>Purred out</u>, the cat fell asleep.

- *Prepositional phrase*: <u>Among cats</u>, Kenneth's cat was one of the hungriest.
- *Infinitive phrase*: <u>To keep his cat happy</u>, Kenneth bought expensive food.
- *Absolute phrase*: <u>Mice running rampant</u>, the cat continued to sleep.
- *Direct object*: <u>His tasty treats</u> this cat liked more than mice or Kenneth.
- *Appositive*: <u>A frequent napper</u>, this cat ignored all the mice.

To avoid monotonous sentences, use a variety of sentence lengths for dramatic effect. (These lengths are only approximates.)

1. **Very short** (three to five words)
2. **Short** (five to fifteen words)
3. **Medium** (fifteen to thirty words)
4. **Long** (thirty to fifty words)
5. **Very long** (fifty or more words)

EDITING TIP

Think of a paragraph like a piece of music. Vary the words, patterns, and lengths. Few writers are more musical than Thoreau. In *Walden* (1854), he often writes short-long-short paragraphs.

He begins with a very short or short sentence; then he alternates medium, long, and very long sentences; finally he ends with a short or very short sentence. Thoreau can make a paragraph swell with melody that lengthens and crescendos to sustained chords that end with a short, sharp cymbal crash.

[**Sentence 1–*5 words*:**] Then to my morning work. [**Sentence 2–*19 words*:**] First I take an axe and pail and go in search of water, if that be not a dream. [**Sentence 3–*13 words*:**] After a cold and snowy night it needed a divining-rod to find it. [**Sentence 4–*66 words*:**] Every winter the liquid and trembling surface of the pond, which was so sensitive to every breath, and reflected every light and shadow, becomes solid to the depth of a foot or a foot and a half, so that it will support the heaviest teams, and perchance the snow covers it to an equal depth, and it is not to be distinguished from any level field. [**Sentence 5–*19 words*:**] Like the marmots in the surrounding hills, it closes its eyelids and becomes dormant for three months or more. [**Sentence 6–*94 words*:**] Standing on the snow-covered plain, as if in a pasture amid the hills, I cut my way first through a foot of snow, and then through a foot of ice, and open a window under my feet, where, kneeling to drink, I look down into the quiet parlor of the fishes, pervaded by a softened light as through a window of ground glass, with its bright sanded floor the same as in summer; there a perennial waveless serenity reigns as in the amber twilight sky, corresponding to the cool and even temperament of the inhabitants. [**Sentence 7–*11 words*:**] Heaven is under our feet as well as over our heads.

> # EDITING TIP, *continued*
>
> Statistics on the paragraph's seven sentences:
>
> 1. **Total word count** = 227 words. Of these, only 15 (7%) have three or more syllables.
> 2. **Sentence patterns** = 1 is a fragment; 2, 4, and 7 begin with subject-verb; 3, 5, and 6 begin with fragments. The sentences alternate kinds of beginnings.
> 3. **Sentence lengths in word counts** = 5, 19, 13, 66, 19, 94, 11. The paragraph follows this variety: very short/medium/short/very long/medium/very long/short.
>
> Traveling in a circle—from a very short sentence, through lengthened middle sentences, then to a short sentence—gives the paragraph symmetry, wholeness, and a great deal of variety.

Revisions: (1) The cat had myriad toys to play with from many pet stores. (2) After eating his food, the cat—a Siamese—ran around the house. Then he washed himself and napped. Kenneth, the cat's companion, also took a catnap. (3) Kenneth drove to the store, bought some cat food, then drove back home. Happy with his food, the cat ate all of it.

STRATEGY 47. Don't repeat monotonous word echoes.

The commission hasn't yet articulated or communicated the issues we strategized and prioritized concerning our determination that there should be a termination of the commission's policy and personnel participation. It is our current judgment that an assessment should be undertaken of management-commission involvement. We also need to assess ourselves vis-à-vis said involvement.

Repetition problem: Both sentences sound ugly because of careless repetitions—of consonants (especially c, p, t), of vowels (articulated, communicated, determination, termination), of endings (commission, determination, termination, participation; strategized, prioritized; judgment, assessment); and of final sentence words (involvement, involvement).

> # EDITING TIP
>
> Words that come from other languages often have three or more syllables and endings like *-ate, -ize, -ment, -sion, -tion*. Padding verbs leads to padded nouns with those monotonous endings: *develop = development; terminate = termination; participate = participation.*
>
> Always try to replace needless big words with plain words: *Less is more.* As you replace big with plain, many of the repetition problems will disappear.
>
> However, one repetition problem that shows up even in plain style is the repeated final word: *Avoid ending two nearby phrases or sentences with the same word.*

Revision: The commission hasn't yet spoken about the main issues we studied: We want it to end its work in policy and personnel. We must assess both our and management's involvement in the commission.

Punctuation Rules

THE APOSTROPHE '

The apostrophe has three uses:

1. **To show possession**
2. **To replace letters**
3. **To form nonstandard plurals**

> ## PUNCTUATION TIP
>
> No other punctuation mark faces as much abuse as the apostrophe. The first problem is failing to use it (thus we see *Walgreens* instead of *Walgreen's*). The second problem is, ironically, using it in words where it doesn't belong *(Open Monday's)*.

To show possession

1. **Use the apostrophe to show possession.**

To know where to place the apostrophe, say the word. Where the word stops, add the apostrophe: the cat—the cat's dish; the cats—the cats' dish.

> Karl's book; both Karls' books (two men named Karl)
>
> everybody's response; someone else's car
>
> city's lights; cities' lights; baby's crib; babies' cribs
>
> the man's hat; the men's hats
>
> the woman's computer; the women's computer
>
> bachelor's degree; master's degree
>
> Paul Smith's house; the Smiths' house
>
> Katie said, "Aren't they at the Smiths'?"
>
> Roger and Bill's book (the one book belongs to both Roger and Bill)
>
> Roger's and Bill's books (each owns a book)
>
> Jean-Luc's singing is enjoyable, and so is Linda's whistling (possessive apostrophe needed for the gerund: a noun that comes from a verb and ends in *-ing*)
>
> the hostess's party; the hostesses' parties
>
> Mrs. Phillips's cell phone

If adding an extra syllable makes the word hard to pronounce, add only the apostrophe.

Mrs. Phillips' cell phone
Athens' famous sights
for goodness' sake

WARNING!

Don't use the apostrophe with seven possessive pronouns: *yours, his, hers, ours, theirs, its* **(versus the contraction** *it's = it is* **or** *it has*)**, and** *whose* **(versus the contraction** *who's = who is* **or** *who has*)**.**

This book is yours; the car is his or hers; the job is ours; the job is theirs. Its color is green. (It's raining outside; it's been raining all afternoon.) Whose responsibility is this? (Who's going to volunteer? Who's volunteered before?)

To replace letters

2. **Use the apostrophe to replace letters.**

it's = it is or it has
shouldn't = should not
they're = they are
the class of '91 = the class of 1991
'til = until
Hallowe'en = Halloween

To form nonstandard plurals

3. **Use the apostrophe to form nonstandard plurals: for letters, numbers used as words, words cited as words, abbreviations, and symbols.**
   CAPITAL LETTERS: Watch your P's and Q's. A's win the pennant.
   LOWERCASE LETTERS: Watch your p's and q's.
   NUMBERS USED AS WORDS: He crosses his 7's. (= sevens)
   He often talks about the 1980's. (= nineteen eighties)
   WORDS CITED AS WORDS: Please practice pronouncing your the's.
   ABBREVIATIONS: The professors all have Ph.D.'s.
   SYMBOLS: I saw +'s and -'s in the grade book.

For this third use, leave out the apostrophe if there's no danger of confusion:

>Watch your Ps and Qs.
>He crosses his 7s.
>He talks often about the 1980s.
>The professors all have Ph.D.s.
>can'ts, don'ts, won'ts
>ifs, ands, or buts; ins and outs

But with confusion, use the apostrophe:

>As win the pennant! (confusion with *As*)
>>A's win the pennant.
>Watch your ps and qs. (confusion with a misprint)
>>Watch your p's and q's.
>Please practice pronouncing your thes. (confusion with a misprint)
>>Please practice pronouncing your the's.
>I saw +s and -s in the grade book (confusion if symbols unclear)
>>I saw +'s and -'s in the grade book.

WARNING!

Remember that most words don't use the apostrophe to form plurals.

WRONG	RIGHT
mens shoe's	men's shoes
open Sunday's	open Sundays
seven month's of the year	seven months of the year

BRACKETS [ ]

Brackets have two uses:

1. **To show an insertion within parentheses**
2. **To show an editor's insertion into a text**

To show an insertion within parentheses

1. **Use brackets to show "parentheses" within parentheses.**

    My friend George Washington (who is not *that* George Washington [the Father of Our Country]) often gets teased about his famous name.

To show an editor's insertion into a text

2. **Use brackets to show that you as editor are supplying missing words or identifying a mistake in the original text.**

    He wrote, "I'll see you at Tom's [cabin]."

    (To clarify, the editor supplies a missing word.)

    "The defendant [Lloyd Turner] was charged with a felony (though later acquitted)."

    (The editor uses brackets and not parentheses for new insertions. In the original text, the writer showed his insertion with parentheses; in the edited text, the editor shows her new insertion with brackets.)

    "We reached our destanation [*sic*] after many wrong detours."

    (By using the Latin word *sic*, the editor identifies a mistake in the original text—"destanation" should be spelled "destination." The Latin sic means *thus: Thus it was written in the original and is not the editor's mistake.* In this case, the editor chooses not to correct the mistake but to signal to the reader that the original text erred.)

    "World War II ended in 1947 [*sic*]."

    (The editor identifies the writer's mistake: World War II ended in 1945, not 1947.)

THE COLON :

The colon has two uses:

1. **To set up material**
2. **To separate a bigger part from a smaller part**

To set up material

1. **Use the colon to set up a list within a sentence.**

    I visited four cities: Omaha, Denver, Salt Lake City, and Dallas.

2. **Use the colon to set up a list in a column.**

    The company needs to focus on four Asian markets:

    China

    Japan

    South Korea

    Thailand

3. **Use the colon to set up an important idea.**

Martin Luther King, Jr., changed the face of America: He spearheaded the modern Civil Rights movement.

Beatriz has a single joy in life: music.

PUNCTUATION TIP

Writers tend to forget the colon. Like the semicolon, the colon gives writing efficiency and professionalism.

For example, it can serve as a space-saving transition to set up an important idea (see **Colon 3**, above). Here, replacing *therefore* with the colon saves a word.

> **WITH TRANSITION WORD:** *Teddy Roosevelt was a keen environmentalist. Therefore, he worked hard to establish a system of national parks.*

> **WITH COLON:** *Teddy Roosevelt was a keen environmentalist: He worked hard to establish a system of national parks.*

---

4. **Use the colon to set up a well-known or long quotation.**

Hamlet said: "To be or not to be."

PUNCTUATION TIP

The comma can also work in the previous sentence, but the colon establishes the fame or seriousness of the quotation.

---

5. **Use the colon to set up a quotation not introduced by a verb (*said, declared, stated*, etc.).**

Many Americans recall a line from John F. Kennedy's most famous speech: "And so, my fellow Americans, ask not what your country can do for you; ask what you can do for your country."

6. **Use the colon to start (to set up) a formal letter.**

Dear Dr. Smith:

Ladies and Gentlemen:

7. **Use the colon to punctuate headers in memos.**

To:

From:

Re:

To separate a bigger part from a smaller part

8. **Use the colon in time references, scriptural references, citation references, and subtitles.**

   3:47 p.m. (separating hour from minute)

   Leviticus 7:14 (separating Bible chapter from verse)

   Boston, MA: Harvard University Press (in APA citation format, separating state abbreviation from publisher)

   Pip's Journey from Snobbery to Salvation: Magwitch and the Lessons of Love in *Great Expectations* (separating title from subtitle)

WARNING!

Be careful with the colon in the next FOUR situations.

---

1. **Do not use the colon AFTER *such as* and *like*.**

   WRONG: He listened to many classical composers, such as: Bach and Brahms.

   RIGHT: He listened to many classical composers, such as Bach and Brahms.

   WRONG: He listened to many classical composers, like: Bach and Brahms.

   RIGHT: He listened to many classical composers, like Bach and Brahms.

2. **Ordinarily, do not use the colon AFTER a <u>verb of being</u> (*am, are, is, were, was, will be*, etc.) or AFTER a <u>preposition</u> (*in, of, by, at*, etc.).**

   WRONG: His favorite foods <u>are</u>: steak and potatoes

   RIGHT: His favorite foods are steak and potatoes.

   WRONG: I want to major <u>in</u>: music and history.

   RIGHT: I want to major in music and history.

   WRONG: The recipe primarily consisted <u>of</u>: zucchini and Indian spices.

   RIGHT: The recipe primarily consisted of zucchini and Indian spices.

   WRONG: The book is <u>by</u>: James McKinley, and it's available <u>at</u>: the bookstore.

   RIGHT: The book is by James McKinley, and it's available at the bookstore.

3. **Do not use the colon INSIDE quotation marks and parentheses.**

   WRONG: Here's why you should read Hemingway's "Soldier's Home:" It dramatizes the pressures that cause us to conform.

   RIGHT: Here's why you should read Hemingway's "Soldier's Home": It dramatizes the pressures that cause us to conform.

WRONG: Here's why you should read Hemingway's best story ("Soldier's Home";) It dramatizes the pressures that cause us to conform.

RIGHT: Here's why you should read Hemingway's best story ("Soldier's Home"): It dramatizes the pressures that cause us to conform.

4. **Capitalize AFTER a colon if a <u>complete sentence</u> follows. Don't capitalize if a fragment follows**.

   COMPLETE SENTENCE: Here's why you should read Hemingway's "Soldier's Home": <u>It dramatizes the pressures that cause us to conform.</u>

   FRAGMENT: Here's what you'll find in Hemingway's "Soldier's Home": a masterly dramatization of the pressures that cause us to conform.

THE COMMA ,

The comma has three uses:

1. **To separate a fragment from the main part of a sentence**
2. **To separate equal sentences or equal sentence parts**
3. **To replace words**

PUNCTUATION TIP

In order, the three most common comma errors are (1) forgetting to use the comma AFTER an introductory fragment, (2) forgetting to use the comma BEFORE a coordinating conjunction to separate two complete sentences, and (3) mistakenly putting a comma between two complete sentences and thus creating a run-on (see **Semicolon 1**, page 420).

To separate a fragment from the main part of a sentence

1. **Use the comma AFTER an <u>introductory fragment</u> to separate it from the main part of a sentence.**

   WRONG: <u>Yes</u> I have many concerns about the merger.

   RIGHT: <u>Yes,</u> I have many concerns about the merger.

   WRONG: <u>After the party fizzled out</u> we walked home.

   RIGHT: <u>After the party fizzled out,</u> we walked home.

2. **Use the comma for a nonessential interrupting fragment to separate it from the main part of a sentence. (An "interrupting fragment" is a fragment inserted into the middle of a sentence. See the following for a discussion of "nonessential" and "essential.")**

Nonessential interrupter

SENTENCE: My father became a Marine.

INTERRUPTING FRAGMENT: who is older than his sister

SENTENCE WITH INTERRUPTING FRAGMENT: My father who is older than his sister became a Marine.

NONESSENTIAL OR ESSENTIAL? If it's nonessential, use commas; if it's essential, don't use commas.

TEST FOR COMMAS: Can you identify the <u>subject</u> (who the father is) by leaving out the interrupting fragment?

ANSWER: Yes. The interrupting fragment offers interesting information, but it's not essential to identifying the subject since we have "my" and only one father.

RULE: If you *don't* need the interrupting fragment to identify the subject, it's nonessential. Therefore, use commas.

THUS: My father, who is older than his sister, became a Marine.

My <u>father</u>, Tom, became a Marine.

(Into *My father became a Marine* insert the interrupting fragment that renames the <u>subject</u>. Since we know it's "*my* father," the fragment is nonessential. Use commas for this nonessential called an "appositive." See **Comma 8**, page 391.)

My brother, likewise, became a Marine.

(Into *My brother became a Marine* insert the interrupting fragment *likewise*; because it's nonessential, use commas.)

My daily schedule, if all goes well, will include an hour at the gym.

(Into *My daily schedule will include an hour at the gym* insert the interrupting fragment *if all goes well*; because it's nonessential, use commas.)

All through the night, because of financial worries, I kept waking up.

(Into *All through the night, I kept waking up* insert the interrupting fragment *because of financial worries*; because it's nonessential, use commas.)

Essential interrupting fragment

SENTENCE: The man is tall.

INTERRUPTING FRAGMENT: who called me last night

SENTENCE WITH INTERRUPTING FRAGMENT: The man who called me last night is tall.

ESSENTIAL OR NONESSENTIAL? If it's essential, don't use commas; if it's nonessential, use commas.

TEST FOR COMMAS: Can you identify the <u>subject</u> (which man you're talking about) by leaving out the interrupting fragment? *The <u>man</u> is tall.*

ANSWER: No. "The man" doesn't identify *which* man is tall. Many men are tall. You need the interrupting fragment **who called me last night** to distinguish this man from all other men.

RULE: If you *need* the interrupting fragment to identify the subject, it's essential. Therefore, don't use commas.

THUS: The man who called me last night is tall.

3. **Use the comma to separate a nonessential final fragment from the main part of a sentence.**

   I saw my brother Tom, who became a Marine.

   (Since the direct object, Tom, is identified, the final fragment is nonessential and requires a comma. Compare to *I saw my brother who became a Marine*. With just one brother, the fragment isn't needed. *I saw my brother, who became a Marine*. With more than one brother, the fragment is needed to distinguish *this* brother from other brothers—and thus the comma isn't used: *I saw my brother who became a Marine*.)

4. **Use the comma to separate a nonessential fragment introduced by *which* from the main part of a sentence.**

PUNCTUATION TIP

Each sentence that follows has a specific, identified subject.

The attic front window, which I must replace, was broken in the hailstorm.

   (Just one attic front window = *which*.)

The White House, which I visited last year, opens its doors to tourists.

   (Just one White House = *which*.)

The Pacific Ocean, which the sailor crossed on a raft, is full of treacherous currents.

   (Just one Pacific Ocean = *which*.)

WARNING!

When you have more than one of something, use *that* without a comma to introduce an essential fragment—a fragment identifying the subject and equal in importance to the main part of the sentence.

The window that was broken in the storm needs to be replaced.

   (*Which* window? One of many—the one that was broken in the storm.)

The house that I visited last year opens its doors to tourists.

   (*Which* house? One of many—the one that I visited last year.)

The ocean that the sailor crossed on a raft is full of treacherous currents.

   (*Which* ocean? One of many—the one that the sailor crossed on a raft.)

To separate equal sentences or equal sentence parts

5. **Use the comma BEFORE the coordinating conjunctions *for, <u>a</u>nd, <u>n</u>or, <u>b</u>ut, <u>o</u>r, <u>y</u>et, <u>s</u>o* (the FAN-BOYS) to separate <u>equal sentences</u>. (They're equal because they're both complete sentences, or independent clauses.)**

   <u>I prepared my taxes in a hurry</u>, for <u>tomorrow was the April 15 deadline.</u>

   <u>I prepared my taxes in a hurry</u>, and <u>I had done the same thing the year before.</u>

   <u>I prepared my taxes</u>, but <u>I put the task off until the last day.</u>

   <u>I prepared my taxes in a hurry</u>, so <u>I hoped that I hadn't made a mistake.</u>

6. **Use the comma to separate *three* or more equal items in a <u>series</u>; last comma = optional.**

   George Clooney is <u>tall, dark(,) and handsome.</u>

7. **Use the comma to separate <u>adjectives</u> that equally describe the same noun.**

   I saw the <u>tired, old</u> man.

   (I saw the <u>old, tired</u> man.)

   # PUNCTUATION TIP

   To test for the comma, try inverting the adjectives. If you can't invert them, they're not equal. Don't use the comma.

   > I saw the <u>old stone</u> fence.

   (The inversion, "<u>stone old</u>," makes no sense because "old" and "stone" don't equally describe "fence.")

   ---

8. **Use the comma to separate an <u>appositive</u> from the noun it renames. (An "appositive" is a word or phrase renaming a *one-of-a-kind* noun that it follows. The appositive is equal to the noun and is a "nonessential interrupting fragment." See Comma 2, page 387.)**

   My wife, <u>Carol</u>, tracks the flight of whooping cranes.

   > (Since you have just *one* wife, she is a *one-of-a-kind* noun. Use commas to set off the appositive that renames it, Carol.)

   My brother, <u>Tom</u>, joined the Marines.

   > (If you have just one brother, use commas. For more than one brother, don't use commas: *My brother Tom joined the Marines, but my brother Joe joined the Air Force.*)

   Jimmy Carter, <u>one of our ex-Presidents</u>, has written a novel.

   > (Since there is just one Jimmy Carter who is an ex-President, use commas.)

9. **Use the comma to separate a final <u>question</u> from the rest of a sentence.**

   It's supposed to rain, <u>isn't it?</u>

   > (The question serves as a balance, equal to the first part of the sentence.)

   You're not really going, <u>are you?</u>

10. **Use the comma to separate <u>balanced, equal phrases</u>.**

    <u>The less</u> I know, <u>the better</u>.

    <u>garbage in</u>, <u>garbage out</u>

    <u>the more</u>, <u>the merrier</u>

    <u>first come</u>, <u>first served</u>

    I like <u>his politics</u>, not <u>his personality</u>.

11. **Use the comma to separate equal items in dates, addresses, geographical sites, and numbers.**

    WRONG: September 11, 2001 is an important date.

    RIGHT: September 11, 2001, is an important date.

    BUT: I will contact him in June 2012 in Chicago. (Don't use the comma with just month and year.)

    WRONG: He lives at 3925 East Johnson, Madison, Wisconsin, 53704. (Never separate state from zip code with the comma.)

    RIGHT: He lives at 3925 East Johnson, Madison, Wisconsin 53704.

    WRONG: I drove to New York, New York and then flew to London, England before taking the train to Paris.

    RIGHT: I drove to New York, New York, and then flew to London, England, before taking the train to Paris.

    WRONG: Please make sure that 6000545 is the correct population.

    RIGHT: Please make sure that 6,000,545 is the correct population.

To replace words

12. **Use the comma to replace <u>words left out</u> of the second half of a parallel sentence.**

    He likes comedies; his wife, dramas.

    (He likes comedies; his wife <u>likes</u> dramas.)

    Americans prefer football; Europeans, soccer.

    (Americans prefer football; Europeans <u>prefer</u> soccer.)

13. **Use the comma to replace *that*.**

    The problem is, Bob can't sing tonight.

    (The problem is that Bob can't sing tonight.)

    Odds are, you won't pass the course if you don't study.

    (Odds are that you won't pass the course if you don't study.)

> # WARNING!
> **Avoid the following TEN comma errors.**

1. **Don't use the comma (or nothing at all) between <u>two complete sentences</u>; you'll cause a run-on.**

   WRONG: <u>I drove to work, I parked my car in the underground garage.</u>

   (**WRONG:** <u>I drove to work I parked my car in the underground garage.</u>)

   RIGHT: I drove to work. I parked my car in the underground garage.

   RIGHT: I drove to work; I parked my car in the underground garage.

   RIGHT: I drove to work, and I parked my car in the underground garage.

PUNCTUATION TIP

A *run-on* is defined by faulty punctuation, not by the length of the sentence. Two problems cause the run-on: (1) Putting a comma between two complete sentences instead of a period, semicolon, or comma plus conjunction. (2) Leaving out *all* punctuation between two complete sentences.

---

2. **Don't use the comma BEFORE a <u>coordinating conjunction</u> if a fragment follows the conjunction.**

   WRONG: Nedra bought groceries, <u>and</u> then gas.

   RIGHT: Nedra bought groceries and then gas.

   WRONG: The girl plays the piano, <u>and</u> sings in the choir.

   RIGHT: The girl plays piano and sings in the choir.

   (**BUT:** The girl plays the piano, <u>and</u> she sings in the choir. See **Comma 5,** page 390.)

3. **Don't use the comma AFTER a <u>coordinating conjunction</u> in sentences like the following.**

   WRONG: <u>But,</u> I think you're wrong about the movie.

   RIGHT: But I think you're wrong about the movie.

   WRONG: <u>And,</u> that's just the beginning of the story.

   RIGHT: And that's just the beginning of the story.

4. **Don't use the comma AFTER *though, although*, and *even although* in sentences like the following.**

   WRONG: Though, your plan has merit, please refigure the budget.

   RIGHT: Though your plan has merit, please refigure the budget.

   WRONG: Brian plans to open a restaurant although, many say he won't succeed.

   RIGHT: Brian plans to open a restaurant although many say he won't succeed.

5. **Don't use the comma AFTER *such as, especially*, or *also* in sentences like the following.**

   WRONG: He visited many famous parks, such as, Yosemite and Glacier.

   RIGHT: He visited many famous parks, such as Yosemite and Glacier.

   WRONG: He liked to visit famous parks, especially, Yosemite and Glacier.

   RIGHT: He liked to visit famous parks, especially Yosemite and Glacier.

   WRONG: He also, liked to visit famous landmarks.

   RIGHT: He also liked to visit famous landmarks.

6. **Don't use the comma to separate a <u>subject</u> from its verb. This error often happens when a verb (like *is* or *was*) comes late in a sentence.**

   WRONG: <u>Everything</u> that the restaurant serves every day of the week, is vegetarian.

   RIGHT: Everything that the restaurant serves every day of the week is vegetarian.

   WRONG: The autographed <u>baseball</u> that my uncle gave me for my birthday, arrived in the mail.

   RIGHT: The autographed baseball that my uncle gave me for my birthday arrived in the mail.

7. **Don't use the comma to separate a <u>verb</u> from its direct object. This error often happens BEFORE *that* or other clause words like *how*.**

   WRONG: John <u>told</u> the group, that he wanted to reorganize our bylaws.

   RIGHT: John told the group that he wanted to reorganize our bylaws.

   WRONG: I never appreciated from my patients' eyes, how much they suffered.

   RIGHT: I never appreciated from my patients' eyes how much they suffered.

8. **Don't use the comma to separate the <u>main part of a sentence</u> from a final fragment that *completes* the main part of the sentence.** (Final fragments often start with clause words like *because, since, though, although, even though, while, despite, in spite of, if, as, before, after, that*, and *how*. Final fragments that complete the main part are essential; those that don't, nonessential.)

   WRONG: <u>Cynthia hoped to enter college</u>, because she wanted to get a pharmacy degree.

   (*Why* did Cynthia hope to enter college? You need *because she wanted to get a pharmacy degree* to complete the sentence by explaining *why*. The *because* is thus *essential*.)

   RIGHT: Cynthia hoped to enter college because she wanted to get a pharmacy degree.

   WRONG: <u>Sidney wanted to study the violin</u>, although she had no musical talent.

   (Sidney's lack of musical talent provides a necessary context for her desire to study the violin. The essential final fragment completes the sentence.)

   RIGHT: Sidney wanted to study the violin although she had no musical talent.

9. **Don't use the comma to separate many internal transitions from the rest of the sentence.**

   WRONG: I, also, must disagree with that.

   RIGHT: I also must disagree with that. (**But:** Also, I must disagree with that.)

   WRONG: I, nevertheless, disagree with that.

   RIGHT: I nevertheless disagree with that. (**But:** Nevertheless, I disagree with that.)

WARNING!

"Right" and "wrong" are not absolutes in this last rule. In general, the shorter the subject *(I, he, she, Bob, Jane)* and the shorter the transition *(too, also, in fact)*, the less likely the comma will be needed. The longer the <u>subject</u> and transition and the greater the emphasis, the more likely you may wish to use it: <u>*President Franklin D. Roosevelt*</u>*, in the same manner, was able to overcome the psychologically crippling effects of polio.*

---

10. **Don't use the comma to separate an intensive pronoun from the rest of the sentence.**

(An intensive pronoun renames the subject with a *-self* word. See **Chapter 10—Easy Grammar**.)

> **WRONG**: I, myself, will take care of planning the party.
>
> **RIGHT**: I myself will take care of planning the party.
>
> **WRONG**: Mrs. Steinberg wanted to speak with the supervisors, themselves.
>
> **RIGHT**: Mrs. Steinberg wanted to speak with the supervisors themselves.
>
> **WRONG**: The President, himself, will speak to the press.
>
> **RIGHT**: The President himself will speak to the press.

THE DASH —

The dash has three uses:

1. **To show an abrupt change in thought**
2. **To sum up another part of the sentence**
3. **To set up an idea by slowing it down**

PUNCTUATION TIP

When you type a dash, type *two* hyphens, not one (word-processing automatically converts two hyphens into a dash). Don't put a space BEFORE or AFTER the dash.

> *old-fashioned* (hyphen)
>
> *The house was old–but we liked it.* (dash)

To show an abrupt change in thought

1. **Use the dash to show an <u>abrupt change</u> in thought.**

   Jon Stewart–<u>I really loved his show!</u>–is my favorite comedian.

   After mixing in the flour–<u>and don't forget the sugar</u>–then add the eggs.

To sum another part of the sentence

2. **Use the dash to <u>sum up</u> material that *follows* the dash.**

   <u>These are the pleasures of vegetable gardening</u>–working the soil, raising healthy crops, and enjoying a bountiful harvest.

3. **Use the dash to <u>sum up</u> material that *precedes* the dash.**

   Working the soil, raising healthy crops, and enjoying a bountiful harvest–<u>these are the pleasures of vegetable gardening</u>.

To set up an idea by slowing it down

4. **Use the dash as a stronger version of the comma, semicolon, colon, and parentheses to <u>set up an idea</u>, often an important one the reader should think about.** (The dash *slows down* the sentence, forcing the reader to pay attention to the idea.)

   You can take the money, <u>if you think you want it</u>.

   > **versus**

   You can take the money–<u>if you think you want it</u>.

   Practice the piano every day; <u>soon you won't have to look at your fingers</u>.

   > **versus**

   Practice the piano every day–<u>soon you won't have to look at your fingers</u>.

   Don't turn the switch on with wet hands: <u>You could be electrocuted</u>.

   > **versus**

   Don't turn the switch on with wet hands–<u>you could be electrocuted</u>.

PUNCTUATION TIP

Capitalize a complete sentence AFTER a colon but not AFTER a dash.

Certain cities appeal to our Romantic imaginations (<u>Shanghai, Tripoli, Istanbul, Rio de Janeiro . . .</u>).

> **versus**

Certain cities appeal to our Romantic imaginations–<u>Shanghai, Tripoli, Istanbul, Rio de Janeiro . . .</u>

LEAST EMPHASIS: My brother (<u>who lives at the North Pole</u>) knows Santa Claus.

AVERAGE EMPHASIS: My brother, <u>who lives at the North Pole</u>, knows Santa Claus.

MOST EMPHASIS: My brother–<u>who lives at the North Pole</u>–knows Santa Claus.

> # WARNING!
> **Place the dash INSIDE the quotation marks.**
>
> *"Maybe–" she said, her voice breaking.*

THE EXCLAMATION POINT !

The exclamation point has one use: *to call attention to an idea.*

1. **Use the exclamation point AFTER an emphatic statement or interjection.**

   Mickey, don't you dare buy that!

   Thief! Murderer!

   Look out—oh, damn!—here comes my brother for his money.

> # PUNCTUATION TIP
> Put the exclamation point INSIDE the quotation marks when it refers to only the quoted material; OUTSIDE when it refers to the whole sentence.
>
> *They shouted, "Four more years! Four more years!"*
>   (Refers to only quoted material.)
> *Stop whistling "Yankee Doodle"!*
>   (The whole sentence, not the song title, is an exclamation; the exclamation point applies to the whole sentence.)

> # WARNING!
> **Don't overuse the exclamation point.**
>
>   **OVERUSED:** Oh, no!!!
>   **BETTER:** Oh, no!

THE HYPHEN -

The hyphen has three uses:

1. **To connect words or parts of words**
2. **To separate parts of words**
3. **To replace words**

PUNCTUATION TIP

Hyphen use changes over time. A two-word compound may begin as *grand mother*, then become *grand-mother*, and end as one word: *grand-mother*. Always consult a recent dictionary to determine if the compound is written as separate words, with the hyphen, or as one word.

To connect words or parts of words

1. **Use the hyphen to connect a prefix to a capitalized root word.**

   anti-Communist   pre-Roman

   non-American   trans-Siberian

   non-Hepatitis B   un-American

   post-Civil War   sub-Saharan

BUT: Don't use the hyphen to connect a prefix to an uncapitalized root word.

nonstop, nonstick, nonviolence; outbrawl, outdance, outscheme; preadvertise, preapply, pre-season; reorient, repave, reprice; subchapter, subtopic, subvariety; uncapitalized, unopposed, unpolished; underfurnished, underrepresented, undertaxed

HOWEVER: Use the hyphen to connect a prefix ending with a vowel to many root words starting with that same vowel.

   anti-inflammatory

   de-emphasize

WARNING!

Always consult a recent dictionary to check for exceptions.

   reentry, cooperation

---

2. **Use the "suspended" hyphen to connect words to a <u>common word</u>.**

   The newsletter printed the names of the first- and second-<u>place</u> winners.

   Many tutors prefer two-, three-, and four-hour <u>sessions</u> with their students.

   The Pentagon contacted eligible <u>service</u>men and -women.

3. **Use the hyphen to connect a letter to a word.**

   A-OK

   U-boat

   H-bomb

   f-stop

   T-shirt

WARNING!

Always consult a recent dictionary to check for exceptions.

C ration, T square

---

4. **Use the hyphen to connect *all-*, *ex-*, *-elect*, *great-*, *-in-law*, and *self-* to words.**

   all-American, all-purpose

   ex-wife, ex-president

   president-elect, mayor-elect

   great-aunt, great-grandmother, great-great-grandmother

   son-in-law, sons-in-law, daughter-in-law, daughters-in-law, mothers-in-law

   self-contained, self-consciousness (**BUT:** selfish, selfhood)

5. **Use the hyphen to connect spelled-out numbers from twenty-one through ninety-nine.**

   thirty-three

   one hundred twenty-eight

6. **Use the hyphen to connect a spelled-out fraction.**

   one-half, one-fourth, two-thirds

   one-half inch

   three-fourths of the assembly

   fifteen thirty-second notes

   BUT: One half of the boys and one half of the girls (Don't use the hyphen with parallel phrases.)

7. **Use the hyphen to connect a compound that characterizes a person or animal.**

   She's a stick-in-the-mud.

   He's a Johnny-one-note.

   Our cat always races to get fed: Leroy's a real Johnny-on-the-spot.

8. **Use the hyphen to connect adjective compounds BEFORE a <u>noun</u>. (These may be constructed from various parts of speech but function as adjectives.)**

   up-to-date <u>styles</u>, eighteenth-century <u>novel</u>

   how-to-do-it <u>book</u>, all-day <u>hike</u>

   first-person <u>novel</u>, twenty-foot <u>ladder</u>,

   go-to kind of <u>guy</u>, turned-up <u>nose</u>,

   worn-out <u>car</u>, around-the-clock <u>attention</u>

   get-well <u>card</u>, thank-you <u>letter</u>

WARNING!

Don't use the hyphen to connect these compounds AFTER a <u>verb</u>.

Those styles <u>are</u> up to date. It <u>is</u> a novel from the eighteenth century.

The book <u>shows</u> how to do it. The hike <u>lasted</u> all day.

The novel <u>is</u> in first person. The ladder <u>looks</u> twenty feet long.

Sam is the kind of guy you <u>can go</u> to. Her nose <u>is turned</u> up.

The car <u>was</u> worn out. She <u>was given</u> attention around the clock.

The card <u>said</u> to get well. The letter <u>said</u> thank you.

WARNING!

Don't use the hyphen to connect well-known compounds or compounds with proper names.

high school teacher

investment banking counselor

social security benefits

Dr. Seuss imitator

Supreme Court justice

Homer Simpson voice

9. **Use the hyphen to connect a <u>noun</u>-adjective compound before a noun or after a verb.**

<u>brain</u>-dead response (the response was <u>brain</u>-dead)

<u>customer</u>-helpful staff (they employ a staff that's <u>customer</u>-helpful)

<u>user</u>-friendly transition (the transition seems <u>user</u>-friendly)

10. **Use the hyphen to connect a <u>noun</u>-participle compound before a noun or after a verb.**

<u>smoke</u>-clogged bar (the bar is <u>smoke</u>-clogged)

<u>habit</u>-forming drug (the drug proved <u>habit</u>-forming)

<u>panic</u>-stricken passengers (the passengers were <u>panic</u>-stricken)

11. **Use the hyphen to connect an adjective-<u>noun-ed</u> compound before a noun or after a verb.**

fair-<u>minded</u> judge (the judge may be fair-<u>minded</u>)

round-<u>faced</u> boy (the boy was round-<u>faced</u>)

deep-<u>rooted</u> desire (the desire is deep-<u>rooted</u>)

12. **Use the hyphen to connect an adjective-<u>participle</u> compound before a noun or after a verb.**

dirty-<u>looking</u> street (the street is dirty-<u>looking</u>)

long-<u>held</u> beliefs (the beliefs are long-<u>held</u>)

rough-<u>talking</u> cowboy (the cowboy is rough-<u>talking</u>)

friendly-<u>appearing</u> dog (the dog is friendly-<u>appearing</u>)

kindly-<u>looking</u> doctor (the doctor appeared kindly-<u>looking</u>)

13. **Use the hyphen to connect an adverb-<u>participle</u> compound BEFORE a noun.**

WARNING!

With this rule, the adverb can't end in *-ly* **(adverbs like** *ever, much, never, often, seldom, soon, well,* etc. **See the list of** Common Short Adverbs Not Ending in *-ly*, page 136).

---

ever-<u>changing</u> world, much-<u>frequented</u> restaurant, never-completed book

often-<u>cited</u> quotation, seldom-<u>seen</u> politician, soon-<u>ignored</u> accomplishments

well-<u>intentioned</u> man, clear-<u>cut</u> answer, hard-<u>hitting</u> storm, fast-<u>moving</u> train

If the adverb-participle compound comes AFTER the verb, one of two things can happen.

1. If the participle belongs to the <u>verb</u>, *don't use the hyphen:*

That quotation <u>is</u> very often <u>cited</u>. (***Cited*** needed to complete verb.)

We <u>have</u> seldom <u>seen</u> that writer. (***Seen*** needed to complete verb.)

2. If the participle doesn't belong to the verb and the compound forms a separate unit, *use the hyphen:*

That quotation appears to be often-cited.

After all these years, the novelist is still seldom-seen.

The answer seems pretty clear-cut.

The storm was hard-hitting.

The train is fast-moving.

> # WARNING!
>
> **Don't use the hyphen to connect an *-ly* <u>adverb</u> to the word that follows.**
>
> > **WRONG:** a frequently-quoted book, our rapidly-dwindling oil
> >
> > **RIGHT:** a frequently quoted book, our rapidly dwindling oil

14. **Use the hyphen to connect both comparative and superlative forms of adverb-participle compounds.**

better-known role, best-known role

longer-running television series, longest-running television series

> # WARNING!
>
> **Don't use the hyphen with *less, least, more,* and *most* in adjective compounds.**
>
> > **WRONG:** less-worthy project, least-expensive candy, more-intelligent man, most-appreciated manager
> >
> > **RIGHT:** less worthy project, least expensive candy, more intelligent man, most appreciated manager

15. **Use the hyphen to connect common word pairs or word compounds before the noun and after the verb.**

itsy-bitsy portion. (the portion was itsy-bitsy)

funny ha-ha joke (the joke was funny ha-ha)

true-false quiz (the quiz will be true-false)

red-hot bargain (the bargain is red-hot)

yes-no answer (the answer seems yes-no)

pass-fail course (the course is pass-fail)

stop-and-go procedures (the procedures were stop-and-go)

do-or-die mentality (the soldier's attitude is do-or-die)

To separate parts of words

16. **Use the hyphen to separate parts of words that might be misread or difficult to read.**

    recreate (as in "take recreation")

    versus

    re-create (as in "create anew")

    recover (as in "regain")

    versus

    re-cover (as in "cover again")

    coop (as in "chicken coop")

    versus

    co-op (as in "cooperative")

    antiintellectual

    versus

    anti-intellectual

    ultraactive

    versus

    ultra-active

To replace words

17. **Use the hyphen to replace *and*, *to*, or *versus*.**

    The liberal-conservative positions (***and***)

    The Denver-New York flight (***to***)

    The Ali-Foreman fight in Zaire (***versus***)

18. **Use the hyphen to replace *through* with a range of numbers or dates.**

    pp. 100-200

    the years 2004-2010

WARNING!

Don't use the hyphen with *from* or *between*; use *to* and *and*.

WRONG	**RIGHT**
from pages 8-10	from pages 8 to 10
between 1941-1945	between 1941 and 1945

ITALICS (UNDERLINING) *ITALICS* (<u>UNDERLINING</u>)

Italics have one use: *to set off special words*

NOTE: Italics = underlining (Underline if you're writing in longhand.)

1. Use italics to set off these titles.

Whole publications that have parts (chapters, articles, columns, features, etc.): books, newspapers, magazines, pamphlets

Each day she reads *The San Francisco Chronicle*.

(Each day she reads the <u>San Francisco Chronicle</u>.)

I subscribe to *The New Yorker*.

(I subscribe to <u>The New Yorker</u>.)

Long works of art that have parts (chapters, acts, episodes, movements, etc.): novels, long plays, long poems, movies, videos, TV and radio shows, ballets, musicals, operas, long musical works with descriptive titles

I read the novel *War and Peace*.

Do you know Carl Nielsen's Symphony No. 4, the *Inextinguishable*?

Paintings, drawings, prints, art installations, sculpture, and performance art

Vermeer's painting *Woman in Blue Reading a Letter*

Michelangelo's statue *David*

I saw Laurie Anderson perform her *Duets on Ice*.

Software and Web sites (but not individual Web pages)

Word still has its fans among desktop publishers.

The Internet Movie Database is my favorite Web site.

Records, DVDs, CDs, and video games

Music of Vienna offers a hundred-year-old boys' choir.

Ships, trains, and airplanes

Our train was the famous *City of San Francisco*.

WARNING!

Don't put a comma BEFORE a title unless you're referring to a *one-of-a-kind* item.

> **WRONG:** I read Hemingway's novel, *The Sun Also Rises*.
>
> (The comma suggests that Hemingway wrote just one novel; since he published seven, the comma should be removed.)
>
> **RIGHT:** I read Hemingway's novel *The Sun Also Rises*.
>
> **RIGHT:** I read Salinger's novel, *The Catcher in the Rye*.
>
> (Since Salinger published just one novel, the comma is correct.)

---

2. **Use italics or quotation marks to set off a special letter or word.**

   The *e* in *mute* is silent.

   We often use the word *really*. (We often use the word really.)

   We often use the word "really."

3. **Use italics to set off foreign words not used in English.**

   C'est pas vrai.

   Lo siento mucho.

   Dein blaues Auge

But don't use italics to set off foreign words that English has adopted.

   aide-de-camp

   enchilada

   angst

WARNING!

See the Warning (page 419) under Quotation Marks and apply all examples to italics.

PARENTHESES ( )

Parentheses have one use: *to show an insertion into a sentence*

1. **Use parentheses to show a parenthetical insertion (that is, material that offers information about the main sentence).**

   The snow blanketed the driveway (a blizzard had blown in over the night), but we managed to back the car out.

   The Academic Advancement Program (AAP) employs many deans.

   John F. Kennedy (the thirty-fifth President of the United States) died in 1963.

PUNCTUATION TIP

If a parenthetically enclosed sentence can stand separate from another sentence, you may want to start the enclosed sentence with a capital letter and place the period INSIDE the final parenthesis.

> *The snow blanketed the driveway. (A blizzard had blown in over the night.)*

---

2. **Use parentheses to show inserted numbers or letters that set up a list.**

   The mayor's concerns are (1) budget, (2) staffing, and (3) reorganization.

   The mayor's concerns are (a) budget, (b) staffing, and (c) reorganization.

3. **Use parentheses to show inserted alternatives.**

   Tell us what date(s) you can attend.

   Choose which class(es) you want.

THE PERIOD .

The period has two uses:

1. **To separate parts by marking the end (of a sentence, an abbreviation, a number, or a letter)**
2. **To replace words**

To separate parts by marking the end (of a sentence, an abbreviation, a number, or a letter)

1. **Use the period to separate one sentence from another.**

The dog barks. The cat meows. The bird chirps.

2. **Use the period to end abbreviations unless they're acronyms (that is, abbreviations pronounced as words) or abbreviations commonly written without periods.**

Mr.	Ph.D.	i.e. (= *id est* = that is)
Mrs.	Oct.	e.g. (= *exempli gratia* = for example)
Dr.	Ms.	etc. (= *et cetera* = and so forth)
Jr.	Sr.	ca. (= *circa* = about, approximately)
Wed.	Esq.	vs. (= *versus* = against, in contrast with)

Acronyms

NATO (**N**orth **A**tlantic **T**reaty **O**rganization)
UNICEF (**U**nited **N**ations **C**hildren's **F**und)
radar (**r**adio **d**etecting **a**nd **r**anging)

All-capital abbreviations usually don't require periods.

FBI, CIA, IBM, LSAT, ACT, WI, NY, CA

But some can go either way.

U.S.A. (USA)   A.D. (AD)
B.C. (BC)

Academic degrees generally use periods.

B.A., B.S., B.Sc., M.A., M.F.A., M.S., LL.B., LL.D., Ph.D., M.D., D.V.M.

And some abbreviations may be variously punctuated and capitalized.

a.m.	am	A.M.	AM
p.m.	pm	P.M.	PM
m.p.h.	mph	M.P.H.	MPH

WARNING!

Consult a recent dictionary to confirm the correct use. (Since dictionaries disagree, you may need to consult more than one.)

---

3. **Use the period to punctuate numbers and letters in outlines and lists. (Here the period "ends" or separates one number/letter from another.)**

I.   1.
  A.   2.
    1.   3.
    2.
  B.

To replace words

4. **Use an ellipsis mark (three periods in a row, with a space BEFORE and AFTER each period) to replace words in quoted material.**

   The senator said: "We must all try to help the poor . . . by giving our share."

   The governor promised to "establish a task force, crack down on welfare abuse, and send the guilty to jail. . . . Then we will have a state to be proud of," he added.

> ## PUNCTUATION TIP
> A final period BEFORE the ellipsis mark signals the end of a sentence.

5. **Use an ellipsis mark to show trailing-off thought.**

   "I'm really not sure . . . if I should . . . or if you should . . ."

> ## WARNING!
> **With an ellipsis mark, be sure to put a space BEFORE and AFTER each period except with the final period before quotations.**
>
> > **WRONG:** "I'm really not sure...if I should...or if you should..."
> > **RIGHT:** "I'm really not sure . . . if I should . . . or if you should . . ."

THE QUESTION MARK ?

The question mark has one use: *to find out about something*

1. **Use the question mark AFTER a <u>direct question</u>.**

   <u>What is your idea</u>?

   She asked, "<u>What is your idea?</u>"

   <u>Are you sure of that</u>?

   He wanted to know, "<u>Are you sure of that?</u>"

2. **Don't use the question mark AFTER an <u>indirect question</u> (which means that the question does not directly address its audience).**

   Sandra wanted to know <u>if she were going</u>. (indirect)

      BUT: Sandra wanted to know, "Are you going?" (direct)

   Don asked his sister <u>whether she wanted to run or swim that night</u>. (indirect)

      BUT: Don asked his sister, "Do you want to run or swim tonight?" (direct)

   Lindsay wondered <u>if the plan would work</u>. (indirect)

      BUT: Lindsay wondered, Will the plan work? (direct)

3. **Use the question mark AFTER questions within a sentence, but don't capitalize the <u>first word</u> of each question because the questions are part of one sentence.**

   Can you tell me what the fare is? when the flight leaves? what gate I should show up at? what stops it makes?

4. **Put the question mark INSIDE the quotation marks when it refers to only the quoted material; put it OUTSIDE when it refers to the whole sentence.**

   The philosopher asked, "What is truth?" (Question mark refers to only quoted material.)

   Do you know the meaning of "truth"? (Question mark refers to whole sentence, which is a question.)

   WARNING!

   Don't overuse the question mark.

      OVERUSED: Are you really sure???
      BETTER: Are you really sure?

QUOTATION MARKS " "

Quotation marks have one use: *to set off special words*

PUNCTUATION TIP

American and British practices differ. Americans generally use double quotation marks; the British generally use single. Americans put quotations OUTSIDE the comma and period; the British, for some situations, put them INSIDE.

---

1. **Use double quotation marks (" ") to set off direct quotations.**

   Leon wrote: "I really enjoy France. The country is beautiful."

WARNING!

When you indent a long quotation for a research paper, don't put quotation marks around it. The indent signals that it's a quotation; quotation marks are thus redundant.

As Dickens tells us,

> It was the best of times, it was the worst of times, it was the age of wisdom, it was the age of foolishness, it was the epoch of belief, it was the epoch of incredulity, it was the season of Light, it was the season of Darkness, it was the spring of hope, it was the winter of despair, we had everything before us, we had nothing before us, we were all going direct to heaven, we were all going direct the other way—in short, the period was so far like the present period, that some of its noisiest authorities insisted on its being received, for good or for evil, in the superlative degree of comparison only. (1)

---

2. **Use single quotation marks (' ') to set off a quotation inside a quotation.**

Bob said, "John said, 'Hello' to me."

3. **Use quotation marks to set off these titles:**

Parts of whole publications: chapters of books; articles, columns, and features of newspapers and magazines; pamphlets

I subscribe to *The New Yorker*, which always contains a column called "The Talk of the Town."

Chapters, acts, episodes, movements, etc., of long artworks that have parts

Chapter I of Stevenson's novel *David Balfour* is "A Beggar on Horseback."
She watched an episode of *South Park* called "Dances with Smurfs."
Nancy loves the "Jupiter" movement of Holst's musical suite *The Planets*.

Parts, sections, features, etc., of software and Web sites

I often check *The Internet Movie Database* for its feature "Celebrity News."

Bands, cuts, parts, sections, features, etc., of records, DVDs, CDs, and video games

The DVD *Music of Vienna* offers Christmas songs like "Silent Night, Holy Night."

Short stories, short plays, short poems, essays, songs, and short pieces of music

Have you read Hemingway's short story "Soldier's Home"?
The boy sang "Tonight," a song from Bernstein's musical *West Side Story*.

WARNING!

Don't put the comma BEFORE a title unless you're referring to a *one-of-a-kind* item.

> **WRONG:** Have you read Hemingway's short story, "Soldier's Home"?
>
> (The comma suggests that Hemingway wrote just one story; since he wrote over sixty, the comma should be removed.)
>
> **RIGHT:** Have you read Hemingway's short story "Soldier's Home"?

---

4. **Use quotation marks (or italics = underlining) to set off a special letter or word.**
   The "e" in "mute" is silent.
   We often use the word "really."
   We often use the word *really*. (We often use the word <u>really</u>.)

5. **Use quotations marks (but not italics) to set off irony.**
   We really appreciated your "help."
   The "election" had only one candidate.

RULES FOR USING QUOTATION MARKS

1. **Always use double quotation marks (" ") unless you're quoting within a quotation; then use single (').**

   Bob said, "John said, 'Hello' to me."

2. **Put quotation marks OUTSIDE the comma, period (with one *exception**), and dash.**

WRONG	RIGHT
"Maybe",	"Maybe,"
"Maybe".	"Maybe."
"Maybe"–	"Maybe–"

   > # *EXCEPTION
   >
   > Within a sentence, when a reference citation follows a quotation, the comma or period goes OUTSIDE the quotation marks.
   >
   > *Smith said that he had "no recollection of the crime" (Harrington 14), but he offered no alibi.*
   >
   > *Smith said that he had "no recollection of the crime" (Harrington 14).*

3. **Put quotation marks INSIDE the semicolon and colon.**

WRONG	RIGHT
"Maybe;"	"Maybe";
"Maybe:"	"Maybe":

4. **Put quotation marks OUTSIDE the question mark or exclamation point when either refers to only the quoted material; INSIDE the question mark or exclamation point when either refers to the whole sentence.**

   The philosopher asked, "What is truth?" (Question mark refers to only quoted material.)

   Do you know the meaning of "truth"? (Question mark refers to whole sentence, which is a question.)

   The philosopher shouted, "That is truth!" (Exclamation point refers to only quoted material.)

   Stop speaking so-called "truths"! (Exclamation point refers to whole sentence, which is an exclamation.)

5. **Use the comma to introduce a quotation that's a complete sentence; capitalize the first word of the quotation.**

   John F. Kennedy said, "And so, my fellow Americans, ask not what your country can do for you; ask what you can do for your country."

6. **Don't use the comma and don't capitalize the first letter of a quotation if it's a fragment (that is, not a complete sentence) that completes a sentence.**

   John F. Kennedy said to "ask what you can do for your country."

7. **Remember to call a quotation a "quotation," not a "quote." "Quote" is a verb; "quotation" is a noun. You "quote a quotation," not "quote a quote."**

WARNING!

Don't use quotation marks (or italics) for the following:

1. **Common religious titles:** the Torah, the Book of Mormon, the Koran, or the Bible (or books of the Bible, like Exodus)

2. **Common public documents:** the Declaration of Independence, the U.S. Constitution, the Gettysburg Address

3. **Common cyberspace terms:** Google, Internet, World Wide Web

4. **Common words or expressions that don't need emphasis:**

   He was being "fresh." (He was being fresh.)

   I felt "out of sorts." (I felt out of sorts.)

   She decided to be "better safe than sorry." (She decided to be better safe than sorry.)

5. **Slang:** "cool," "hot," "wasted" (cool, hot, wasted)

6. **Nicknames:** "Mr. Money," "Nana" (Mr. Money, Nana)

7. **An attempt at humor:**

   I really had "egg on my face" when I forgot my credit card was "maxed out."

   (I really had egg on my face when I forgot my credit card was maxed out.)

THE SEMICOLON ;

The semicolon has two uses:

1. **To substitute for the period to separate related sentences**
2. **To separate items that have internal punctuation**

PUNCTUATION TIP

In 1 and 2 that follow, the semicolon = the period; in 3, the semicolon = a punctuation mark midway between the comma and the period.

To substitute for the period to separate related sentences

1. **Use the semicolon (and not the comma) to separate related sentences.**

   I saw a famous French movie; it's called *La grande illusion.*

   Be sure to check the stove; I think I left the burner on.

   My daughter lives in Madison; my son lives in San Diego.

WARNING!

In the previous three sentences, using the comma instead of the semicolon will cause run-ons.

---

2. **Use the semicolon to separate related sentences linked with a <u>transition</u>. (See the transition chart on page 59.)**

   Eric stayed in Barcelona for a year; <u>consequently</u>, his Spanish improved considerably.

   Frank Sinatra was a good actor; <u>however</u>, it is as a singer that he is better known.

To separate items that have internal punctuation

3. **Use the semicolon to <u>separate series</u> units that have internal punctuation.**

                          1   2

   WRONG: We went to <u>New York, New York,</u> <u>Detroit, Michigan,</u>

            3

   and <u>Seattle, Washington.</u>

   RIGHT: We went to New York, New York; Detroit, Michigan; and Seattle, Washington.

   (Each of the three units in the series has its own comma between city and state, that is, "internal punctuation." Replace the commas *between* units with semicolons to avoid confusion.)

1

WRONG: This semester, she will study *Jane Eyre*, by Charlotte

2

Brontë, *Great Expectations*, by Charles Dickens, *Huckleberry Finn*,

3   4

by Mark Twain, and *Heart of Darkness*, by Joseph Conrad.

RIGHT: This semester, she will study *Jane Eyre*, by Charlotte Brontë; *Great Expectations*, by Charles Dickens; *Huckleberry Finn*, by Mark Twain; and *Heart of Darkness*, by Joseph Conrad.

WARNING!

Review the use of the semicolon in the following FIVE situations.

---

1. **The semicolon goes OUTSIDE the quotation marks and parentheses.**

   WRONG: I heard a song called "Fugue for Tinhorns;" Frank Loesser wrote the words and music.

   RIGHT: I heard a song called "Fugue for Tinhorns"; Frank Loesser wrote the words and music.

   WRONG: I heard a song by Frank Loesser (an American composer of Broadway shows;) it's called "Fugue for Tinhorns."

   RIGHT: I heard a song by Frank Loesser (an American composer of Broadway shows); it's called "Fugue for Tinhorns."

2. **Don't capitalize the first word AFTER the semicolon unless it's a <u>proper noun</u>.**

   WRONG: I saw the man in downtown Detroit; He was a resident.

   RIGHT: I saw the man in downtown Detroit; he was a resident.

   RIGHT: I saw the man in downtown Detroit; Bob was a resident.

3. **Don't use the semicolon to set up a <u>list</u>, either within a sentence or for a column (use the colon or dash).**

   WRONG: I visited four cities; Omaha, Denver, Salt Lake City, and Dallas.

   RIGHT: I visited four cities: Omaha, Denver, Salt Lake City, and Dallas.

   RIGHT: I visited four cities—Omaha, Denver, Salt Lake City, and Dallas.

4. **Don't use the semicolon AFTER an <u>introductory fragment</u> (use the comma).**

   WRONG: Although I was too busy to notice; it was raining all day.

   RIGHT: Although I was too busy to notice, it was raining all day.

5. **Don't use the semicolon BEFORE a <u>nonessential final fragment</u> (use the comma).**

   WRONG: It was raining all day; although I was too busy to notice.

   RIGHT: It was raining all day, although I was too busy to notice.

THE SLASH /

The slash has three uses:

1. **To show alternatives**
2. **To separate one part from another**
3. **To connect compounds**

To show alternatives

1. **Use the slash to show alternatives.**
   and/or
   either/or
   yes/no

To separate one part from another

2. **Use the slash with dates.**
   3/9/2017

3. **Use the slash to separate lines of poetry in a quotation.**
   In the first three lines of sonnet 116, "Let me not to the marriage of true minds / Admit impediments; love is not love / Which alters when it alteration finds," Shakespeare's narrator anchors the poem in legal language.

> # WARNING!
> **If the original poem capitalizes each new line, you must capitalize each new word AFTER the slash.**

To connect compounds

4. **Use the slash instead of *to* to connect compounds like the following.**
   the 2017/2018 budget
   the November/December issue

Spelling and Mechanics Rules

Spelling
Capitalization
Abbreviations
Numbers

SPELLING

You can handle most spelling problems with a spell-checker. But spell-checkers won't help with:

- **Typing errors that don't look wrong (net when you mean next)**
- **Compound words that should be written as one word (black bird = blackbird)**
- **Compound words that need hyphens (old-fashioned dress)**
- **Spellings of proper nouns (Carrie, Keri, or Cary?)**
- **Many homonyms**

Homonyms are words that sound alike, or almost alike, like *it's* and *its* and *your* and *you're*. Each of the sentences below has an error because of sound-alike confusion.

Yet one program's spell-checker recognized only *one* error ("even though"), and a second spell-checker recognized only *nine*. (An asterisk marks the nine errors; corrections for each error follow in parentheses.)

What is the affect of global warming? *(effect)*

***How does global warming effect you?** *(affect)*

Someday she hopes to retire to an aisle in the Pacific. *(isle)*

She took a seat on one side of the isle. *(aisle)*

I have to site every reference in my research paper. *(cite)*

***I went eventhough I didn't want.** *(even though)*

She calls her mother everyday. *(every day)*

Those are my every day clothes. *(everyday)*

***She goes to highschool.** *(high school)*

***Did you see it's color?** *(its)*

I think its raining. *(it's)*

He needed some lose change. *(loose)*

Please don't loose that money. *(lose)*

She disagrees with the principal of the decision. *(principle)*

He's the principle of the school. *(principal)*

He is my oldest sun. *(son)*

The son comes up when the moon goes down. *(sun)*

***I'm suppose to volunteer.** *(supposed)*

Bob is taller then Peggy. *(than)*

***Than we ate breakfast.** *(then)*

He went to there house. *(their)*

I went they're. *(there)*

***Their going to the party.** *(they're)*

I use to volunteer. *(used)*

***Whose going to the party?** *(who's)*

***Who's house is that?** *(whose)*

Did you see you're mother? *(your)*

I hope your going to the party. *(you're)*

Obviously, you can't rely on spell-checkers to catch every error. To catch the errors the spell-checker misses, try the following:

- Keep an alphabetized list of the words you always misspell next to the computer.
- Check the hyphen rules for compound words in Chapter 16—Punctuation Rules.
- Enter the spelling of proper nouns and other special words into the spell-checker vocabulary so it will check them.
- Check the list of homonyms and near-homonyms below.
- Check Chapter 18—Word Confusions (with definitions of the words below included in a longer list of Word Confusions).

The following list has two kinds of word-pair confusions. The words in **bold** are homonyms or near-homonyms that pose spelling problems. The words in *italics* are word-pair confusions that can cause problems with spelling, word usage, or both. (The asterisked* words are the most frequently made errors.)

**ability/capacity*	**beside/besides**
accept/except	**capital/capitol**
adapt/adopt	**censor/censure**
adverse/averse	**cite/sight/site**
advice/advise	**climactic/climatic**
affect/effect	**coarse/course**
all ready/already	**complement/compliment**
all right/alright	**compose/comprise*

*all together/altogether	*conscience/conscious
allude/refer	*continual/continuous*
allusion/illusion	*criterion/criteria*
*a lot/alot	*data/datum*
alternate/alternative	*decent/descent
among/between	*definitely/defiantly*
amount/number	*disinterested/uninterested*
anxious/eager	disassemble/dissemble
any one/anyone	*each other/eachother
*a part/apart	elicit/illicit
*a while/awhile	eminent/immanent/imminent
as/because	*every day/everyday
every one/everyone	principal/principle
fewer/less	quiet/quite
imply/infer	rational/rationale
ingenious/ingenuous	*respectfully/respectively*
*its/it's	role/roll
know/no	some one/someone
*lead/led	*some time/sometime/sometimes
lend/loan	*than/then*
lie/lay	*their/there/they're
*loose/lose	*thorough/through*
masterful/masterly	*to/too/two
may be/maybe	verbage/verbiage
meantime/meanwhile	*weather/whether
moral/morale	*where/when*
nauseated/nauseous	*who's/whose
oral/verbal	woman/women
passed/past	*you're/your

CAPITALIZATION

> # WARNING!
> A spell-checker won't catch capitalization errors. Enter words with capitals into your spell-checker.

Capitalization rules break into two broad groups:

- Group One—Capitalization Rules for a Particular Person, Group, Quality, Place, or Purpose
- Group Two—Capitalization Rules for Words and Sentences

GROUP ONE—CAPITALIZATION RULES FOR A PARTICULAR PERSON, GROUP, QUALITY, PLACE, OR PURPOSE

Proper nouns and adjectives refer to a *particular* person, group, quality, place, or purpose. Common nouns and adjectives refer to *any* person, group, quality, place, or purpose.

PROPER NOUNS/ADJECTIVES	COMMON NOUNS/ADJECTIVES
PARTICULAR PERSON	**ANY PERSON**
Pronoun "I"	you
Bob Smith, Hillary Clinton	a man, a woman
Uncle James, Grandma Janet (BUT: my uncle James, my grandma Janet)	an uncle, a grandmother
ex-Mayor Jones and Senator Greene	a mayor and a senator
President Trump	a president (**BUT:** *The President of the United States* is always capitalized)
Professor Hayes, Dr. Cummings (Lloyd Hayes, Professor of Music; Margo Cummings, M.D.)	a professor, a doctor
Director of Advertising (used in an letter address)	a director of advertising
PARTICULAR GROUP	**ANY GROUP**
First Baptist Church, Rotarians	a church, a group
Catholic, Boy Scout	a church member, a group member
University of Wisconsin-Madison	a university or college

Fuller Plastics Company	a company (**BUT:** Capitalize when representing a specific company/group: *the Company, the University, the State*)
Committee on Equal Pay	a committee
Indiana State Legislature	a state legislature
Supreme Court of the United States	a supreme court of the land
Army, Navy, Air Force, Congress	an army, a navy, an air force, a congress
Federal Reserve Board	a federal agency
PARTICULAR QUALITY PERSONIFIED	**ANY QUALITY**
Nature, Beauty, Youth, Old Age	nature, beauty, youth, old age
PARTICULAR PLACE	**ANY PLACE**
Hudson River, Death Valley	a river, a desert
New York City, Chicago	a city
Empire State, Windy City	a state or city nickname
the South, the Far West, the East (points on the compass)	driving south, going west, east of Pittsburgh (general directions)
PARTICULAR PURPOSE DOCUMENT	**ANY DOCUMENT**
Declaration of Independence, Treaty of Versailles, Occupational Safety and Health Act, the Constitution	a declaration, a treaty, an act, a constitution
PARTICULAR MONTH OR DAY	**ANY MONTH OR DAY**
March, Friday, Memorial Day (BUT: Don't capitalize seasons, decades, centuries—*winter, nineteen-sixties, nineteenth century*)	a month, a day of the week, a holiday
PARTICULAR TRADEMARKED PRODUCT	**ANY PRODUCT**
Chevrolet, Apple, Red Bull	a car, a computer, an energy drink
PARTICULAR CULTURAL TYPE	**ANY TYPE**
Swiss watch, Italian food, Hmong, African-American	a watch, a food, a language, a culture
PARTICULAR CULTURAL WORD COMPOUND	**ANY WORD COMPOUND**
French-Canadian Pact, anti-America	a two-country pact, anticountry

PARTICULAR TIME IN HISTORY	ANY TIME IN HISTORY
Dark Ages, Renaissance, D-Day, Neolithic, World War II	a period of cultural stagnation, an era of artistic flowering, a major battleground invasion, an age of polished stone tools, a war
PARTICULAR NAME OF A SHIP, AN AIRPLANE, A TRAIN, AND A SPACECRAFT	**ANY SHIP, AIRPLANE, TRAIN, AND SPACECRAFT**
Titanic, Concorde, Orient Express, Sputnik (also italicized or underlined)	an ocean liner, a jet, a luxury train, a satellite
PARTICULAR DEITY	**ANY DEITY**
God, Jesus, Buddha, Ahura Mazda	a creator, a savior
MEMBER OF A PARTICULAR RELIGION	**MEMBER OF ANY RELIGION**
Christian, Jewish, Buddhist, Zoroastrian	a born-again, an evangelical
PARTICULAR HEAVENLY BODY	**ANY HEAVENLY BODY**
Mars, Saturn, Big Dipper (BUT: Don't capitalize sun and moon unless grouped with other heavenly bodies)	a planet, a constellation
PARTICULAR NAME IN BOTANY OR ZOOLOGY (GENERA)	**ANY PLANT OR ANIMAL**
Tulipa fosteriana, Panthera leo	a tulip, a lion

WARNING!

In binomial (or Latin) scientific names, capitalize the genus (*Tulipa, Panthera*) but not the species (*fosteriana, leo*). Both genus and species should be italicized or underlined: *Tulipa fosteriana, Panthera leo.*

GROUP TWO—CAPITALIZATION RULES FOR WORDS AND SENTENCES

First word of a sentence

The sky is blue.

First word of a fragment

No. Maybe. (**BUT:** He'd been saying "no" all week.)

First word of a direct quotation

He said, "The sky is blue."

First word of a sentence (but not a fragment) after a colon

Eat more green food: It's good for your health.

(**BUT:** Eat more green food: broccoli, spinach, and kale.)

First word in a list

We have three goals:

a. **Exercising**

b. **Eating good foods**

c. **Losing weight**

(**BUT:** Letters are not capitalized in a list.)

First word of an independent question within a sentence

I ask myself, Am I doing the right thing?

(**BUT:** Am I doing the right thing? should I change my ways? what is the answer?)

First, last, and main words in a title or subtitle

(**BUT:** Except for the first and last words in a title, don't capitalize *a, an, the*; prepositions; to with a verb; and coordinating conjunctions.

The Old Man and the Sea

Of a Fire on the Moon

"The Only Way Is Up: A Tool to Change Your Life"

A Farewell to Arms

A Good Day to Die

---

*EXCEPTION

In a title, capitalize a preposition used as a part of a verb phrase: *Petey, the Dog Who Jumped Up the Mountain.*

First word after a dash or colon in a title or subtitle

(This rule applies as well to *a, an, the*; prepositions; *to* with a verb; and coordinating conjunctions.)

"Six Ways to Happiness—And Financial Security"

"Mailer's Greatest Novel: *An America Dream*"

CAPITALIZATION TIP

"The" in a title: If "the" belongs to the title of a publication and is printed on the cover, capitalize it. But if the official cover title doesn't use "the," don't capitalize it.

The New Yorker

The Atlantic

The New York Times

BUT: *the National Enquirer*

WARNING!

If you use MLA rules, follow the title rules above. If you use APA rules, remember that, in a citation, APA capitalizes just the first word and proper nouns of a title. (See MLA/APA tab.)

First word in a letter's salutation or complimentary close

Dear Mr. Smith:

My dear friend,

Sincerely yours,

Truly yours,

Academic subjects or fields of study that come from proper names

English, Swedish, French, Freudian analysis, Pythagorean geometry (**BUT**: grammar, language, psychology, math)

Names of academic courses using catalogue numbers

Grammar 100, Language 233, Psychology 699, Math 400

Academic degrees—abbreviations

Rita Rupp, M.D.

Kevin Hardwick, B.A, M.A., Ph.D.

Place names—abbreviations
Washington, D.C. (District of Columbia)

Other abbreviations, with or without periods
M.J. (Michael Jordan); B.S. (Bachelor of Science)
NATO, FBI, CIA, WHO-TV

With letters and numbers
Exhibit C, Drawer M, Figure Z
Flight 221, Section II, Figure 14

ABBREVIATIONS

WARNING!

In academic writing, don't abbreviate unless a convention allows it; avoid texting and e-mail abbreviations in all formal writing.

Abbreviations break into two broad groups:

- **Group One—Abbreviations of one word (dept. = department; Mr. = mister)**
- **Group Two—Abbreviations of more than one word (a.m. = *ante meridiem*; FBI = Federal Bureau of Investigation)**

Whether Group One or Group Two, abbreviations cause two problems:

- **Problem One—When do you use capital letters?**
- **Problem Two—When do you use periods?**

PROBLEM ONE

Capitalize an abbreviation when it refers to a proper noun or adjective but not when it refers to a common noun or adjective (see page 429).

Federal Bureau of Investigation = FBI (a *particular* group)
United States of America = USA (a *particular* place)
department = dept. (*any* group. **BUT**: The Department of Administration = DOA)
professor = prof. (*any* person. **BUT**: Prof. Hutchins)
sons of bitches = s.o.b.'s (*any* people)

PROBLEM TWO

Use periods with abbreviations according to common usage:

- The preferred usage of the person, organization, etc., or preferred convention (FBI [see page 429] BUT: Mr. and Jr.)
- The usage given in a recent dictionary

WARNING!

Abbreviations cause problems. Good writers *always* consult the dictionary for every abbreviation. Is it *am, a.m., AM,* or *A.M.?* The dictionary says all four are acceptable. If the dictionary gives a preference, use that. Whichever form you choose, use it consistently.

Conventional (acceptable) abbreviations in academic writing

Titles of a Particular Person

> Mr. and Mrs. Curtiss
>
> Ms. Carter
>
> Dr. Adams
>
> St. Cecilia
>
> Jerry Conwell, M.A., Ph.D.
>
> Bill Rogers, Sr. (Use comma if person uses comma in name.)

Other than these abbreviated titles, write out *senator, professor, sergeant, colonel*, etc. Capitalize when they appear before a name but not after.

Senator Abraham Stein (**BUT:** Abraham Stein, a senator)

First and Middle Names

If a person abbreviates his or her first and/or middle names, do likewise. Otherwise, spell out the name as conventionally written.

> A.J. Liebling
>
> J.K. Rowling
>
> B. Traven
>
> ZZ Packer (no periods used in the author's spelling of her name)
>
> Arthur Conan Doyle (not A.C. Doyle)
>
> Edgar Allan Poe (not E.A. Poe)

Particular Groups Whose Trademarked Name Is Abbreviated

> Tiffany & Co.
>
> Hollister Co.
>
> Warner Bros.
>
> Jos. A Bank
>
> Macy's, Inc. (*But no comma in trademarked name:* Liz Claiborne Inc.)

WARNING!

If the abbreviation is not part of the trademarked name, write out *company* **(not co.),** *corporation* **(not corp.), and** *incorporated* **(not inc.).**

Words Commonly Abbreviated

> 78°F (for Fahrenheit), 50°C (for Celsius)
>
> No. 98 (for a particular numbered thing)
>
> 16-mm film, 35-mm movie
>
> UN, UNICEF, WHO, YMCA, YWCA, IBM, UPS, NAACP, FBI, CIA, AFL-CIO, CNN, ABC, NBC, CBS, MSNBC, a.m., p.m., mph, mpg, BC/BCE, AD/CE, academic titles, Latin abbreviations (*e.g.*—for example; *i.e.*—that is; *cf.*—compare; *etc.*—and so forth; *et al.*—and others; *N.B.*—note well; *P.S.*—postscript)

WARNING!

In most academic writing, don't abbreviate the following.

> *Common shorthand terms:* w/, w/o, c/o, FYI, N/A, HR
>
> *Places*: California (not Calif. or CA), Puerto Rico (not PR)
>
> *People*: Robert (not Robt.), Charles (not Chas.), Elizabeth (not Eliz.) Joseph (not Jos.)
>
> *Months of the year:* January (not Jan.), December (not Dec.)
>
> *Days of the week:* Sunday (not Sun.), Saturday (not Sat.)
>
> *Holidays*: Christmas (not Xmas), Memorial Day (not Mem. Day)
>
> *Measurements:* inch (not in.), pound (not lb), ounce (not oz), foot (not ft)
>
> *Dollar sign:* five dollars (not $5)

BUT:

> 1. Use the dollar sign when the written-out version is three or more words: $129 million (not one million, two hundred twenty-nine dollars)

2. Use the dollar sign with a series of figures: The costs were $5, $78.92, and $1,832.24.

3. Use the dollar sign in charts, tables, graphs, and figures.

Percent sign: five percent (not 5%; however, don't write out a series of percentages—use abbreviations: The breakdowns were 5%, 10%, and 85%.) **BUT:** Use the percent in charts, tables, graphs, and figures.

Courses: political science (not poli. sci.), organic chemistry (not o. chem.)

Page, chapter, section, and page continuation references: page (not p. or pp.), chapter (not chap.), section (not. sect.), continued (not cont.) **BUT:** Use these abbreviations in non-Body material: parenthetical citations, footnotes, index, etc.

Text references to a figure or illustration: see Figure 1 (not Fig. 1), see Illustration A (not Illus. A) **BUT:** Use these abbreviations in non-Body material: parenthetical citations, footnotes, indexes, etc.

The United States of America and Other Countries: Don't use U.S. unless it precedes a <u>noun</u>: U.S. <u>Senate</u>. Formal writing always writes out the United States or the United States of America. Likewise, write France, not. Fr.; Germany, not Ger.

Usage Rules

1. **If a sentence ends with an abbreviation period, don't use two periods. Delete one.**

   WRONG: He was proud of his Ph.D..

   RIGHT: He was proud of his Ph.D.

2. **Don't use periods with U.S. Post Office abbreviations.**

   WI, CA, NY (*not* W.I., C.A., or N.Y.)

3. **Don't write out the first use of a common abbreviation: DNA (not deoxyribonucleic acid). However, an uncommon abbreviation should be written out with first use:** The Academic Advancement Program (not AAP).

PARENTHESES TIP

Many writers clumsily overwork the parenthetical abbreviation: If the written-out first use comes within a sentence or two of the second use, don't use the parentheses.

> **CLUMSY:** *The Academic Advancement Program (AAP) has been active since 1966. AAP serves minority, disadvantaged, and first-generation students.*

> **BETTER:** *The Academic Advancement Program has been active since 1966. AAP serves minority, disadvantaged, and first-generation students.*

4. **Add "s" to form the plural of one-word abbreviations, with or without a period.**

   mo = mos   yr = yrs
   apt = apts   dept = depts
   bldg. = bldgs.   fig. = figs.

   BUT: Units of measure use the singular for both singulars and plurals.

1 in	2 in	1 oz	6 oz
1 yd	4 yd	1 qt	10 qt

5. **Add "s" plus an apostrophe to form the plural of lowercase phrase abbreviations that use periods.**

   c.o.d.'s   f.o.b.'s

6. **Add "s" to form the plural of capitalized abbreviations, with or without the period.**

   M.D.s, Ph.D.s
   ABMs, ABCs

7. **Add an apostrophe (and "s" as needed) to form singular possessives of an abbreviation.**

   Tiffany & Co.'s spring sale   Margo Cummings, M.D.'s office address
   Hollister Co.'s Website   the M.D.s' convention
   Warner Bros.' newest release   Bill Rogers, Sr.'s home

NUMBERS

> # WARNING!
>
> **Texting and e-mailing cause many writers to substitute Arabic numbers (*3, 4, 5*) for written-out numbers (*three, four, and five*). With academic writing, follow the rules below.**

Numbers break into four broad groups:

- **Group One—Numbers as Words**
- **Group Two—Numbers as Figures**
- **Group Three—Numbers as Figures *Plus* Words**
- **Group Four—Numbers as Words *or* Figures**

In addition to the rules for Groups One through Four, there are also **Three Miscellaneous Number Rules** (see page 443).

GROUP ONE—NUMBERS AS <u>WORDS</u>

1. **Write out numbers that you can say in one or two words.***
   WRONG: Yolanda completed the first 3 assignments. (number = one word)
   RIGHT: Yolanda completed the first <u>three</u> assignments.
   * A hyphenated number, like twenty-two, counts as one word.

2. **Use words for indefinite numbers.**
   WRONG: 100s of demonstrators, 1,000s of dollars, in her 30s
   RIGHT: <u>hundreds</u> of demonstrators, <u>thousands</u> of dollars, in her <u>thirties</u>

3. **Use words when numbers start a sentence.**
   WRONG: 8 boys left on a canoe trip.
   RIGHT: <u>Eight</u> boys left on a canoe trip.

4. **Use words with a hyphen when a fraction is used by itself.**
   <u>Two-thirds</u> of the class was late.
   About <u>seven-eighths</u> of the orchestra was out of tune.
   BUT: She estimated that 3 1/2 yards wouldn't be enough. (number + fraction = use figure)
   BUT: <u>Three and one-half</u> yards won't be enough. (Don't start a sentence with a figure.)

GROUP TWO—NUMBERS AS FIGURES

5. **Use figures for numbers that take three words or more to express.**
   WRONG: Yolanda had <u>one hundred twenty-five</u> assignments. (number = <u>three words</u>; a hyphenated number counts as one word)
   RIGHT: Yolanda had 125 assignments.

6. **Use figures when they identify people and things.**
   Edward II   Route 66
   Channel 9   Chanel No. 5

7. **If a page of text presents a series of numbers (e.g., to show numerical evidence), use all figures instead of words.**

GROUP THREE—NUMBERS AS FIGURES PLUS <u>WORDS</u>

8. **Combine figures and words for money amounts in the millions, billions, and trillions.**
   The President asked for $40 <u>million</u> in aid.
   Congress is expected to cut $90 <u>billion</u> from the budget; so far it has cut 1.3 <u>billion</u>.

9. **When writing an address or numbered street name, sometimes use words, sometimes use figures, sometimes a combination.**

   He lives at 221 South Maple Street. (use figures for a street address)

   I went shopping on <u>Fifth</u> Avenue. (use <u>words</u> for streets *under* ten)

   I went shopping at 321 <u>Fifth</u> Avenue. (use a combination of figures and <u>words</u>)

   I went shopping at 304 West 44 Street. (or 44th Street; use figures for streets *over* ten)

10. **With two numbers before a NOUN, use a <u>word</u> for the shorter one and a figure for the longer. Use either if the numbers are equal.**

    The inspector found 152 <u>ten-dollar</u> BILLS in the mud.

    The company stored <u>five</u> 100-pound CRATES in the basement.

    We will have a party for <u>nine</u> 21-year-old BIRTHDAYS.

    The woman lifted <u>five</u> 10-pound WEIGHTS *or* 5 <u>ten-pound</u> WEIGHTS.

GROUP FOUR—NUMBERS AS <u>WORDS</u> OR FIGURES

11. **When writing about time with a.m. or p.m., always use figures.**
    WRONG: I will see you at <u>two</u> a.m.; we'll start the meeting at <u>three</u>.
    RIGHT: I will see you at 2 a.m.; we'll start the meeting at 3 a.m.

12. **With time periods, use words or figures.**
    19th century **OR** nineteenth century; 1800s **OR** the eighteen hundreds
    WRONG: 19th-century novels are often very long.
    RIGHT: Nineteenth-century novels are often very long.
    (Spell out the number when it begins a sentence.)

13. **Follow Rule 1 and use both <u>words</u> or both figures—don't mix.**
    WRONG: Yolanda completed the first <u>three</u> of the 125 assignments.
    RIGHT: Yolanda completed the first 3 of the 125 assignments.
    RIGHT: Yolanda completed the first <u>three</u> of the first <u>twelve</u> assignments.
    WRONG: Congress cut $8 <u>million</u> and $9,124,470.
    RIGHT: Congress cut $8,000,000 and $9,124,470.

Three Miscellaneous Number Rules

1. **When the day FOLLOWS the month, don't add "st," "d," or "th" to the day.**
   WRONG: We hope to see you at the March 14th retreat.
   RIGHT: We hope to see you at the March 14 retreat.
   WRONG: Please contact us by December 2d.
   RIGHT: Please contact us by December 2.

2. **When the day FOLLOWS the month and year, add a comma.**

   WRONG: John F. Kennedy was shot on November 22 1963.

   RIGHT: John F. Kennedy was shot on November 22, 1963.

   ALSO RIGHT: John Kennedy was shot on 22 November 1963.

> # NUMBER TIP
>
> Use a comma after the year if the sentence continues.
>
> **WRONG:** John F. Kennedy was shot on November 22, 1963 in Dallas.
>
> **RIGHT:** John F. Kennedy was shot on November 22, 1963, in Dallas.

3. **Don't use periods with Roman numerals except in outlines.**

   He read Chapter III in the morning and Chapter IV in the afternoon.

   Instruments of the Orchestra

   I. Strings

   II. Woodwinds

   III. Brass

   IV. Percussion

   V. Keyboard

MLA *and* APA *Citations*

Where do I start?

Let's start with the two kinds of citations you need to cite sources in a research project:

1. The list of citations you place at the end (called *Works Cited* or *References*)
2. The parenthetical citations you place in the text (called *in-text*)

Let's learn how to format both kinds of citations in two different citation styles.

MLA and APA are the commonest citation styles, and many professors don't care what approach you use as long as it's consistent—no mixing of MLA and APA. The main thing is to give credit to every source that you consult.

What, specifically, is *a "source"?*

A source is anything you consult to support your project's claims—like a scholarly study that backs up your thesis. Common sources are books and periodicals, but to those you can add a map, the Internet Movie Database, a CD or DVD, a census report, a comic book, an artwork in a museum, a tweet or posting, a YouTube video … You can also add a person, like an expert you interview in person or by email.

So with MLA or APA, you have citation rules for every kind of source?

Just about. The *Less-Is-More Handbook* offers citation models for seventy-nine types of sources, in both MLA and APA, from books to movies to postings. But it's impossible to keep up with every new source. Technology moves too fast.

However, you can use these seventy-nine citation models *as* models for special sources. For example, how do you cite a Blue-ray Disc? Logic says it's just like citing a DVD. Or how do you cite a TED talk?

So you can write citations, MLA and APA both want to know more or less the same information. To gather this information, the eighth edition (2016) of the *MLA Handbook* (often abbreviated *MLA8*) suggests asking the following questions about your source, in this order:

1. Who's the *author*?
2. What's the *title*?
3. If it's a *part of a whole* (like a story in a book), what's the title of the whole? (MLA calls this whole a "container" because it contains parts.)
4. Who are the other *contributors* (like editors, illustrators, translators, actors)?
5. What *version* is it?
6. What *number* is it?

7. **Who's the *publisher* (in other words, who's responsible for it?)**

8. ***When* was it published?**

9. ***Where* did you find it (like the page in a book or Web site, the hour/minute/second of a movie frame)?**

Once you answer these questions, you can plug the information into a citation—either MLA or APA. You won't always need to answer all nine questions. You answer as many as a reader needs to find the source.

For example, a reader could track down the TED talk with just the following:

MLA

    1.   **2.**   **3.**   **8.**
Cuddy, Amy. "Your Body Language Shapes Who You Are." TED, June 2012,

                                  9.
www.ted.com/talks/amy_cuddy_your_body_language_shapes_
who_you_are.

APA

   1.   **8.**   **2.**
Cuddy, A. (2012, June). *Your body language shapes who you are* [Video file].

                              9.
Retrieved from https://www.ted.com/talks/amy_cuddy_your_body_
language_shapes_who_you_are

The MLA citation differs from the APA, but the information is approximately the same:

    Author? = 1.
    Title? = 2.
    When published? = 8.
    Where found? = 9.

For this source, MLA wants to know the container (**3.**), but APA doesn't. And APA wants to know the source's medium ("Video file"), though MLA doesn't.

So note: Depending on the kind of source, MLA sometimes asks questions about a source that APA doesn't. And vice versa.

If you can't find a specific model in the seventy-nine models below, improvise, using the closest model.

       TWO FORMATS TO KNOW BEFORE YOU START:

1. **Page Format—Works Cited and References**

2. **Entry Format—Works Cited and References**

1. PAGE FORMAT

MLA

1. Start Works Cited on a new page one inch from the top.
2. Double-space from the running head; center Works Cited (don't italicize or underline; use normal capitalization; don't put a period after it).
3. Double-space throughout.
4. Use a hanging indent: for each entry, type the first line flush left; indent each succeeding line one-half inch.
5. Alphabetize each entry by last name; if no author, by first word of title (excluding *A, An, The*).

APA

1. Start References on a new page one inch from the top.
2. Double-space from the running head; center References (don't italicize or underline; use normal capitalization; don't put a period after it).
3. Double-space throughout.
4. Use a hanging indent: for each entry, type the first line flush left; indent each succeeding line one-half inch.
5. Alphabetize each entry by last name; if no author, by first word of title (excluding *A, An, The*).

WARNING!

MLA and APA format each entry in very different ways. Do not mix styles.

2. ENTRY FORMAT

MLA

One author

Last name, First name, Middle initial.

Smith, John J.

(Invert author's name; use middle initial if stated; place period after entry.)

Two authors

Last name, First name, Middle initial., and First name Middle initial. Last name.

Smith, John J., and Mary R. Smith.

(Invert first author; separate with commas; place period after entry.)

Three or more authors

Last name, First name, et al.

Smith, John J., et al.

(Invert first author; use first author and et al.; *separate with commas; place period after entry.)*

Corporate (Group) Author

World Health Organization.

(Place period after entry.)

Titles: Book chapters, articles, Web pages

Capitalize the first letter of all words except the following unless they start or conclude a title: **the, a, an;** prepositions: **at, by, between,** etc.; these conjunctions: **for, and, nor, but, or, yet, so;** and **to** in infinitives *(The Way to Win).*

"Article Title: Subtitle."

"The Slow Death of the Planet: The Next Step."

(Use quotation marks; place period after title if it's the first title in your citation.)

Titles: Books, journals, magazines, newspapers, Web sites

Capitalize the first letter of all words except the following unless they start or conclude a title: **the, a, an;** prepositions: **at, by, between,** etc.; these conjunctions: **for, and, nor, but, or, yet, so;** and **to** in infinitives *(The Way to Win).*

Book Title: Subtitle.

The Warming of the Planet: A Guide to Climate Change.

(Italicize; place period after title if it's the first title in your citation.)

Place of publication

For books, cite only if an edition is published in another country (e.g., a British or Canadian edition that varies from the American) or if the publisher is not generally known.

London,

(Place comma after entry.)

Publisher

Use full name of publisher but omit *Co., Corp., Inc., Ltd.,* **and such words from business titles. However, do abbreviate academic presses:**

Farrar, Straus and Giroux, *not* **Farrar, Straus, and Giroux, Inc.**

UP of Mississippi *(University Press of Mississippi),*

U of Chicago P *(University of Chicago Press),*

(Place comma after entry.)

Publication Date (Year or month/year or day/month/year, depending on source)

1951.

(Ordinarily, place comma after date but see exceptions in Seventy-Nine Citation Models, below.)

APA

One author

Last name, First initial., Middle initial.

Smith, J. J.

(Use middle initial if stated; do not place a second period after entry.)

Two to seven authors

Last name, First initial., Middle initial., & Last name, First initial., Middle initial.

Smith, J. J., & Smith, M.

Smith, J. J., Smith, M., & Jones, P.

(Use comma and ampersand [&]; do not place a second period after entry.)

Eight or more authors

Smith, J. J., Smith, M., Smith, R. J., Smith, P., Smith, A. C., Smith, B. T., ... Jones, B.

(List first six authors, ellipsis, last author; do not place a second period after entry.)

Group author

World Health Organization.

(Place period after entry.)

Publication Date

(2017). [Book]

(2017, June). [Magazine]

(2017, 19 June). [Daily newspaper, blog, etc.]

(Place after author; place period after parentheses.)

Titles: Books, book chapters, articles, Web articles, Web pages

Capitalize only the first word and proper nouns in titles and subtitles; capitalize book volume numbers.

Book title: Subtitle.

The warming of the planet: A guide to climate change (Vol. 1).

　　(Italicize; place period after entry.)

Article title: Subtitle.

　　(Don't italicize or use quotation marks.)

Book chapters, articles, Web articles, Web pages: Subtitle

The slow death of the planet: And then what?

(Place comma after entry unless title includes a punctuation mark.)

Titles: Journals, magazines, newspapers; Web sites, online journals, online newspapers, reference databases

Capitalize the first letter of all words except the following unless they start or conclude a title: **the, a, an,** prepositions, and these conjunctions: **for, and, nor, but, or, yet, so.**

Journal Title,

The Journal of Social Media,

(Italicize; place comma after entry unless title includes a punctuation mark.)

Place of publication

For nonperiodicals, use first city stated on title page, comma, state postal abbreviation.

Boston, MA:

(Place a colon after entry.)

Omit state with a university press that uses a state name.

Columbia: University of South Carolina Press.

(Place colon after city.)

If publisher is located outside the United States, give country.

Dublin, Ireland: University College Dublin Press.

(Place colon after country.)

Use short form of publisher (leave out *Inc., Co.,* etc.) but write out *Books* or *Press.*

Publisher

Harvard University Press.

(Place a period after entry.)

WARNING!

MLA omits repeated digits in consecutive page numbering: 213-15; 1789-91. **APA retains the digits:** 213-215; 1789-1791.

FORMAT GUIDE

WORKS CITED (MLA) AND REFERENCES (APA)

Sources exist in three forms:

1. **Only in print**
2. **Both in print and online**
3. **Only online**

Many of the sources you consult will exist both in print and online. It's important, however, not to neglect sources only in print. Old textbooks, obscure government reports, pulp novels and magazines, political and advertising ephemera, archival collections, early audio and visual productions: Many fertile research sources haven't been scanned or uploaded and can't be found online. **Try not to limit your search for sources to what you find on the computer.**

Nevertheless, given that many college research projects rely solely on computer searches, each entry of your Works Cited or References list will probably end with an online address:

MLA

> David, Larry. "Wandering Bear." *Curb Your Enthusiasm*, produced by Jeff Garlin, DVD version, season 4, episode 8, HBO Home Entertainment, 29 Feb. 2004. *Amazon Prime*, www.amazon. com/gp/video/detail/B0172URD64?ref_=aiv_dp_season_select.

APA

> David, L. (Writer-Director). (2004, February 29). Wandering bear [Television series episode]. In Garlin, J. (Producer), *Curb your enthusiasm*. Retrieved from http://www.amazon.com/gp/video/ detail/B0172URD64?ref_=aiv_dp_season_select

Therefore, please take note:

Many of the seventy-nine citation models below can be written in one of two ways:

1. **As a print citation**
2. **As an online citation**

MLA

1. **For sources that exist both in print and online, begin with the print citation (see 1-63, below) but add the DOI (preferred if available) or URL:**

   > Last name, First name. *Book Title in Italics: Subtitle If Any.* Publisher, year of publication. *Title of Web Site or Database in Italics*, doi.

   > Last name, First name. *Book Title in Italics: Subtitle If Any.* Publisher, year of publication. *Title of Web Site or Database in Italics*, URL.

   For the DOI (*digital object identifier*, a unique number assigned to a database article, document, or book):
   - **Find the DOI in the database citation, abstract, or full-text format**
   - **Don't capitalize DOI: doi**
   - **Put a colon after with no space: doi:10.1000/1000000**
   - **Put a period at end of DOI**

   For the URL (*uniform resource locator*, the address of a Web source):
   - **Omit *http://* or *https://* but give rest of address**
   - **Put a period at end of URL**

If using a library or subscription database, add the name of the database in italics and the DOI or URL:

> Last name, First name. "Title in Quotations: Subtitle If Any." *Journal Title in Italics*, vol. 54, no.3, Mar. 2017, pp. 135-54. *Project Muse*, doi:10.1000/1000000.

> Last name, First name. "Title in Quotations: Subtitle If Any." *Journal Title in Italics*, vol. 54, no.3, Mar. 2017, pp. 135-54. *ProQuest*, URL.

2. **For sources that exist only or primarily online, see 64-79, below.**

APA

1. **For sources that exist both in print and online, begin with the print citation (see 1-63, below) but add the DOI:**

    - **Find the DOI in the database citation, abstract, or full-text format**
    - **Don't capitalize DOI: doi**
    - **Put a colon after with no space: doi:10.1000/1000000**
    - **Don't put a period at end of DOI**

    For books and reports, omit city and publisher and replace with DOI:

    > Last name, Initial. (Year of publication). *Title in italics: Subtitle if any.* doi:10.1000/1000000

    For journals, keep all information and add DOI:

    > Last name, Initial., & Last name, Initial. (Year of publication). Title without quotations: Subtitle if any. *Journal Title in Italics*, 56, 213-216. doi:10.1000/1000000

    If the source has no DOI, write:

    Retrieved from http:// [rest of URL]

    - **Break the URL *before* periods and slashes; don't use hyphens**
    - **Don't put a period at the end of the URL**

    For books and reports, omit city and publisher and replace with URL:

    > Last name, Initial. (Year of publication). *Title in italics: Subtitle if any.* Retrieved from http:// [rest of URL]

    For journals, keep all information and add URL:

    > Last name, Initial., & Last name, Initial. (Year of publication). Title without quotations: Subtitle if any. *Journal Title in Italics*, 56, 213-216. Retrieved from http:[rest of URL]

2. **For sources that exist only or primarily online, see 64-79, below.**

SEVENTY-NINE CITATION TYPES

BOOK

1. One Author
2. Two Authors
3. Two to Seven Authors
4. Three or More Authors
5. Eight or More Authors
6. An Organization as Group Author
7. Same Author of More than One Book
8. Same Author of More than One Book in Same Year
9. Republished (Reprinted) Book
10. Second or Later Revised Edition
11. One Author with Translator
12. One Author with Translator and Editor
13. Unknown Author with Translator
14. Translation of Part of Book
15. Title within Title
16. One Work or Collected Works of One Author in One Book with Editor(s)
17. Anthology or Scholarly Collection with Editor(s)
18. One Work in Anthology or Collected Works with Editor(s)
19. Reprinted Article in Scholarly Collection with Editor(s)
20. Books in Volumes—with and without Editor(s)
21. Book in Series
22. Article in Reference Book (Dictionary, Encyclopedia, etc.)
23. Foreword, Preface, Introduction, Afterword
24. Illustrated Book with Introduction
25. Graphic Narrative
26. Religious Text (Bible, Qur'an, etc.)

MASTER'S THESIS OR PH.D. DISSERTATION

27. Master's Thesis or Ph.D. Dissertation
28. Dissertation Abstract (Citing Abstract Listed in *Dissertation Abstracts International*)

SCHOLARLY JOURNAL

29. Article in Journal Paginated by Volume
30. Article in Journal Paginated by Volume and Issue

MAGAZINE AND NEWSPAPER

31. Magazine Article with Author
32. Newspaper Article with Author
33. Unsigned Magazine or Newspaper Article
34. Unsigned Editorial in Magazine or Newspaper
35. Letter to Editor in Magazine or Newspaper
36. Review in Magazine or Newspaper
37. Article in Series in Magazine or Newspaper
38. Advertisement in Magazine or Newspaper
39. Cartoon or Comic Strip

REPORT, PAMPHLET, CONFERENCE PROCEEDINGS, PAPER PRESENTATION, OR POSTER SESSION

40. Report or Pamphlet
41. Article (Paper) in Published Conference Proceedings
42. Paper Presentation or Poster Session

GOVERNMENT PUBLICATION

43. Government Publication

PRINT INTERVIEW

44. Interview in Magazine or Newspaper

UNPUBLISHED SOURCE

45. Letter
46. Manuscript or Typescript Other than Letter

TELEVISION, RADIO

47. Television Broadcast
48. Radio Broadcast

FILM, DVD, VIDEO

49. Film—Seen in Theatre
50. Film—DVD or Videocassette

SOUND RECORDING (CD, LP, MUSIC DOWNLOAD/MP3 FILE)

51. CD or LP—Composer or Performer Emphasized First
52. Digital File Download: Audio, Image, Video, Movie (e-book, JPEG, MP3, PDF, etc.)

CD-ROM, DVD-ROM, VIDEO OR COMPUTER GAME, COMPUTER SOFTWARE

53. CD-ROM or DVD-ROM
54. Video/Computer Game or Specialized Computer Software Program

PODCAST

55. Podcast

LECTURE, POWERPOINT, SPEECH, READING

56. Lecture

ORAL INTERVIEW

57. Oral (Unpublished) Interview
58. Broadcast Interview—Television or Radio

LIVE PERFORMANCE

59. Play, Music Concert, Ballet, Opera, Dance

WRITTEN MUSICAL COMPOSITION

60. Longer Composition: Symphony, Ballet, Opera, etc.
61. Shorter Composition: Song, Short Instrumental Piece, etc.

ARTWORK (PAINTING, DRAWING, ETCHING, SCULPTURE, PHOTO-GRAPH, ETC.)

62. Artwork

MAP OR CHART

63. Map or Chart

ENTIRE WEB SITE

64. Entire Web Site

SECTION OF WEB SITE

65. Section of Web Site

ARTICLE IN ONLINE JOURNAL

66. Article in Online Journal

ARTICLE FROM ONLINE MAGAZINE OR NEWSPAPER

67. Article from Online Magazine or Newspaper

ONLINE BOOK

68. Online Book

ONLINE POEM OR SHORT STORY

69. Online Poem or Short Story

ONLINE REFERENCE WORK

70. Online Reference Work

WIKI

71. Wiki

BLOG (WEB LOG)

72. Entire Blog
73. Posting on a Blog

POSTINGS ON A WEB PAGE

74. Discussion Group Posting
75. Comments Posted on a Web Page

E-MAIL

76. E-mail

SOCIAL MEDIA

77. Social Media (Twitter, Facebook, Google+, etc.)

YOUTUBE AND MOVIE-/VIDEO-STREAMING SITES

78. YouTube
79. Movie-/Video-Streaming Sites (Netflix, Hulu, Amazon Prime, etc.)

SEVENTY-NINE CITATION MODELS

BOOK

1. One Author

MLA

> Last name, First name. *Title in Italics: Subtitle If Any.* Publisher, year of publication.
>
> Smith, John J. *The Warming of the Planet: A Guide to Climate Change.* Alfred A. Knopf, 2012.

APA

> Last name, Initial. (Year of publication). *Title in italics: Subtitle if any.* City of publication, State Abbreviation: Publisher.
>
> Smith, J. J. (2012). *The warming of the planet: A guide to climate change.* New York, NY: Knopf.

(With DOI, omit city and publisher:

> Smith, J. J. (2012). *The warming of the planet: A guide to climate change.* doi:10.1000/1000000

See the Rules for Online Sources, page TBD. No period follows DOI in entry.)

2. Two Authors

MLA

> Last name, First name, and First name Last name. *Title in Italics: Subtitle If Any.* Publisher, year of publication.

3. Two to Seven Authors

APA

> Last name, Initial., Last name, Initial., & Last name, Initial. (Year of publication). *Title in italics: Subtitle if any.* City of publication, State Abbreviation: Publisher.

4. Three or More Authors

MLA

> Last name, First name, et al. *Title in Italics: Subtitle If Any.* Publisher, year of publication.

5. Eight or More Authors

APA

> Last name, Initial., Last name, Initial., Last name, Initial., Last name, Initial., Last name, Initial., Last name, Initial., … & Last name, Initial. (Year of publication). *Title in italics: Subtitle if any.* City of publication, State Abbreviation: Publisher.

(After six authors, use ellipsis to omit remaining authors except last author.)

6. **An Organization as Group Author**
   MLA

   > Group name. *Title in Italics: Subtitle If Any.* Publisher, year of publication.

   APA

   > Group name. (Year of publication). *Title in italics: Subtitle if any.* City of publication, State Abbreviation: Publisher.

7. **Same Author of More than One Book**
   MLA

   > Last name, First name. *Title in Italics: Subtitle If Any.* Publisher, year of publication.
   >
   > ---. *Title in Italics: Subtitle If Any.* Publisher, year of publication.

   (Type three hyphens followed by period; alphabetize by title.)

8. **Same Author of More than One Book in Same Year**
   APA

   > Last name, Initial. (Year of publication a). *Title in italics: Subtitle if any.* City of publication, State Abbreviation: Publisher.
   >
   > Same last name, Initial. (Year of publication b). *Title in italics: Subtitle if any.* City of publication, State Abbreviation: Publisher.

   (Use lowercase letter for each book published in same year: 2012a, 2012b, etc.)

9. **Republished (Reprinted) Book**
   MLA

   > Last name, First name. *Title in Italics: Subtitle If Any.* Year of original publication. Publisher, year of new publication.

   (If the republished book has been issued under a new title, add reprint information.)

   > Last name, First name. *Title in Italics: Subtitle If Any.* Publisher, year of new publication, rpt. of *Title in Italics: Subtitle If Any.* Year of original publication.

   APA

   > Last name, Initial. (Year of publication). *Title in italics: Subtitle if any* (Initial. Last name, Ed.). City of publication, State Abbreviation: Publisher. (Original work published [year])

   (No period follows.)

10. **Second or Later Revised Edition**
    MLA

    > Last name, First name. *Title in Italics: Subtitle If Any.* 2nd ed., Publisher, year of publication.

    APA

    > Last name, Initial. (Year of publication). *Title in italics: Subtitle if any* (2nd ed.). City of publication, State Abbreviation: Publisher.

11. **One Author with Translator**

    MLA

    > Last name, First name. *Title in Italics: Subtitle If Any.* Translated by First name Last name, Publisher, year of publication.

    APA

    > Last name, Initial. (Year of publication). *Title in italics: Subtitle if any* (Initial. Last name, Trans.). City of publication, State Abbreviation: Publisher. (Original work published [year])

    (No period follows.)

12. **One Author with Translator and Editor**

    MLA

    > Last name, First name. *Title in Italics: Subtitle If Any.* Translated by First name Last name, edited by First name Last name, Publisher, year of publication.

    For APA, use *Ed.* for one editor and *Eds.* for more than one. (See Model 17.)

    APA

    > Last name, Initial. (Year of publication). *Title in italics: Subtitle if any* (Initial. Last name, Ed.). (Initial. Last name, Trans.). City of publication, State Abbreviation: Publisher.

13. **Unknown Author with Translator**

    MLA

    > *Title in Italics: Subtitle If Any.* Translated by First name Last name, Publisher, year of publication.

    APA

    > *Title in italics: Subtitle if any.* (Year of publication). (Initial. Last Name, Trans.). City of publication, State Abbreviation: Publisher.

14. **Translation of Part of Book**

    MLA

    > Last name, First name. "Title in Quotations: Subtitle If Any." Translated by First name Last name, *Title in Italics: Subtitle If Any*, edited by First name Last name and First name Last name, Publisher, year of publication.

    APA

    > Last name, Initial. (Year of publication). Title without quotations: Subtitle if any (Initial. Last name, Trans.). In Initial. Last name & Initial. Last name (Eds.), *Title in italics: Subtitle if any* (pp. 10-15). City of publication, State Abbreviation: Publisher.

15. **Title within Title**

    For both MLA and APA, if quoting a title within a title, like *Shakespeare's Pupils: The School of* Hamlet, don't italicize or put into quotations a title that ordinarily would be.

    MLA

    Last name, First name. *Title in Italics with* Title within Title: *Subtitle If Any*. Publisher, year of publication.

    APA

    Last name, Initial. (Year of publication). *Title in italics with* Title within title: *Subtitle if any*. City of publication, State Abbreviation: Publisher.

    (Capitalize first word of Title within title.)

16. **One Work or Collected Works of One Author in One Book with Editor(s)**

    MLA

    Last name, First name. *Title in Italics: Subtitle If Any*. Edited by First name Last name, Publisher, year of publication.

    APA

    Last name, Initial. (Year of publication). *Title in italics: Subtitle if any* (Initial. Last name, Ed.). City of publication, State Abbreviation: Publisher.

17. **Anthology or Scholarly Collection with Editor(s)**

    MLA

    Last name, First name, and First name Last name, editors. *Title in Italics: Subtitle If Any*. Publisher, year of publication.

    APA

    Last name, Initial., & Last name, Initial. (Eds.). (Year of publication). *Title in italics: Subtitle if any*. City of publication, State Abbreviation: Publisher.

18. **One Work in Anthology or Collected Works with Editor(s)**

    MLA

    Last name, First name. "Title of Work in Quotations: Subtitle If Any." *Title of Anthology: Subtitle If Any*, edited by First name Last name, Publisher, year of publication, pp. 254-63.

    (Include page numbers of selection after year of publication: pp. 254-63.)

    APA

    Last name, Initial. (Year of publication). Title of work without quotations: Subtitle if any. In Initial. Last Name & Initial. Last Name (Eds.), *Title of anthology in italics: Subtitle if any* (pp. 254-263). City of publication, State Abbreviation: Publisher.

19. **Reprinted Article in Scholarly Collection with Editor(s)**

MLA

> Last name, First name. "Title of Article in Quotations: Subtitle If Any." *Title of Journal Where First Printed in Italics*, vol. 18, year of original publication, pp. 40-51, rpt. in *Title in Italics: Subtitle If Any*, edited by First name Last Name, Publisher, year of publication, pp.154-62.

(If the article first appeared in a journal, include journal volume number [18] and page numbers [pp. 40-51] as well as page numbers [pp. 154-62] in book where reprinted [*rpt.*].)

APA

> Last name, Initial. (Year of publication). Title without quotations: Subtitle if any. In Initial. Last Name & Initial. Last Name (Eds.), *Title of collection in italics: Subtitle if any* (pp. 154-162). City of publication, State Abbreviation: Publisher. (Reprinted from *Title in italics: Subtitle if any*, pp. 9-15, by Initial. Last name, Ed., year of publication, City of publication, State Abbreviation: Publisher)

(No period follows.)

20. **Books in Volumes–with and without Editor(s)**

MLA

> Last name, First name. *Title in Italics: Subtitle If Any*. Edited by First name Last name, vol. 2, Publisher, year of publication.

(If your project refers to just one volume, write vol. 2.)

But:

> Last name, First name. *Title in Italics: Subtitle If Any*. 2nd ed., Publisher, year of publication. 4 vols.

(If your project refers to two or more volumes, write *4 vols.*, etc..) The in-text citation will state which volume used: 4: 251.)

APA

> Last name, Initial. (Year of publication). *Title in italics: Subtitle if any* (Initial. Last name, Ed.). (Vol. 2). City of publication, State Abbreviation: Publisher.

(If your project refers to just one volume, write Vol. 2.)

> Last name, Initial. (Year of publication). *Title in italics: Subtitle if any* (Initial. Last name, Ed.). (Vols. 1-4). City of publication, State Abbreviation: Publisher.

(If your project refers to more than one volume, write Vols. 1-4.)

21. **Book in Series**

MLA

> Last name, First name. *Title in Italics: Subtitle If Any*. Publisher, year of publication. Title of Series 56.

(The series title is not italicized or put into quotations. Include series number if stated.)

APA

Last name, Initial. (Year of publication). *Title in italics: Subtitle if any*. City of publication, State Abbreviation: Publisher. (*Title of Series in Italics 56*)

(Capitalize key words in a Title of Series. Include series number if stated; no period follows.)

22. **Article in Reference Book (Dictionary, Encyclopedia, etc.)**

MLA

Last name, First name. "Title in Quotations: Subtitle If Any." *Title in Italics: Subtitle If Any*, 5th ed., Publisher, 2010, p 203.

Or

"Title in Quotations: Subtitle If Any." *Title in Italics: Subtitle If Any*, 2nd ed., Publisher, 2011, pp. 1021-2.

(Use title if article has no author.)

APA

Last name, Initial. (Year of publication). Title without quotations: Subtitle if any. In Initial. Last name (Ed.), *Title in italics: Subtitle if any* (Vol. 18, pp. 143-144). City of publication, State Abbreviation: Publisher.

Or

Title without quotations: Subtitle if any. (Year of publication). In Initial. Last name (Ed.), *Title in italics: Subtitle if any* (2nd ed., p. 898). City of publication, State Abbreviation: Publisher.

23. **Foreword, Preface, Introduction, Afterword**

MLA

Last name, First name. Foreword. *Title in Italics: Subtitle If Any*, by First name Last name, Publisher, year of publication, pp. xx-xxvi.

(Include page numbers after year of publication: *pp. xx-xxvi.* **After author's name, include foreword title if given:** Last name, First name. "Title in Quotations: Subtitle If Any." Foreword.**)**

APA

Last name, Initial. (Year of publication). Foreword. In Initial. Last name, *Title in italics: Subtitle if any* (pp. xx-xxvi). City of publication, State Abbreviation: Publisher.

(If specific title is given, write Last name, Initial. (Year of publication). Title without quotations: Subtitle if any [Foreword]. In Initial. Last name, **and then continue rest of reference.)**

24. **Illustrated Book with Introduction**

MLA

Last name, First name. *Title in Italics: Subtitle If Any*. Introduction by First name Last name, illustrated by First name Last name, Publisher, year of publication.

APA

Last name, Initial. (Year of publication). *Title in italics: Subtitle if any* (Initial. Last name, Introd.). (Initial. Last name, Illus.). City of publication, State Abbreviation: Publisher.

25. **Graphic Narrative**

MLA

> Last name, First name, artist. *Title in Italics: Subtitle If Any.* Written by First name Last name, Publisher, year of publication.

***Or* (depending on whether project primarily discusses artist or writer)**

> Last name, First name, writer. *Title in Italics: Subtitle If Any.* Art by First name Last name, Publisher, year of publication.

APA

> Last name, Initial. (Artist). (Year of publication). *Title in italics: Subtitle if any* [Graphic novel]. Initial. Last name (Writer). City of publication, State Abbreviation: Publisher.

***Or* (depending on whether project primarily discusses artist or writer)**

> Last name, Initial. (Writer). (Year of publication). *Title in italics: Subtitle if any* [Graphic novel]. Initial. Last name (Artist). City of publication, State Abbreviation: Publisher.

26. **Religious Text (Bible, Qur'an, etc.)**

MLA

> *Title in Italics: Subtitle If Any.* Translated by name of group, edited by First name Last name and First name Last name, Publisher, year of publication.

(For a large work with many translators, state name of group translating: *World Bible Society.***)**

APA

(Religious and standard classical works are cited in-text parenthetically but not in References. See Guide to Formatting In-Text Citations: MLA and APA, 17 **and** 37.**)**

MASTER'S THESIS OR PH.D. DISSERTATION

27. **Master's Thesis or Ph.D. Dissertation**

MLA

> Last name, First name. *Title in Italics: Subtitle If Any.* Dissertation. Name of University, year dissertation accepted.

(Use short forms of the university name: U of Iowa, Iowa State U.**)**

APA

> Last name, Initial. (Year dissertation accepted). *Title in italics: Subtitle if any* (Doctoral dissertation, Name of University). Retrieved from http://

(No period follows.)

28. Dissertation Abstract (Citing Abstract Listed in *Dissertation Abstracts International*)

MLA

> Last name, First name. *Title in Italics: Subtitle If Any.* Dissertation. Name of University, year dissertation accepted, *Dissertation Abstracts International.* vol. 50, no.2, 2005, p. 1321.

(Give *Dissertation Abstracts International* volume number [50], issue number [2], year of publication [2005], and page number [1321]).

APA

> Last name, Initial. (2005). Title without quotations: Subtitle if any. *Dissertation Abstracts International: Section B. Sciences and Engineering,50*(2), 1321.

(Spell out *Dissertation Abstracts International*, stating section letter and category. Italicize volume [50] but not issue number [2].)

SCHOLARLY JOURNAL

> # WARNING!
>
> **MLA gives dates as the following:** 27 Sept. 2010. **APA gives dates as the following: 2010, September 27. In MLA, abbreviate all months except May, June, July. In APA, spell out all months.**

29. Article in Journal Paginated by Volume

Each issue within a volume continues consecutive page numbering—i.e., each new issue doesn't begin with *page 1.*

APA

> Last name, Initial., & Last name, Initial. (Year of publication). Title without quotations: Subtitle if any. *Journal Title in Italics, 56,* 213-216.

(Use normal capitalization with periodical titles: *The Journal of Social Media*. Include volume number [56] and page numbers [213-216]. Note: Don't use *p.* with journals and magazines. Note: Volume number is italicized; don't include issue number.)

30. Article in Journal Paginated by Volume and Issue

Each issue is paginated with a new *page 1.*

MLA

> Last name, First name. "Title in Quotations: Subtitle If Any." *Journal Title in Italics*, vol. 54, no. 3, year of publication, pp. 135-54.

(Include volume number [54], issue number [3], and page numbers [135-54]. If the journal includes only issue numbers, write *Journal Title in Italics*, no. 104, 2010, pp. 1-5.)

APA

> Last name, Initial. (Year of publication). Title without quotations: Subtitle if any. *Journal Title in Italics, 54*(3), 135-154.

(Note: Volume number is italicized, but issue number is not: *54*[3]**.)**

MAGAZINE AND NEWSPAPER

31. **Magazine Article with Author**

    For MLA, for a weekly or twice-monthly magazine, include date and page numbers.

    MLA

    > Last name, First name. "Title in Quotations: Subtitle If Any." *Magazine in Italics*, 18 Jan. 2010, pp 45-51.

    For MLA, for a monthly or every-other-month magazine, include month, year, and page number.

    > Last name, First name. "Title in Quotations: Subtitle If Any." *Magazine in Italics*, Dec. 2010, pp. 75+.

    (For an article that isn't printed on consecutive pages—that is, it skips pages—cite the first page it begins on with a plus sign.)

    For APA, for a weekly or twice-monthly magazine, include volume [56] and also issue number [3] if each issue starts numbering with page 1.

    APA

    > Last name, Initial. (2011, June 18). Title without quotations: Subtitle if any. *Magazine in Italics, 56*(3), 18-19.

    (Note: Don't use *p.* **for page number.)**

    For APA, for a monthly or every-other month magazine, include year and month, volume [91] and also issue number [2] if each issue starts numbering with page 1.

    APA

    > Last name, Initial. (2011, June). Title without quotations: Subtitle if any. *Magazine in Italics, 91*(2), 18.

    (Note: volume number is italicized for all magazines, but issue number is not: *91*[2]**.)**

32. **Newspaper Article with Author**

    MLA

    > Last name, First name. "Title in Quotations: Subtitle If Any." *Newspaper in Italics*, 6 June 1995, late ed., pp. D3+.

    (Include the section letter [D], the first page the article begins on [3], and the plus sign [+] to show that the article doesn't continue on consecutive pages—that is, the article skips pages.)

APA

Last name, Initial. (1995, June 6). Title without quotations: Subtitle if any. *Newspaper in Italics*, pp. D3, D5, D6.

(Note: If the article doesn't continue on consecutive pages, list each page it appears on. Note: With newspapers, include *p.* or *pp.* for page numbers.)

33. **Unsigned Magazine or Newspaper Article**

For MLA, for magazine follow Model 31 but replace author with title; for newspaper:

MLA

"Title in Quotations: Subtitle If Any." *Newspaper in Italics*, 9 Dec. 1993, late ed., p. B6.

(Add which edition if more than one.)

For APA, for magazine follow Model 31 but replace author with title; for newspaper:

APA

Title without quotations: Subtitle if any. (1993, December 9). *Newspaper in Italics*, p. B6.

34. **Unsigned Editorial in Magazine or Newspaper**

For MLA, for magazine follow Model 31 but replace author with title and add *Editorial* (no italics) plus period after title; for newspaper:

MLA

"Title in Quotations: Subtitle If Any." Editorial. *Newspaper in Italics*, 3 Mar. 2012, p. A8.

For APA, for magazine follow Model 31 but replace author with title and add *Editorial* (no italics) in brackets after title; for newspaper:

APA

Title without quotations: Subtitle if any [Editorial]. (2012, March 3). *Newspaper in Italics*, p. A8.

35. **Letter to Editor in Magazine or Newspaper**

For MLA, for magazine follow Model 31 and add *Letter* (no italics) after name; for newspaper:

MLA

Last name, First name. Letter. "Title in Quotations: Subtitle If Any." *Newspaper in Italics*, 18 Apr. 2009, p. A7.

For APA, for magazine follow Model 31 and add *Letter to the editor* (no italics) in brackets after title; for newspaper:

APA

Last name, Initial. (2005, March 1). Title without quotations: Subtitle if any [Letter to the editor]. *Newspaper in Italics*, p. A7.

36. **Review in Magazine or Newspaper**
    MLA

    Last name, First name. "Title in Quotations: Subtitle If Any." Review of *Title in Italics: Subtitle If Any*, by First name Last name. *Magazine in Italics*, 8 Sept. 2010, pp. 118-22.

    Last name, First name. "Title in Quotations: Subtitle If Any." Review of *Film in Italics*, directed by First name Last name. *Newspaper in Italics*, 3 Jan. 1974, p. B13.

    For APA, for magazine follow Model 31 and add *Review of* (no italics) in brackets after title; for newspaper:

    APA

    Last name, Initial. (1974, January 3). Title without quotations: Subtitle if any [Review of the book *Title in italics*, by Initial. Last name]. *Newspaper in Italics*, p. 75.

37. **Article in Series in Magazine or Newspaper**
    For MLA, for newspaper, follow Model 32. If title changes for each installment in a series, add this description: Pt. 3 of a series, Title without Quotations: Subtitle If Any, begun 7 Sept. 2008. For magazine:
    MLA

    Last name, First name. "Title in Quotations: Subtitle If Any." *Magazine in Italics*, 28 Sept. 2008, pp. 78-81, pt. 3 of a series, Title without Quotations: Subtitle If Any, begun 7 Sept. 2008.

38. **Advertisement in Magazine or Newspaper**
    For MLA, for magazine or newspaper, use same model, inserting *Advertisement* (no italics).
    MLA

    Name of Product Advertised. Advertisement. *Magazine in Italics*, 11 Oct. 1965, p. 18.

39. **Cartoon or Comic Strip**
    For MLA, for magazine or newspaper, insert *Cartoon* or *Comic Strip* (no italics).
    MLA

    Last name, First name. "Title If Any in Quotations." Cartoon. *Magazine in Italics*, 3 Feb. 2001. p. 78.

REPORT, PAMPHLET, CONFERENCE PROCEEDINGS, PAPER PRESENTATION, OR POSTER SESSION

40. **Report or Pamphlet**
    MLA

    Last name, First name. *Title in Italics: Subtitle If Any*. Publisher, year of publication.
    APA

    Last name, Initial., & Last name, Initial. (Year of publication). *Title in italics: Subtitle if any* (Report No. 555-067). City of publication, State Abbreviation: Publisher.

    (With DOI, omit city, state abbreviation, and publisher.)

41. Article (Paper) in Published Conference Proceedings

MLA

Last name, First name. "Title in Quotations: Subtitle If Any." *Conference Proceedings in Italics*, edited by First name Last name, City of publication, Publisher, year of publication. pp. 6-12.

APA

Last name, Initial. (Year of publication). Title without quotations: Subtitle if any. In Initial. Last name (Ed.), *Conference proceedings in italics* (pp. 6-12). City of publication, State Abbreviation: Publisher.

42. Paper Presentation or Poster Session

MLA

Last name, First name. "Title in Quotations: Subtitle If Any." Name of Session, Name of Organization, Location, 18 Jan. 2009. Poster session.

APA

Last name, Initial. (2010, February). *Title in italics: Subtitle if any.* Paper or poster session presented at the 2010 Name of Organization, City, State Abbreviation.

GOVERNMENT PUBLICATION

43. Government Publication

MLA

Last name, First name. *Title in Italics: Subtitle If Any.* Name of Government Agency Issuing Document, Government Printing Office, year of publication.

Or (if no author)

Name of Government Agency Issuing Publication. *Title in Italics: Subtitle If Any*, Government Printing Office, year of publication.

APA

Last name, Initial. (Year of publication). *Title in italics: Subtitle if any.* Washington, DC: Government Printing Office.

Or (if no author)

Name of Government Agency Issuing Publication. (Year of publication). *Title in italics: Subtitle if any.* Washington, DC: Government Printing Office.

PRINT INTERVIEW

44. Interview in Magazine or Newspaper

MLA

Last name, First name. "Title in Quotations: Subtitle If Any." *Magazine in Italics*, 6 Mar. 2009, pp. 56-65.

APA

Last name, Initial. (2009, December). Title without quotations: Subtitle if any. *Magazine in Italics*, 35, 77-87.

UNPUBLISHED SOURCE

45. Letter

MLA

Last name, First name. Letter to the author. 8 Nov. 2005. Manuscript.

(Use *manuscript* to show handwritten form; *typescript* to show typed form.)

APA

Last name, Initial. (2005, November 8). [Letter to First name Last name]. Copy in possession of First name Last name.

(Include letter in References if retrievable. Otherwise, include in only parenthetical citation.)

46. Manuscript or Typescript Other than Letter

MLA

Last name, First name. *Title If Any in Italics: Subtitle If Any.* 1951. Typescript, Box 18, Memoirs of First name Last name, Name of Library, City.

(If no title, describe the manuscript/typescript in clear terms: novel, poetry collection, diary, notebooks, memoirs, etc.)

APA

Last name, Initial. (1951). *Title if any in italics: Subtitle if any* [Unpublished memoir]. Smith Memoirs (Box 18). Library, City, State Abbreviation.

(If there is no title or it does not clearly describe the source, immediately after title include bracketed description: unpublished novel, poetry collection, diary, notebook, memoir, etc. If the source has a library description that identifies it, such as Smith Collection **or** Smith Memoirs, **include that after the bracketed description.)**

TELEVISION, RADIO

47. Television Broadcast

MLA

"Title of Episode in Quotations." *Program Series in Italics*, directed by First name Last name, performances by First name Last name, First name Last name, and First name Last name, NBC, WHO, Des Moines, 18 Nov. 2001.

(Give as much information as needed: written by, directed by, performed by, narrated by, etc.)

APA

Last name, Initial. (Writer), & Last name, Initial. (Director). (2001, November 18). Title of episode without quotations [Television series episode]. In Initial. Last name & Initial. Last name (Producers), *Program series in italics*. City, State Abbreviation: Home Box Office.

48. Radio Broadcast

MLA

"Title in Quotations." *Program Series in Italics*, narrated by First name Last name, National Public Radio, WNPR, City,
16 June 2010.

APA

Last name, Initial. (Narrator). (2010, June 16). Title without quotations: Subtitle if any. In Initial. Last name (Executive producer), *Program series in italics* [Radio program]. City, State Abbreviation: National Public Radio.

FILM, DVD, VIDEO

49. Film—Seen in Theatre

MLA

Last name, First name, director. *Film Title in Italics*. Performances by First name Last name and First name Last name, Studio, year of release.

(Here emphasizing director first and performers second; studio: M-G-M, Warner Bros., etc.)

Or

Film Title in Italics. Directed by First name Last name, performances by First name Last name and First name Last name, Studio, year of release.

APA

Last name, Initial. (Director), & Last name, Initial. (Producer). (Year of release). *Film title in italics* [Motion picture]. Country of origin: Studio.

(Country of origin = studio's home country.)

50. Film—DVD or Videocassette

MLA

Last name, First name, director. *Film Title in Italics*. Performances by First name Last name and First name Last name, year of original release, DVD distributor, year of DVD release, disc 4.

APA

Last name, Initial. (Director), & Last name, Initial. (Producer). (Year of DVD release). *Film title in italics* [DVD]. Country of origin: Studio. (Original release date)

(No period follows.)

SOUND RECORDING (CD, LP)

51. CD or LP— Composer or Performer Emphasized First
MLA

> Last name, First name. "Title of Selection in Quotations." *Title of CD in Italics*, performance by First name Last name, CD manufacturer, year of release.

APA

> Last name, Initial. (Year of copyright). Title of selection without quotations. On *Title of CD in italics* [CD]. City, State Abbreviation: CD manufacturer.

52. Digital File Download: Audio, Image, Video, Movie (MP3, e-book, JPEG, PDF, etc.)
MLA

> Last name, First name. "Selection in Quotations." *Title in Italics*, year of release. MP3 file.
>
> Last name, First name. *Title in Italics*. Kindle ed., Publisher, year of publication.

APA

> Last name, Initial. (Year of release). Title without quotations [MP3]. Available from Organization Name.

CD-ROM, DVD-ROM, VIDEO OR COMPUTER GAME, COMPUTER SOFTWARE

53. CD-ROM or DVD-ROM
For MLA, for a nonperiodical CD-ROM or DVD-ROM:
MLA

> Last name, First name. *Title in Italics*. Version number, Publisher, year of release.

For MLA, for a periodical (journal, magazine, or newspaper) CD-ROM or DVD-ROM:

> Last name, First name. "Title in Quotations: Subtitle If Any." *Periodical in Italics*. 9 Mar. 2009, pp. 14+, *Name of CD-ROM in Italics*, Publisher.

APA

> Last name, Initial. (Year of CD-ROM release). Title without quotations: Subtitle if any. On *Title in italics* [CD-ROM]. City of publication, State Abbreviation: Publisher. (Original publication date)

(No period follows.)

54. **Video/Computer Game or Specialized Computer Software Program**

    For both MLA and APA, it isn't necessary to cite common products. Cite only specialized.

    MLA

    > *Title of Software in Italics.* Version Number, Publisher, year
    >   of release.

    APA

    > Title of Software in Capitals (Version number) [Computer software]. (Year of release). City of
    >   software vendor, State Abbreviation: Software vendor.

PODCAST

55. **Podcast**

    For MLA, for downloaded files:

    MLA

    > Last name, First name. "Title in Quotations: Subtitle If Any." *Site Title in Italics*, episode 212, 9
    >   Dec. 2011. MP3 file.

    For MLA, for files available through an open Web site:

    > Last name, First name. "Title in Quotations: Subtitle If Any." *Site Title in Italics*, 8 May 2007,
    >   URL.

    APA

    > Last name, Initial. (Producer/Host). (2010, June 18). *Site Title in Italics* [Audio podcast]. Avail-
    >   able from Organization Name.

    (Use normal capitalization with Web site titles and italicize.)

LECTURE, POWERPOINT, SPEECH, READING

56. **Lecture**

    MLA

    > Last name, First name. "Title in Quotations: Subtitle If Any." Name of Organization, 5 June
    >   2011, location. Lecture. [*or, if PowerPoint,* Slide 5.]

    **(Indicate the type of oral presentation: Lecture, PowerPoint, Reading, Address, Keynote
    Address, etc.)**

    APA

    > Last name, Initial. (2011, June 5). *Title in italics: Subtitle if any.* Lecture presented at Name of
    >   Organization. City, State Abbreviation. Retrieved from http://

    (Indicate the type of oral presentation: Lecture, Reading, Address, Keynote Address. **Include in**
    References **only if retrievable. No period follows** *Retrieved from.***)**

ORAL INTERVIEW

57. Oral (Unpublished) Interview

MLA

Last name, First name. Personal interview. 5 Mar. 2011.

Or

Last name, First name. Telephone interview. 5 Mar. 2011.

(Use Last name, First name of person interviewed: *Obama, Barack*.)

APA

(Use only in-text parenthetical citation since APA does not include nonretrievable sources in *References*. See Guide to Formatting In-Text Citation: MLA and APA, 12 **and** 32.**)**

58. Broadcast Interview—Television or Radio

MLA

Last name, First name. Interview by First name Last name, *Program Series in Italics*, ABC, WABC, City, 9 May 2004.

APA

Last name, Initial. (Interviewer). (2004, May 9). Interview with First name Last name. *Program series in italics* [Radio program]. City, State Abbreviation: National Public Radio.

(Alphabetize under interviewer's last name.)

LIVE PERFORMANCE

59. Play, Music Concert, Ballet, Opera, Dance, Performance Art

MLA

Title in Italics. By First name Last name, directed by First name Last name, performances by First name Last name and First name Last name, Name of Theater, 7 Sept. 2011, City.

(Usual listing of live performance: Emphasizes title first.)

Last name, First name. *Title in Italics*. Directed by First name Last name, performances by First name Last name and First name Last name, Name of Theater, 7 Sept. 2011, City.

(Emphasizes author first.)

APA

Use only in-text parenthetical citation since APA does not include nonretrievable sources in *References*. A typical in-text citation: (Title of live performance, location, date).

WRITTEN MUSICAL COMPOSITION

60. **Longer Composition: Symphony, Ballet, Opera, etc.**

    MLA

    Last name, First name. *Title in Italics.* Year of composition, Publisher, year of publication.

    APA

    Last name, Initial. (Year of publication). *Title of score in italics* [Opera]. City of publication, State Abbreviation: Publisher. (Year of composition)

    (No period follows.)

61. **Shorter Composition: Song, Short Instrumental Piece, etc.**

    MLA

    Last name, First name. "Title in Quotations." Year of composition, Publisher, year of publication.

    APA

    Last name, Initial. (Year of publication). Title without quotations [Song for voice]. City of publication, State Abbreviation: Publisher. (Year of composition)

    (No period follows.)

ARTWORK (PAINTING, DRAWING, ETCHING, SCULPTURE, PHOTO-GRAPH, ETC.)

62. **Artwork**

    MLA

    Last name, First name. *Title of Artwork in Italics.* Year of completion, Gallery/Owner, City. Medium.

    (Medium = oil on canvas, oil on wood, charcoal, watercolor, etc. If no title, provide brief description: Early twentieth-century oak arts-and-craft chair with barley-twist arm supports.)

    APA

    Last name, Initial. (Year of completion). *Title of artwork in italics* [Medium]. Gallery/Owner, City, State Abbreviation.

    (Medium = oil on canvas, oil on wood, charcoal, watercolor, etc. If no title, provide brief description: Early twentieth-century oak arts-and-craft chair with barley-twist arm supports.)

MAP OR CHART

63. **Map or Chart**

    MLA

    Title of Map in Italics. Map. Publisher, year of publication.

    Or

    "Title of Map in Quotations." Map. *Title in Italics*, by First name Last name, Publisher, year of publication. p. 29.

    APA

    Title of map in italics [Map]. (Year of publication). City of publication, State Abbreviation: Publisher.

WARNING!

For MLA, if an online source has no date, don't write *n.d.* Rather, give an indication of possible date: *circa 2011.* Or *2011(?).*

For APA, if an online source has no date, write *n.d.*

ENTIRE WEB SITE

64. **Entire Web Site**

    MLA

    Site Title in Italics. 18 May 2012, URL.

    Or

    Last name, First name, editor. *Site Title in Italics.* Site Sponsor, URL. Accessed 30 May 2012.

    (If author or editor is given, begin with that. If site sponsor is important to identify source, add that. Give access date for source material regularly updated. Period follows.)

    APA

    Site Title in Italics. (2012, May 18). Retrieved from http://

    Or

    Last name, Initial. (Ed.). (2012, May 18). *Site Title in Italics.* Retrieved from http://

    (No period follows.)

SECTION OF WEB SITE

65. Section of Web Site

MLA

"Title in Quotations." *Site Title in Italics*, URL. Accessed
30 June 2012.

(Give access date for source material regularly updated. Period follows.)

Or

Last name, First name. "Title in Quotations." *Site Title in Italics*, 18 May 2012, URL.

APA

Title without quotations. (2012, May 18). *Site Title in Italics*. Retrieved from http://

Or

Last name, Initial. (2012, May 18). Title without quotations. *Site Title in Italics*. Retrieved from
http://

(No period follows.)

ARTICLE IN ONLINE JOURNAL

66. Article in Online Journal

MLA

Last name, First name. "Title in Quotations: Subtitle If Any." *Journal Title in Italics*, vol. 8, no.
4, 2010, pp. 15-28, DOI or URL.

APA

Last name, Initial., & Last name, Initial. (2010). Title without quotations: Subtitle if any. *Journal Title in Italics*, 8(4), 15-28. Retrieved from http://

(No period follows.)

ARTICLE FROM ONLINE MAGAZINE OR NEWSPAPER

67. Article from Online Magazine or Newspaper

MLA

Last name, First name. "Title in Quotations: Subtitle If Any." *Magazine Title in Italics*, 31 Dec.
2010, DOI or URL.

APA

Last name, Initial. (2011, July 3). Title without quotations: Subtitle if any. Newspaper *Title in
Italics*. Retrieved from http://

(No period follows.)

ONLINE BOOK

68. Online Book

MLA

> Last name, First name. *Title in Italics: Subtitle If Any.* Publisher, year of original publication. *Site Title or Database in Italics*, DOI or URL.

APA

> Last name, Initial. (Year of original publication). *Title in italics: Subtitle if any.* Retrieved from http://

Or

> Last name, Initial. (Year of original publication). *Title in italics: Subtitle if any.* doi:10.1000/1000000

(No period follows.)

ONLINE POEM OR SHORT STORY

69. Online Poem or Short Story

MLA

> Last name, First name. "Title in Quotations." Publisher, year of original publication. *Site Title or Database in Italics*, DOI or URL. Site Sponsor, Publisher, year of site publication, URL.

APA

> Last name, Initial. (Year of original publication). Title without quotations. *Site Title in Italics.* Retrieved from http://

(No period follows.)

ONLINE REFERENCE WORK

70. Online Reference Work

MLA

> "Title of Entry in Quotations." *Site Title in Italics*, year of publication, DOI or URL.

APA

> Title of entry without quotations. (n.d.) In *Title in italics* (2nd ed.). Retrieved from http://

(No period follows.)

WIKI

71. Wiki

MLA

"Title with Quotations." *Wiki Title in Italics*, 14 Apr. 2009, URL. Accessed 9 Sept. 2009.

(Give access date for source material regularly updated. Period follows.)

APA

Title without quotations. (2009, April 14). Retrieved September 9, 2009, from Name of Wiki: http://

(Give access date for source material regularly updated. No period follows.)

BLOG (WEB LOG)

72. Entire Blog

MLA

Last name, First name. *Blog Title in Italics*. 19 Feb. 2012, URL. Accessed 21 Mar. 2012.

(Give access date for source material regularly updated. Period follows.)

APA

Last name, Initial. (2012, February 19). *Blog Title in Italics* [Web log]. Retrieved March 21, 2012, from http://

(Give access date for source material regularly updated. No period follows.)

73. Posting on a Blog

MLA

Last name, First name. "Title in Quotations." *Blog Title in Italics*, June 2017, 2:15 a.m., URL. Accessed 9 Sept. 2012.

(Give access date for source material regularly updated. Period follows.)

APA

Last name, Initial. (2012, June 4). Title without quotations [Web log post]. Retrieved September 9, 2012, from http://

(Give access date for source material regularly updated. No period follows.)

POSTING ON A WEB PAGE

74. Discussion Group Posting

MLA

Online Name *or* Last Name, First name. "Title in Quotations." *Discussion Group in Italics*, Site Sponsor, 2 Aug. 2011, 1:14 p.m., URL. Accessed 4 Aug. 2011.

(Give access date for source material regularly updated. Period follows.)

APA

Last name, Initial. (2011, August 2). Title without quotations [Online discussion group post]. Retrieved August 4, 2011, from http://

(Give access date for source material regularly updated. No period follows.)

75. **Comment Posted on Web Page**

MLA

Name [*Or* Last name, First Name]. Comment on "Title in Quotations." *Site Title in Italics*, 29 Aug. 2017, 3:31 a.m., URL.

APA

Last name, Initial. (2017, August 29, 3:31 a.m.). Title without quotations [Online comment post]. Retrieved from http://

E-MAIL

76. **E-mail**

MLA

Last name, First name. "Re: Subject in Quotations." Received by First name Last name, 18 Mar. 2017.

APA

APA considers e-mail a nonretrievable source and hence includes it only for in-in-text citations, not for References.

SOCIAL MEDIA

77. **Social Media (Twitter, Facebook, Google+, Etc.)**

In MLA, pseudonyms and usernames are acceptable.

MLA

@Name [*Or* Last name, First name]. "Entire tweet in quotations, #Subject." *Twitter*, 23 May 2017, 8:53 a.m., twitter.com address.

APA

Last name, Initial [@Name]. (2017, 23 May). Entire tweet [Tweet]. Retrieved from http://twitter.com

(No period follows.)

YOUTUBE AND MOVIE-/VIDEO-STREAMING SITES

78. **YouTube**

MLA

[*If author*] Last name, First name. "Title in Quotations." *YouTube*, uploaded by First name Last name, upload date if given, **URL.** Accessed 8 Mar. 2017.

(Give access date for source material regularly updated. Period follows.)

APA

YouTube user name. (upload date if given; if not given, n.d.) Title [YouTube Channel].
    Retrieved March 8, 2017, from http://youtube.com

(Give access date for source material regularly updated. No period follows.)

79. **Movie-/Video-Streaming Sites (Netflix, Hulu, Amazon Prime, etc.)**

For any movie or video Web-streaming source like YouTube, follow the YouTube model, adding relevant information (e.g., for television, episode and season) as needed.

MLA

David, Larry. "Wandering Bear." *Curb Your Enthusiasm*,
    produced by Jeff Garlin, DVD version, season 4, episode 8,
    HBO Home Entertainment, 29 Feb. 2004. *Amazon Prime*,
    www.amazon.com/gp/video/detail/B0172URD64?ref_
    =aiv_dp_season_select.

(Period follows.)

APA

David, L. (Writer-Director). (2004, February 29). Wandering bear [Television series episode].
    In Garlin, J. (Producer), *Curb your enthusiasm*. Retrieved from http://www.amazon.com/gp/
    video/detail/B0172URD64?ref_=aiv_dp_season_select

(No period follows.)

HOW TO FORMAT IN-TEXT CITATIONS

GENERAL RULES

For giving in-text credit to sources of information for your project, you must write a citation. You write this citation inside parentheses; it can have several forms, depending on whether you use MLA or APA and whether you do or don't state the author's name in a sentence in the text.

If you *do* state the author's name in the text:

MLA

On the one hand, as film scholar David Webber claims, D.W. Griffith is the racist who in *The Birth of a Nation* glorified the Ku Klux Klan (12).

Citation = parentheses with page number only.

(12)

APA

On the one hand, as film scholar David Webber (2015) has claimed, D.W. Griffith is the racist who in *The Birth of a Nation* glorified the Ku Klux Klan.

Citation = parentheses after author's name with date of publication

(2015).

If you *don't* state the author's name in the text—and save it till the parentheses:

MLA

On the other hand, Griffith is the pioneer technician whose "brilliant editing set the standard for films to come" (Webber 12).

Citation = author's last name plus page number—no comma.

(Webber 12)

APA

On the other hand, Griffith is the pioneer technician whose "brilliant editing set the standard for films to come" (Webber, 2015, p. 12).

When using quotations or making specific references, add p. (page) or para. (paragraph).

(Webber, 2015, p. 12) *or* (Webber, 2015, para. 13)

Otherwise, write the following:

Citation = author's last name plus year of publication—separated by comma

(Webber, 2015).

And note:

When you refer to sources, MLA uses present-tense signal phrases ("claims"); APA uses past-tense or present-perfect ("has claimed").

Specific Rules

All your in-text citations won't be a simple author and page (MLA) or author and year (APA). Complexities develop putting together various combinations—one author, more than one author, unknown author, etc. —with various kinds of publications—book, anthology, the Bible, e-mail, etc.

GUIDE TO FORMATTING IN-TEXT CITATIONS

MLA and APA

a. You *Do* State the Author in the Text

1. One Author Stated in Text
2. Two or More Sources by Same Author Stated in Text
3. Two Authors Stated in Text (MLA)
4. Two Authors Stated in Text (APA)
5. Three or More Authors Stated in Text (MLA)
6. Three to Five Authors Stated in Text (APA)
7. Six or More Authors Stated in Text (APA)
8. An Organization as Group Author Stated in Text
9. Two or More Separate Sources Stated in Text
10. Nonprint (Web, Social Media, etc.) Author Stated in Text

w. You *Do* State the Author in the Text

1. One Author Stated in Text

MLA: According to Elliott, the rising whooping crane population has encountered several "life-threatening setbacks" (47).

For APA, use *p.* plus page number for quoted words but also specific but unquoted references to a text.

APA: Elliott (2012) shows that the rising whooping crane population has encountered several "life-threatening setbacks" (p. 47).

2. Two or More Sources by Same Author Stated in Text

For MLA, use a short version of title in citation to distinguish source from author's other works.

MLA: The newest models, argues Dvorsky, will be "accessible from your cell phone" ("Appliances" 26).

For APA, if more than one publication by author in the same year, letter the sources in the citation and in References.

APA: A current projection (Dvorsky, 2012a) claims that the newest models will be "accessible from your cell phone" (p. 26).

3. Two Authors Stated in Text (MLA)

MLA: A pioneering study by Harkins and Stafford explores how nineteenth-century artist William Daniell undertook a series of sketching voyages around the coast of Great Britain to gain admittance to the Royal Academy (18).

4. Two Authors Stated in Text (APA)

Use *and* (not *&*) in text.

APA: A pioneering study by Harkins and Stafford (1997) explores how nineteenth-century artist William Daniell undertook a series of sketching voyages around the coast of Great Britain to gain admittance to the Royal Academy.

5. Three or More Authors Stated in Text (MLA)

Use the first author plus *et al.* (without italics).

MLA: Bobbs et al. claim that passing a single-payer system will cause a dramatic fall in insurance costs (184-86).

6. Three to Five Authors Stated in Text (APA)

List all authors in first citation; in later citations, use first author plus *et al.* (without italics).

APA: Bobbs, Fitch, Gunderman, and Hernandez (2005) claim that passing a single-payer system will cause a dramatic fall in insurance costs.

and

APA: According to the study by Bobbs et al. (2005), the single-payer system has been successfully instituted in Massachusetts.

7. **Six or More Authors Stated in Text (APA)**

APA: An investigation by Henshaw et al. (2010) of Milwaukee's redlining has revealed a sordid history of racial intolerance.

8. **An Organization as Group Author Stated in Text**

MLA: The World Health Organization has published a study demonstrating that malnutrition has ravaged the sub-Saharan continent (43).

For APA, in first citation, spell out group author with parenthetical abbreviation (WHO); in later citations, abbreviate: WHO (2008).

APA: The World Health Organization (WHO) has published a study (2008) demonstrating that malnutrition has ravaged the sub-Saharan continent.

9. **Two or More Separate Sources Stated in Text**

For both MLA and APA, separate with semicolon.

MLA: The dissertation by Claussen and the book by McBride and Peters simultaneously point out that Ned Rorem made "major creative breakthroughs" while living in Africa (313; 128).

For APA, in parenthetical citation, use & instead of *and* when referring to paired authors.

APA: The dissertation by Claussen (2011) and the book by McBride and Peters (2011) simultaneously point out that Ned Rorem made "major creative breakthroughs" while living in Africa (p. 313; p. 128).

10. **Nonprint (Web, Social Media, etc.) Author Stated in Text**

Cite page number if using a PDF format; otherwise, identify according to available identifiers:

For MLA, author or title and/or section (*sec.* or *secs.*) or paragraph number (*par.* or *pars.*) following a heading. For a movie or video, if referring to a frame, shot, or scene, give the time in hours/minutes/seconds.

MLA: "Great Depression Games" reminds us that Monopoly is no doubt Parker Brothers' most famous game from the 1930s (Parker Brothers heading, par. 6).

MLA: Movie director Schoenberg shows a dog tormented by a trio of Italian schoolboys (01:03:14-54).

For APA, author or title and/or section (*section* or *sections*) or paragraph number (*para.* or *paras.*) following a heading. For a movie or video, if referring to a frame, shot, or scene, give the time in hours/minutes/seconds.

APA: "Great Depression Games" (2012) reminds us that Monopoly is no doubt Parker Brothers' most famous game from the 1930s (Parker Brothers heading, para. 6).

APA: Movie director Schoenberg (2015, 01:03:14-54) shows a dog tormented by a trio of Italian schoolboys).

11. **Lecture or Public Presentation Author Stated in Text**

For both MLA and APA, if more than one lecture or presentation, use identifying date.

MLA: Dr. Baldridge claims that Istanbul as a source of romantic imagery has made its way into a number of spy novels (9 Sept. 2012).

APA: Dr. Baldridge (lecture, 2012, September 9) claims that Istanbul as a source of romantic imagery has made its way into a number of spy novels.

12. **Personal Interview, Telephone Interview, or E-mail Author Stated in Text**

For MLA, if more than one communication from same source, use identifying date.

> **MLA:** To summarize Stanton-Crosby, significant advances have been made in treating macular degeneration with blood-vessel inhibitors (24 June 2009).

For APA, any nonretrievable source like e-mail or personal interview is cited within the text but not included in References. Identify as *personal communication* (no italics) with date.

> **APA:** To summarize C.K. Stanton-Crosby (personal communication, June 24, 2009), significant advances have been made in treating macular degeneration with blood-vessel inhibitors.

13. **Republished Author Stated in Text**

For MLA and APA, with a text that has gone through many editions, give the page number of the text consulted but also a chapter, part, or line number.

> **MLA:** In *Gulliver's Travels*, Swift tells how Gulliver says of a farmer whom he encounters, "[He] by this time was convinced I must be a rationale Creature" (87; pt. 2, ch. 1).

For APA, with a text that has gone through many editions, also give original publication date as well as date of text consulted. (Abbreviate *Part* but not *Chapter*.)

> **APA:** In *Gulliver's Travels*, Swift (1735/1976) tells how Gulliver says of a farmer whom he encounters, "[He] by this time was convinced I must be a rationale Creature" (Pt. 2, Chapter 1, p. 87).

14. **Author of Multivolume Work Stated in Text**

For MLA, give both volume and page number (don't write *volume* or *page*).

> **MLA:** We are told by Stanley, "Among our Egyptians there was one called Ali Effendi, a captain, who complained of heart disease" (2: 226).

For APA, give both volume and page number (but write *Vol.* and *p.*).

> **APA:** We are told by Stanley (1890), "Among our Egyptians there was one called Ali Effendi, a captain, who complained of heart disease" (Vol. 2, p. 226).

15. **Author in Anthology Stated in Text**

> **MLA:** Whittington's "Swamp Search" is typical of the crime stories published in *The Black Lizard Anthology of Crime* for pulp lines like "She had me all clobbered, but I wanted her worse than ever" (33).

For APA, with a text that has gone through many editions, also give original publication date as well as date of text consulted.

> **APA:** Whittington's "Swamp Search" (1957/1987) is typical of the crime stories published in *The Black Lizard Anthology of Crime* for pulp lines like "She had me all clobbered, but I wanted her worse than ever" (p. 33).

16. **Unknown Author Stated in Text**

> **MLA:** "Nursing Home Laws Needed" blows the whistle on how the nursing home industry often escapes "rigorous oversight" (2).

> **APA:** "Nursing Home Laws Needed" (2009) blows the whistle on how the nursing home industry often escapes "rigorous oversight" (p. 2).

17. **A Religious Work (Bible, Qur'an, etc.): Unknown Author Stated in Text**

    For MLA and APA, use the edition/translation. Spell out names in text.

    MLA: Lamentations 5.10 gives the reader yet another metaphor: "Our skin is as hot as an oven with the burning heat of famine" (*The Holy Bible, New Revised Standard Version*).

    For APA, cite classical work like the Bible in the text but not in References; don't italicize.

    APA: Lamentations 5:10 (The Holy Bible, New Revised Standard Version) gives the reader yet another metaphor: "Our skin is as hot as an oven with the burning heat of famine."

18. **An Indirect Source: Author Stated in Text**

    For MLA and APA, give page number in parentheses. Do not abbreviate *quoted*.

    MLA: As quoted in Murray, Hamwell often insists that, in the words of the famous Irish playwright, "I can resist everything except temptation" (334).

    APA: As cited in Murray (1982), Hamwell often insists that, in the words of the famous Irish playwright, "I can resist everything except temptation" (p. 334).

19. **Encyclopedia or Other Reference Book: Author Stated in Text**

    For both MLA and APA, if the reference book doesn't provide the author of an entry, use entry title ("Lemon").

    MLA: The history note on "Lemon" on the etymology of the word reveals the tree's origins in the Middle East.

    APA: The history note on "Lemon" (1992) on the etymology of the word reveals the tree's origins in the Middle East.

20. **A Long Quotation: Author Stated in Text**

    For MLA, set off quotations longer than four typed lines:

    - indent *one inch* from flush left
    - double-space
    - don't use quotation marks unless the passage quotes a quotation
    - don't indent the first line unless (1) the passage is longer than one paragraph and (2) the first paragraph in the original is indented
    - indent each new paragraph *one-fourth inch*
    - place a period at the end of the quotation, and then one space after, type the parenthetical citation: page number (no period follows)

    > Klare notes that historians will credit Algeria for the recent unrest in the Middle East:
    >
    > > On January 5, young protestors in Algiers, Oran, and other major cities blocked roads, attacked police stations and burned stores in demonstrations against soaring food prices. Other concerns–high unemployment, pervasive corruption, lack of housing–also aroused their ire, but food costs provided the original impulse. As the epicenter of youthful protest moved elsewhere … the food price issue was subordinated … but it never disappeared. (7–8)

For APA, set off quotations forty words or more:

- indent *one-half inch* from flush left
- double-space
- don't use quotation marks unless the passage quotes a quotation
- indent each new paragraph one more *one-half inch*
- place a period at the end of the quotation, and then one space after, type the parenthetical citation: page number (no period follows)

> Klare (2011) notes that historians will credit Algeria for the recent unrest in the Middle East:
>
> > On January 5, young protestors in Algiers, Oran, and other major cities blocked roads, attacked police stations and burned stores in demonstrations against soaring food prices. Other concerns–high unemployment, pervasive corruption, lack of housing–also aroused their ire, but food costs provided the original impulse. As the epicenter of youthful protest moved elsewhere ... the food price issue was subordinated ... but it never disappeared. (pp. 7–8)

b. You *Don't* State the Author's Name in the Text

3. One Author Not Stated in Text

MLA: The rising whooping crane population has encountered several "life-threatening setbacks" (Elliott 47).

For APA, use *p.* plus page number for quoted words but also specific (but unquoted) references to a text.

APA: The rising whooping crane population has encountered several "life-threatening setbacks" (Elliott, 2012, p. 47).

4. Two or More Sources by Same Author Not Stated in Text

For MLA, use a short version of title in citation to distinguish source from author's other works.

MLA: The newest models will be "accessible from your cell phone" (Dvorsky, "Appliances" 26).

For APA, if more than one publication by author in the same year, letter the sources in the citation and in References.

APA: The newest models will be "accessible from your cell phone" (Dvorsky, 2012a, p. 26).

5. Two Authors Not Stated in Text (MLA)

MLA: Nineteenth-century artist William Daniell undertook a series of sketching voyages around the coast of Great Britain to gain admittance to the Royal Academy (Harkins and Stafford 18).

6. **Two Authors Not Stated in Text (APA)**

Use the *&* to replace *and* in citation.

> **APA:** Nineteenth-century artist William Daniell undertook a series of sketching voyages around the coast of Great Britain to gain admittance to the Royal Academy (Harkins & Stafford, 1997).

7. **Three or More Authors Not Stated in Text (MLA)**

Use the first author plus *et al.* (without italics).

> **MLA:** Passing a single-payer system will cause a dramatic fall in insurance costs (Bobbs et al. 184-86).

8. **Three to Five Authors Not Stated in Text (APA)**

List all authors in first citation; in later citations, use first author plus *et al.* (without italics). Use *&* to replace *and* in citation.

> **APA:** Passing a single-payer system will cause a dramatic fall in insurance costs (Bobbs, Fitch, Gunderman, & Hernandez, 2005).

9. **Six or More Authors Not Stated in Text (APA)**

> **APA:** An investigation of Milwaukee's redlining has revealed a sordid history of racial intolerance (Henshaw et al., 2010).

10. **An Organization as Group Author Not Stated in Text**

> **MLA:** Malnutrition has ravaged the sub-Saharan continent (World Health Organization 43).

For APA, in first citation, spell out group author with bracketed abbreviation [WHO]; in later citations, abbreviate: (WHO, 2008).

> **APA:** Malnutrition has ravaged the sub-Saharan continent (World Health Organization [WHO], 2008).

11. **Two or More Separate Sources Not Stated in Text**

For both MLA and APA, separate with semicolon. Alphabetize sources.

> **MLA:** Two simultaneous studies both point out that Ned Rorem made "major creative breakthroughs" while living in Africa (Claussen 313; McBride and Peters 128).

For APA, in parenthetical citation, use *&* instead of *and* when referring to paired authors.

> **APA:** Two simultaneous studies both point out that Ned Rorem made "major creative breakthroughs" while living in Africa (Claussen, 2011, p. 313; McBride & Peters, 2011, p. 128).

12. **Nonprint (Web, Social Media, etc.) Author Not Stated in Text**

Cite page number if using a PDF format; otherwise, identify according to available identifiers:

For MLA, author or title and/or section (*sec.* or *secs.*) or paragraph number (*par.* or *pars.*) following a heading. For a movie or video, if referring to a frame, shot, or scene, author or title plus give the time in hours/minutes/seconds.

> **MLA:** Monopoly is no doubt Parker Brothers' most famous game from the 1930s ("Great Depression Games," Parker Brothers heading, par. 6).

MLA: The movie's shot startling for its brutality, we watch a dog tormented by a trio of Italian schoolboys (Schoenberg, 01:03:14-54).

For APA, author or title and/or section (*section* or *sections*) or paragraph number (*para.* or *paras.*) following a heading. For a movie or video, if referring to a frame, shot, or scene, author or title plus give the time in hours/minutes/seconds.

APA: Monopoly is no doubt Parker Brothers' most famous game from the 1930s ("Great Depression Games," 2012, Parker Brothers heading, para. 6).

APA: The movie's shot startling for its brutality, we watch a dog tormented by a trio of Italian schoolboys (Schoenberg, 2015, 01:03:14-54).

13. Lecture or Public Presentation Author Not Stated in Text

For both MLA and APA, use name of lecturer or presenter. If more than one lecture or presentation, use identifying date.

MLA: Istanbul as a source of romantic imagery has made its way into a number of spy novels (Baldridge, 9 Sept. 2012).

APA: Istanbul as a source of romantic imagery has made its way into a number of spy novels (Baldridge, 2012, September 9).

14. Personal Interview, Telephone Interview, or E-mail Author Not Stated in Text

For MLA, use author's last name. If more than one communication from same source, use identifying date.

MLA: Significant advances have been made in treating macular degeneration with blood-vessel inhibitors (Stanton-Crosby, 24 June 2009).

For APA, any nonretrievable source like e-mail or personal interview is cited within the text but not included in References. Use author's initials and don't invert name. Identify as *personal communication* (no italics) with date.

APA: Significant advances have been made in treating macular degeneration with blood-vessel inhibitors (C. K. Stanton-Crosby, personal communication, June 24, 2009).

15. Republished Author Not Stated in Text

For MLA and APA, with a text that has gone through many editions, give the page number of the text consulted but also a chapter, part, or line number.

MLA: In *Gulliver's Travels*, Gulliver says of a farmer whom he encounters, "[He] by this time was convinced I must be a rationale Creature" (Swift 87; pt. 2, ch. 1).

For APA, with a text that has gone through many editions, also give original publication date as well as date of text consulted. (Abbreviate *Part* but not *Chapter*.)

APA: In *Gulliver's Travels*, Gulliver says of a farmer whom he encounters, "[He] by this time was convinced I must be a rationale Creature" (Swift 1735/1976, Pt. 2, Chapter 1, p. 87).

16. **Author of Multivolume Work Not Stated in Text**

    For MLA, give both volume and page number (don't write *volume* or *page*).

    MLA: We are told, "Among our Egyptians there was one called Ali Effendi, a captain, who complained of heart disease" (Stanley 2: 226).

    For APA, give both volume and page number (but write *Vol.* and *p.*).

    APA: We are told, "Among our Egyptians there was one called Ali Effendi, a captain, who complained of heart disease" (Stanley, 1890, Vol. 2, p. 226).

17. **Author in Anthology Not Stated in Text**

    For both MLA and APA, use the author of the piece consulted, not the editor of the anthology; use the page number from the anthology.

    MLA: "Swamp Search" is typical of the crime stories published in *The Black Lizard Anthology of Crime* for pulp lines like "She had me all clobbered, but I wanted her worse than ever" (Whittington 33).

    For APA, with a text that has gone through many editions, also give original publication date as well as date of text consulted.

    APA: "Swamp Search" is typical of the crime stories published in *The Black Lizard Anthology of Crime* for pulp lines like "She had me all clobbered, but I wanted her worse than ever" (Whittington, 1957/1987, p. 33).

18. **Unknown Author Not Stated in Text**

    For MLA, use full or short form of a title.

    MLA: The nursing home industry often escapes "rigorous oversight" ("Nursing Home Laws Needed" 2).

    For APA, shorten a title to two or three words, leaving out *The, A,* and *An*. Use quotation marks or italics as appropriate; capitalize key words for parenthetical citation but not for References.

    APA: The nursing home industry often escapes "rigorous oversight" ("Nursing Home Laws," 2009, p. 2).

19. **A Religious Work (Bible, Qur'an, etc.): Unknown Author Not Stated in Text**

    For MLA and APA, use the edition/translation plus book, chapter, and verse. Spell out names in text, but in citation, abbreviate books with long names.

    MLA: The reader is given yet another metaphor: "Our skin is as hot as an oven with the burning heat of famine" (*The Holy Bible, New Revised Standard Version*, Lam. 5.10).

    For APA, cite classical work like the Bible in the text but not in References; no page numbers required because such texts are normally numbered; don't italicize.

    APA: The reader is given yet another metaphor: "Our skin is as hot as an oven with the burning heat of famine" (The Holy Bible, New Revised Standard Version, Lam. 5:10).

20. An Indirect Source: Author Not Stated in Text

For MLA, use *qtd. in* ("quoted in") to show that your source is quoting or paraphrasing another source.

> **MLA:** Hamwell often insists that, in the words of the famous Irish playwright, "I can resist everything except temptation" (qtd. in Murray 334).

For APA, use *as cited in* to show that your source is quoting or paraphrasing another source.

> **APA:** Hamwell often insists that, in the words of the famous Irish playwright, "I can resist everything except temptation" (as cited in Murray, 1982, p. 334).

21. Encyclopedia or Other Reference Book: Author Not Stated in Text

For both MLA and APA, if the reference book doesn't provide the author of an entry, put the entry title in quotations (and alphabetize by title in Works Cited or References). Don't use page numbers for reference books that list entries alphabetically.

> **MLA:** The history note on the etymology of the word reveals the tree's origins in the Middle East ("Lemon").

> **APA:** The history note on the etymology of the word reveals the tree's origins in the Middle East ("Lemon," 1992).

22. A Long Quotation: Author Not Stated in Text

For MLA, set off quotations longer than four typed lines:

- **indent *one-half inch* from left margin**
- **double-space**
- **don't use quotation marks unless the passage quotes a quotation**
- **don't indent the first line even if the first paragraph in the original is indented**
- **indent each new paragraph *one-fourth inch*, place a period at the end of the quotation and then one space after, type the parenthetical citation: author and page number (no period follows)**

> It may turn out that historians will credit Algeria for the recent unrest in the Middle East:
>
> > On January 5, young protestors in Algiers, Oran, and other major cities blocked roads, attacked police stations and burned stores in demonstrations against soaring food prices. Other concerns–high unemployment, pervasive corruption, lack of housing–also aroused their ire, but food costs provided the original impulse. As the epicenter of youthful protest moved elsewhere ... the food price issue was subordinated ... but it never disappeared. (Klare 7-8)

For APA, set off quotations forty words or more:

- indent *one-half inch* from flush left
- double-space
- don't use quotation marks unless the passage quotes a quotation
- indent each new paragraph one more *one-half inch*
- place a period at the end of the quotation and then the parenthetical citation: author, date, and page number (no period follows)

> It may turn out that historians will credit Algeria for the recent unrest in the Middle East:
>
>> On January 5, young protestors in Algiers, Oran, and other major cities blocked roads, attacked police stations and burned stores in demonstrations against soaring food prices. Other concerns–high unemployment, pervasive corruption, lack of housing–also aroused their ire, but food costs provided the original impulse. As the epicenter of youthful protest moved elsewhere ... the food price issue was subordinated ... but it never disappeared. (Klare, 2011, pp. 7-8)

ENDNOTES AND FOOTNOTES

Occasionally, as you put a project together, you may want to say something more about a point. But a problem develops: If you bring up the new material, it won't fit the flow of your project. It will veer off at a tangent.

But scholars have developed a solution for such tangents: endnotes and footnotes.

The endnote (which comes at the end of the project) or the footnote (which comes at the foot of the page) will allow you to expand on a point without breaking into the forward, logical movement of your prose. Here's how to handle endnotes (MLA calls them "Notes") and footnotes (APA calls them "Footnotes"):

For referring to endnotes or footnotes,

1. Use superscripts.
2. Number notes (endnotes or footnotes) in the same order that they appear in the text. Note that APA uses the superscript to number notes (no period follows).
3. Superscripts follow all punctuation except the dash. With the dash—like here[1]—the superscript comes before.

MLA: Ortiz makes no such claim.[1]

> ### Notes
>
> 1. In fact, Ortiz argues to the contrary. See Ortiz in *The Way to the Border* (2009) and earlier articles that clearly state his position on immigration policies.

APA: Ortiz makes no such claim.[1]

> ### Footnotes
>
> [1]In fact, Ortiz argues to the contrary. See Ortiz in *The Way to the Border* (2009) and earlier articles that clearly state his position on immigration policies.

CPSIA information can be obtained
at www.ICGtesting.com
Printed in the USA
FFHW01n1802130718
47409692-50619FF

9 781524 936907